KRISHNAMURTI IN AMERICA

New Perspectives on the Man and his Message

KRISHNAMURTI IN AMERICA

New Perspectives on the
Man and his Message

DAVID EDMUND MOODY

ALPHA CENTAURI PRESS
OJAI, CALIFORNIA

KRISHNAMURTI IN AMERICA: NEW PERSPECTIVES ON THE MAN
AND HIS MESSAGE

Copyright © 2020 by David Edmund Moody
First Edition 2020

Published by Alpha Centauri Press
Ojai, California

For more information about J. Krishnamurti (1895-1986) please see:
www.jkrishnamurti.org.

Author services by Pedernales Publishing, LLC.
www.pedernalespublishing.com

Library of Congress Control Number: 2019917929

ISBN 978-1-7342278-1-9 Hardcover Edition
ISBN 978-1-7342278-2-6 Paperback Edition
ISBN 978-1-7342278-0-2 Digital Edition

Printed in the United States of America

For Mina and Leif and all
the children of the world

CONTENTS

PREFACE

K rishnamurti's life was conducted on three continents. India was the land of his birth and the country to which he returned many times, but he established residences with deep roots in England and the United States as well. The frequency and extent of his travels were among the defining characteristics of his career.

One of the challenges facing Krishnamurti's biographers is the necessity to bring into balance the geographical components of his life. The first and only authorized biography was composed by his lifelong friend, the English novelist Mary Lutyens. Her work appeared in three volumes, published in 1975, 1983, and 1988. She provided the factual foundation for all subsequent research, but the center of gravity of her perspective was located in England. Pupul Jayakar composed a biography published in 1986 that supplements the record provided by Lutyens with respect to people and events in India. Neither author was well acquainted with his life in the United States.

During the years subsequent to the appearance of the work of Lutyens and Jayakar, vast quantities of new information about Krishnamurti have appeared in the form of numerous memoirs and other forms of documentary evidence. Much of this information illuminates his life in America, including the people and organizations responsible for arranging his talks and publishing his books. Prolonged lawsuits and Krishnamurti's private relationships were also subjects of much of this new material. The present volume incorporates these findings and corrects the geographic imbalance in the existing record.

The lack of geographic proportionality has been matched by a certain degree of distortion in how Krishnamurti's philosophy is characterized. Lutyens was raised in a theosophical environment that she never entirely relinquished, and her work expresses traces and remnants of that background. Jayakar's perspective is steeped in her familiarity with the philosophical and religious traditions of India, and she casts Krishnamurti in the role of the ancient seer and sage. Neither author examines his teaching entirely on its own terms, without regard for any background or traditional point of view.

Due in part to the orientation of the existing biographies, Krishnamurti's philosophy continues to be viewed through a haze of inaccurate images and associations. A front-page article in the *New York Times* (December 9, 2017) exemplified these false impressions. There he was described as a "renowned Indian guru" and as the "anointed messiah" of a spiritual organization, one who transformed the valley in which he lived into "a mecca for New Age pilgrims."

This way of characterizing Krishnamurti's work is based on his life before the age of thirty-four, whereas for more than half a century thereafter, he followed another course entirely. One objective of this book is to convey his life and work in a more accurate and revealing manner, one in which the thrust of his philosophy is recognized, not as a mystical, religious, or Eastern point of view, but rather as a revolutionary new understanding of ordinary consciousness and daily life.

The large body of public statements that represents Krishnamurti's teaching speaks for itself and needs no assistance to enable an understanding of it. But the public reception of his work remains limited or shaped by inaccurate images, and much time may be required before the actuality of his message breaks through and dispels the false associations. This book is written in an effort to advance that day by a few years and to move the compass needle toward true north by a few degrees. If it succeeds, the primary beneficiary will be the individual human being throughout the world for whom his message was intended.

David Edmund Moody
Ojai, California
December 1, 2019

A NOTE REGARDING NAMES

In the culture into which Krishnamurti was born, the family name precedes the individual's given name. Thus, his father was Jiddu Narianiah; his brother was Jiddu Nityananda; and he was Jiddu Krishnamurti. For most of his life, he was known primarily by his given name only, but in more formal contexts, he was called J. Krishnamurti. In his childhood, his name was usually abbreviated to Krishna.

It is the custom in India to attach the suffix "ji" to the name of some individuals as an expression of affection and respect. Thus, for most of his adult life, people often called him Krishnaji. This was the name by which he was most commonly addressed in person by those close to him.

For purposes of referring to himself, Krishnamurti often employed the initial K by itself. His associates occasionally adopted this form as well, especially if they were referring to him in his capacity as a teacher or philosopher, rather than in a more personal, informal sense. His primary biographer, Mary Lutyens, alternated between referring to him as Krishnamurti and as K.

In this book, the name Krishnamurti is used almost exclusively, although Krishna is employed to refer to him in his youth. Krishnaji conveys too much familiarity for the present context, and K represents a more specialized usage appropriate for those within his immediate circle or well acquainted with his work. However, the reader will note occasional references to K and to Krishnaji in quotations from the work of others.

Another issue involves what to call the vast record of Krishnamurti's books, talks, and dialogues. Krishnamurti himself generally referred to them as his teaching or teachings. The difficulty with that usage is not in its literal meaning but its overtones. For an American audience, to refer to an individual's views as his or her teaching has a slightly foreign ring and is associated with the expressions of a guru or a religious authority. That is an association that Krishnamurti strongly disavowed: he insisted that he was not any kind of guru or figure of authority.

Krishnamurti was reluctant to call his work a philosophy. That word suggested to him a set of theories, ideas, and conclusions developed through a process of logic and analysis. But if we can take the word in a looser, less rigorous sense, it seems to be appropriate. In this book, as applied to Krishnamurti's views, *philosophy* is meant to convey a comprehensive set of observations and insights pertaining to consciousness and the human condition.

A third alternative is to refer to Krishnamurti's teaching as his work. That is a neutral term without baggage or unfortunate connotations, although it is somewhat vague and lacking in color or clarity.

In this book, the terms *teaching*, *philosophy*, and *work* are used interchangeably to refer to Krishnamurti's expression of his point of view. *Philosophy* is the generic term most commonly employed, while *teaching* tends to be reserved to refer more precisely to the actual exposition given in talks and dialogues. *Work* is used as an occasional alternative where specificity is not necessary.

Chapter One

THE TWO BROTHERS

It was the illness of his younger brother, Nityananda, that brought Krishnamurti to American shores. The year was 1922, and the symptoms of Nitya's tuberculosis had been following an erratic course for fourteen months. The brothers were en route to Switzerland from Australia, but they decided to travel east in order to stop at a valley in California known for the healing properties of its climate. At the time of their visit, they had no way of knowing that the valley would become, not a stepping stone, but their home.

Krishnamurti was twenty-seven years old, and Nitya was twenty-four. They arrived at the port of San Francisco and spent a day in Berkeley at the University of California. Krishnamurti's impressions of the students were favorable. "There was not that aloofness that exists between the godly Englishman and the humble Indian," he wrote; and he added, "One breathed the air of freedom."

The brothers proceeded by train to the Ojai (OH-hi) valley, some four hundred miles south and fifteen miles inland from the sea. A few weeks after they arrived, Nitya described Ojai in a letter to a friend. "In a long and narrow valley of apricot orchards and orange groves is our house, and the hot sun shines down day after day," he said, "but of an evening the cool air comes from the range of hills on either side."

Far beyond the lower end of the valley runs the long, perfect road from Seattle in Washington down to San Diego in

Southern California, some two thousand miles, with a ceaseless flow of turbulent traffic, yet our valley lies happily, unknown and forgotten, for a road wanders in but knows no way out. The American Indians called our valley the Ojai or the nest, and for centuries they must have sought it as a refuge.

At the time the two brothers arrived in Ojai, they had been steeped for thirteen years in the esoteric philosophy of Theosophy. The Theosophical Society (TS), formed in New York in 1875, was the brainchild of Helena Blavatsky, the Russian émigré and author of *The Secret Doctrine*. Her controversial book was an encyclopedic compilation of mystical and occult literature drawn from an indiscriminate mixture of religious traditions. The TS owed much of its success to the guidance and influence of a single convert, Annie Besant. She was a woman renowned for her speaking skills, energy, and formidable advocacy on behalf of working women, the independence of India, and other progressive causes far in advance of her time. As president of the TS, Besant declared that its foremost mission was to identify and nurture the next manifestation of what she called the World Teacher. Such an individual would speak to all of humanity in a time of global darkness and elevate the consciousness of the world.

In 1909, two years after her ascension to the presidency of the TS, Besant determined that fourteen-year-old Krishnamurti was destined to fulfill the role of World Teacher. He and his brother Nitya were living with their father in primitive quarters adjacent to the theosophical compound at Adyar, on the southeastern coast of India. The two brothers were inseparable, in part because their mother had died a few years earlier. Besant effectively adopted them both and removed them to England, where they were raised in the homes of wealthy theosophists and educated by private tutors.

Krishnamurti later maintained that he was never deeply influenced by theosophical doctrines, but in his youth he acquiesced to the role into which he had been cast. He absorbed the language and appeared to accept the outlook of the TS as his own. By his early or mid-twenties, however, he had begun to exhibit a restless dissatisfaction with his life and the course that had been charted for him by others. When he and Nitya arrived in Ojai, it was his first opportunity in many years to escape the presence and pressure of the network of people, the atmosphere, and the somewhat oppressive milieu of the Theosophical Society. The time was ripe for something more authentic to emerge from within. His inward sense of dissatisfaction, the spirit of freedom he sensed at Berkeley, and the beauty and isolation of the Ojai Valley, combined to create a potent opportunity for something radically new to occur.

Much of what we know about the young brothers was conveyed by the mother and daughter, Emily and Mary Lutyens. Emily was the daughter of the Earl of Lytton, who served for four years as the chief administrator of India on behalf of Great Britain. As a member of the nobility, the Earl's daughter was endowed with the title Lady. Born in 1874, Lady Emily married Edwin Lutyens when she was twenty-three and he was twenty-eight. Considered the most outstanding English architect during his lifetime, Lutyens was largely responsible for designing New Delhi, the capital of India. Upon its completion, the city was commonly called Lutyens' Delhi.

Emily and Edwin Lutyens had five children during the first eleven years of their marriage. The youngest of these was Mary, born in 1908. She grew up to become a prolific novelist and the biographer of her father and of the art critic John Ruskin. Later she served as the only authorized biographer of Krishnamurti.

Lady Emily composed the first detailed memoir of Krishnamurti, *Candles in the Sun*, published in 1957 and dedicated to

Mary. In the first paragraphs, she describes her conversion to Theosophy at the age of thirty-six:

> I had then been married to Edwin Lutyens for thirteen years, and the youngest of my five children was two. When I married I was still an orthodox Christian, a member of the Church of England. I read the Bible daily and attended church regularly, and I had hoped that my husband would join me in these observances, but he was not an orthodox believer.
>
> At first this lack of religious sympathy between us distressed me very much, but gradually I came to realize that I, with my orthodox religion, was a much more intolerant and narrow-minded person than he without it, and this realization had the effect of gradually modifying my views and giving me a wider outlook on religious ideas which paved the way for Theosophy.

When Annie Besant brought "the boys," as they were called, to England in 1910, Emily was among those waiting on the dock to greet them. And so began her deep and sustained devotion to Krishnamurti, a relationship of almost equal significance to him. She opened the doors of her home and her heart without reservation or qualification, and her observations represent one of our primary sources for understanding the nature and qualities of the brothers in their youth.

While Emily's devotion to Krishna, as he was known, was maternal and religious in nature, Mary was in love with Nitya in a more romantic way. Her memoir of her early years with the brothers, *To Be Young*, revolves largely around her infatuation with Nitya from the age of six to seventeen. The two memoirs together provide an intimate and revealing set of observations.

In spite of the disparity in the ages of mother and daughter, and in the objects of their affection, they paint a remarkably similar portrait of the brothers. The boys exhibited an infectious sense of spontaneity and good cheer, devoid of affectation or consciousness of Krishna's exalted mission. They liked to play with and tease the children with an affectionate spirit, and their company was appreciated for its own sake, not for their reputation or what they represented. Of the two brothers, Nitya was demonstrably sharper and more intellectually astute. He excelled in his academic work and was much admired by his tutors, while Krishna was likely to be bored by his studies and lacking in focus or concentration. Their differences, however, were less pronounced than their common qualities of impeccable grooming, good taste in clothes, sensitivity in manners, and easy acquiescence to the highly unusual and potentially burdensome expectations placed upon them.

While Krishna carried the primary responsibility of gradually moving into the role of World Teacher, Nitya's participation was considered indispensable. Among their several siblings, the bond of these brothers was the strongest, and no one else was remotely as important to Krishna as Nitya. It was understood from the beginning that he would never have agreed to participate in any theosophical activities if Nitya were not an integral part of the proceedings, and Nitya was amenable to do so. He fully embraced his role as ally and acolyte to his older brother.

The central conceit of Theosophy, as described by Emily, lay in the idea of spiritual progress along a prescribed path. This notion was held to correspond with the secret or occult beliefs of many religions, so Theosophy deemed itself to be a kind of hub or nexus of the collective wisdom of all religious traditions. As a practical matter, what distinguished Theosophy was the claim of its leading figures to have access to clairvoyant powers that enabled them to assess the spiritual progress of any individual. A crucial element in this ongoing drama was the participation of a handful of otherworldly men who had perfected themselves spiritually and transcended normal earthly constraints of time and place. These Masters of Wisdom could be consulted by those with clairvoyant powers in a nonmaterial domain called the astral plane, usually at night, in a state of mind otherwise known as dreaming.

A strange and significant series of events occurred just a few weeks after the brothers arrived in Ojai. What happened has been enmeshed from the beginning in descriptions laden with theosophical images and interpretations, and it is important to disentangle the facts from the speculative network of ideas in which it has been viewed. To do so is essential in order to understand not only what occurred at the time, but also what it signified in terms of the life of Krishnamurti and the meaning of his work.

The primary account we have of what took place was composed by Nitya in a long letter addressed to Annie Besant. Fortunately, much of what he wrote was objective in nature, and his theosophical interpolations are not too difficult to distinguish from the facts. In any case, the overall effect of the sequence of events was profound, "leaving us all so changed," he wrote, "that now our compass has found its lodestar."

The unusual episode began, according to Nitya, on a Thursday evening and came to a conclusion shortly after sundown on Sunday. The first sign of trouble was a painful swelling or lump, as if of a contracted muscle, in the back of Krishna's neck. This served as prelude to the events that began in earnest the next morning.

What happened for the next three days consisted of an odd combination of physical and psychological symptoms without any discernible cause or source. Krishna's body ached and he suffered from erratic alterations in his subjective sense of temperature, ranging from intense shivering to burning heat. He tried to stay in bed, but sometimes impulsively got up, only to fall to the floor. His symptoms curiously subsided at mealtimes, but if he had anything to eat, he could not keep it down. This syndrome fluctuated in intensity, enabling him to sleep at night, but it gradually increased over the course of the three days.

Coupled with the physical symptoms was an equally strange set of changes in his state of mind. He often seemed not unconscious but psychologically absent in the normal sense. A distinctly childlike persona emerged instead, confused about where he was or calling out for his mother.

By the end of the third day, some of the behavioral changes became even more pronounced. Although his room and his bed were kept very clean, he "began to complain bitterly of the dirt, the dirt of the bed, the intolerable dirt of the house, the dirt of everyone around, and in a voice full of pain said that he longed to go to the woods." He sat sobbing in a corner of his room and would not let anyone come near him. "Suddenly he announced his intention of going for a walk alone, but from this we managed to dissuade him, for we did not think that he was in any fit condition for nocturnal ambulations."

At dusk on Sunday, Nitya and two friends were sitting with Krishna on the porch of his one-bedroom house, Pine Cottage. "The sun had set an hour ago and we sat facing the far-off hills, purple against the pale sky in the darkening twilight." Nitya had the feeling that the three-day episode was approaching "an impending climax.... In front of the house a few yards away stands a young pepper tree, with delicate leaves of a tender green, now heavy with scented blossoms." One of the friends suggested to Krishna that he go and sit under the tree, and, after an initial hesitation, he did so.

> Now we were in a starlit darkness and Krishna sat under a roof of delicate leaves black against the sky. He was still murmuring unconsciously, but presently there came a sigh of relief and he called out to us, "Oh, why didn't you send me out here before?"

Nitya's observations of what followed that evening are steeped in theosophical imagery and accordingly are not too meaningful to anyone who does not subscribe to that philosophy. He sensed the arrival of a "Great Presence," and he believed he heard "divine music softly played" emanating from a distant source. He claimed that the face of one of his friends lit up in rapture; but then she fell into a "swoon," and when she awoke she could no longer remember what she had observed.

Krishnamurti also wrote an extended account of what he had experienced. His subjective recollections form a curious counterpoint to Nitya's observations, dovetailing with and alternately departing from them. Most poignant among his memories was the metaphor of "a man mending the road," a rather humble but apt adumbration of the whole of his subsequent career. The parable of the man mending the road surely deserves a place of honor within the spiritual literature of the world.

> On the first day while I was in that state and more conscious of the things around me, I had the first most extraordinary experience. There was a man mending the road; that man was myself; the pickaxe he held was myself; the very stone which he was breaking up was a part of me; the tender blade of grass was my very being, and the tree beside the man was myself. I almost could feel and think like the roadmender, and I could feel the wind passing through the tree, and the little ant on the blade of grass I could feel. The birds, the dust, and the very noise were a part of me.
>
> Just then there was a car passing by at some distance; I was the driver, the engine, and the tires; as the car went further away from me, I was going away from myself. I was in everything, or rather everything was in me, inanimate and animate, the mountain, the worm, and all breathing things. All day long I remained in this happy condition.

This experience is not easy to reconcile with the outward symptoms described by Nitya, but the conclusions of the two accounts correspond with one another rather well:

I began to come to myself under the pepper tree which is near the house. There I sat cross-legged in the meditation posture…. There was such profound calmness both in the air and within myself, the calmness of the bottom of a deep unfathomable lake. Like the lake, I felt my physical body, with its mind and emotions, could be ruffled on the surface but nothing, nay nothing, could disturb the calmness of my soul.

Even shorn of its theosophical associations, the outcome of the three-day episode was clearly transcendental in its depth and dimensions:

I have drunk at the clear and pure waters at the source of the fountain of life and my thirst was appeased. Nevermore could I be thirsty, never more could I be in utter darkness. I have seen the Light. I have touched compassion which heals all sorrow and suffering; it is not for myself, but for the world.

One of the friends present to witness the events was Mr. Warrington, an officer of the TS in America. He told Nitya that "some process" was going on in Krishna's body, "as a result of influences directed from planes other than physical." Whether or not its source was in planes other than physical, the term "process" has remained attached ever since to descriptions of whatever was taking place. Over the years, the term has acquired an added significance due to the fact that the process continued in an attenuated and somewhat muted form. A few weeks after the three-day event, the process resumed for an hour or two most evenings for a period of several months, and it recurred in a similar fashion at intervals for the next two or three years. And although it continued to abate somewhat in duration and intensity, the process remained an intermittent occurrence for the rest of Krishnamurti's life. Its nature and meaning also remain mysterious and unresolved.

Nitya was visiting Lady Emily in England when, at the age of twenty-three, he coughed and brought up blood, the first distressing symptoms of tuberculosis. She notified Krishna who was staying at that time with a theosophical family in France. The family recommended a doctor in Paris who claimed to be able to cure any disease with diet, and Nitya was soon under his care. A few months later the brothers traveled to Switzerland where a renowned specialist in tuberculosis declared that Nitya had been cured. Thereafter they went to India for four months and then to Sydney, Australia, where Nitya suffered a relapse.

The doctor in Sydney advised that the climate there was too damp and recommended that Nitya return to Switzerland for further treatment. That was the brothers' eventual destination when they decided to travel first to Ojai, where the climate was said to be conducive to the treatment of tuberculosis. The brothers remained in Ojai for almost a full year. It was the longest period of time they had stayed continuously in one place since they had left India thirteen years earlier. Even so, they would not have left Ojai were it not for the fact that Nitya was once again declared cured.

The brothers set off for a TS convention in Chicago in June 1923 before returning to England, where Emily saw them for the first time in many months. She had read the accounts of Krishna's experience under the pepper tree, and she was "a little apprehensive that I might feel shy in his presence now that he had attained a new spiritual stature." But she found to her "unspeakable joy" that he was "exactly the same."

In October, the brothers returned to Ojai for another eight months before traveling back to England in June 1924. It was the first time that Mary, now sixteen years old, had seen Nitya in nearly two years, and she was unsure whether she would respond with the same passion she had felt earlier. "Five minutes in Nitya's company and I was hopelessly bewitched and enslaved again. I rebelled against my thralldom but could not escape from it."

The brothers stayed for several weeks with Emily, Mary, and a few other friends at Pergine, a mountain resort in Italy, before setting off from Venice to Bombay. It was on this ocean voyage, wrote Mary, that, "leaning side by side on the rail of the deck one evening, watching the sunset, Nitya told me that he loved me. He did not kiss me but he held my hand against his heart, and I reached the summit of human happiness."

But her happiness soon encountered a bitter reality:

A couple of days before we arrived in Bombay, Nitya told me when we met on deck as usual after tea that he had coughed up blood that morning, but had not yet told Krishna or anyone else about it. I could see that he was very upset, but I did not realize the full significance of what he had told me.

The brothers were in India from November until March 1925. While they were there, Nitya stayed by himself in the mountains but remained feverish throughout that time. When he returned to travel with Krishna back to Sydney, Emily reported that he looked "very gaunt and sunken, and Krishna was greatly worried about him. He was very ill during the whole of the voyage."

Upon their arrival in Sydney, Nitya went straight again to a mountain setting where Krishna remained with him most of the time. Emily wrote,

Later Krishna came down from the hills and I went into Sydney by ferry to meet him. I was full of my [theosophical activities] and was deeply hurt because he merely seemed bored by it all. We were completely out of tune. I had been living intensely for the last few weeks in a kind of ecstatic dream while he had been in the depressing atmosphere of

Nitya's illness. He was dreadfully worried about Nitya and only wanted to talk about him, and was probably hurt in his turn by my apparent callousness. The truth is that I was convinced that the Masters would look after Nitya and that there was really nothing to worry about.

The brothers returned to Ojai again in June 1925. Normally they would have attended a convention of the TS scheduled for August in Holland, but Nitya was too ill to travel, and Krishna was too concerned about him to leave. But by late October, Nitya's condition had somewhat improved, and Krishna's participation was considered indispensable for the fiftieth anniversary "Grand Jubilee" convention of the TS scheduled in November. As a result, he left Nitya in the care of others and travelled to England on his way to India.

On November 3, Krishna, Lady Emily, Annie Besant, and several others left England for Rome and prepared to set sail for India. On November 7, they received a telegram reporting that Nitya was suffering from the flu. News of such an illness must have been disturbing and ominous in view of the existing fever and lung conditions associated with tuberculosis. Nevertheless, Krishna and the others maintained an unshakeable faith that Nitya's welfare was in the hands of the Masters of Wisdom, who would never allow him to die. They knew this on general principle; but, in addition, Krishna had had a dream in which one of the Masters personally assured him that Nitya's fate was secure.

On November 13, the party reached Port Said on the Red Sea, and another telegram arrived that evening. Even in a message so brief, one can discern the distinctive tenor of Nitya's voice: "Flu rather more serious. Pray for me."

That night the ship on which they sailed entered the Suez Canal during a thunderstorm. The next morning there arrived the cable announcing Nitya's death. Mary, now age seventeen, was in Sydney at the time. She received a telegram sent from Port Said: "Nitya peacefully passed away. Love. Mother. Krishna."

Krishnamurti's grief was intense but not prolonged. For days he wept alone in his cabin and cried out for his brother. His suffering was acute, but he said later that he faced the fact of death without escaping or looking away, and it had a transformative effect. His faith in the Masters was now broken, and the sequence of events was set in motion that would lead to his irrevocable break with Theosophy. When he arrived in Bombay ten days later, he had incorporated within himself the reality of what had occurred. "I still miss him; I shall always miss him physically, but I feel that he and I are working together, that we are walking along the same path, on the same mountain side, seeing the same flowers, the same creatures, the same blue sky."

In short, Krishna considered that he and Nitya were now and forever inseparable, "for I and my brother are one."

Three and a half years had elapsed from the time the two brothers arrived in Ojai until Nitya died in 1925. During that period, they were in Ojai for twenty-four months altogether, distributed over three intervals, far more time than they spent in any other location. This three-and-a-half-year period represented the central transition point of Krishnamurti's life. His first fourteen years had been spent in India; the next thirteen years were located largely in England; but beginning in 1922, the center of gravity shifted, and now Ojai became his primary home. He continued to travel throughout the world on an annual basis, and he rejected any form of nationality beyond the minimum required to secure a passport. But whenever his schedule permitted, it was Ojai to which he returned, and there that he spent more time by far than any other place for the rest of his life.

It was not only in a geographical sense that the center of gravity of Krishnamurti's life underwent a fundamental transition during this period of time. The strange three-day episode that began a few weeks after he arrived in Ojai has been the subject of much speculation, largely revolving around a theosophical interpretation, replete with interventions by the Masters and other spiritual beings.

But if we regard it from a more objective vantage point, the primary factor precipitating the episode was manifestly the new environment in which he found himself. For the first time in his adult life, Krishnamurti was removed from the theosophical atmosphere, expectations, and personalities in which he had been immersed for thirteen years. It is difficult not to conclude that coming to America, a land completely divorced from his past, with all of its associations, triggered the sequence of events that culminated in a new vision of life under the pepper tree.

America would be forever associated too with the loss of Nitya. The brothers came to Ojai in the hope that it would be conducive to his health. Although that hope was ultimately not realized, it may well be that Nitya's life was prolonged by Ojai's healing climate. In any case, his death in America, coupled with Krishnamurti's absence, sealed an association with the inadequacy of the premise on which Nitya's promised survival was based. America was the crucible in which an old structure of ideas began to dissolve.

In Ojai the break with the past began, both literally and symbolically, and after 1925 a new direction emerged for Krishnamurti's life. For the time being, the new direction was only implicit; but, with the strength of a gathering storm, it grew ever so gradually until it burst into public view in the summer of 1929. At that time, the implicit became explicit; and the break with the past became categorical and irrevocable.

Chapter Two

ANNIE BESANT

Henry Steel Olcott, one of the two founders of the Theosophical Society, was descended from six generations of Olcotts in Massachusetts and New Jersey. Born in 1832, he gained entry into New York University at the age of fifteen, but he had to drop out due to a reversal in his father's business affairs. He went to work on a farm in Ohio, where he excelled in the application of scientific principles to agriculture. Prior to the Civil War, Olcott became an authority on varieties of sugar plants in anticipation of a disruption in the supply from the South. His treatise on Chinese and African sugar canes, written at age twenty-five, was published in seven editions.

During the Civil War, Olcott was commissioned to root out corruption among the contractors and suppliers upon whom the Army depended for services. He investigated speculators and swindlers for three years and earned a reputation for perseverance and integrity in the pursuit of men possessed of money, influence, and dubious motivations. At the conclusion of the war, he left the military with the rank of colonel. As a result of his stellar wartime performance, Olcott was selected to serve on the three-man commission appointed to investigate the circumstances surrounding the assassination of President Lincoln.

In the years following the war, Olcott married and fathered four children. In 1868, he gained admission to the bar and went into legal practice on his own. His clientele included the New York Stock

Exchange, the City of New York, and the Treasury Department of the United States.

Even as his law practice prospered, a restless curiosity induced Olcott to pursue other interests, including the subject of "spiritualism." Manifestations of the existence of an unseen world had been prevalent on the American scene since 1848, when a family in upstate New York reported a knocking sound in their house whose source could not be determined. A more sensational demonstration of mysterious entities began to occur in 1874 at the Eddy household in Vermont. Olcott's accounts of these events for the *New York Daily Graphic* did'much to bring them to the attention of the public.

The events in question were taking place on a nightly basis on the second floor of the farmhouse owned by the Eddy brothers. Behind a curtain at the end of a long room, a medium seated himself and went into a trance. Once he was installed, a variety of spirit individuals appeared from behind the curtain and proceeded to dance in strange costumes and to speak in peculiar dialects. The Eddy brothers did not charge for attendance at these performances, so there was no apparent financial incentive for fraud.

Olcott's letters to the New York newspapers attracted a variety of visitors to the farm. By virtue of her colorful dress and manner, one of these captured his attention immediately: on an afternoon in October 1874, Olcott made the acquaintance of Helena Blavatsky, forty-three years old. Born Helena Petrovna van Hahn, her parents both had aristocratic blood in their lineage; her father was a military officer, and her mother was a successful novelist. When Helena was eleven, her mother died, and her teenage years were spent in the home of her wealthy grandparents. There she found a large collection of books on mythology, comparative religion, and the occult, and she began to acquire her voluminous knowledge in these areas.

Helena was strong-willed and impetuous. At the age of seventeen, she provoked and accepted an offer of marriage from Nicifor

Blavatsky, a wealthy landowner, official of the neighboring district, and twenty years her senior. Helena tried to back out of her agreement, but her family refused to allow it. She ran away before the wedding and again on her wedding day, but both times she was captured and returned to her fate. Three months after her marriage, but before it could be consummated, Helena ran away for good.

Blavatsky's travels over the next twenty-five years included sojourns in Egypt, India, Tibet, France, Canada, the United States, and Mexico, all underwritten by funds forwarded by her father in Russia. Her driving passion throughout her travels was to investigate hidden realities and, if possible, to make personal contact with sources of ancient wisdom. In both respects, she assured Henry Olcott, her efforts had been rewarded.

Helena Blavatsky was a burlesque dramatist on a stage of her own creation, a vaudeville pantomimist of the mind. She was a guerilla warrior on a psychological plane: her aim was to mock the arrogant certainty of Western materialism, and she had no compunctions about resorting to fraudulent tricks to advance that purpose. Foremost among these were the letters she composed, ostensibly written by Masters of Wisdom and addressed to her associates and to herself. She proffered the letters as if they had materialized into her hands out of thin air. Even Henry Olcott was taken in by her performances.

Blavatsky introduced Olcott to a world far richer in ideas and personalities than anything he had imagined. Within a few months of their acquaintance, he rented an apartment for her in New York City. Although their relationship was platonic—he called her "Old Horse," to her delight—Olcott was her most frequent visitor. He continued with his law practice while she wrote articles for outlets interested in occult affairs; and, in the evenings, they entertained visitors who shared their otherworldly interests.

One night in August 1875, an architect named George Felt gave a lecture in Blavatsky's apartment on "The Lost Canon of Proportion in Egypt," a rich vein of wisdom lost to the modern world. At the conclusion of the lecture, Olcott proposed the formation of a social organization for the ongoing investigation of related topics. Blavatsky agreed, and the Theosophical Society was born.

"Theosophy" derives from the Greek for "divine wisdom." As it developed, the stated objectives of the Society were threefold: to work toward the universal brotherhood of man; to explore the underlying unity among the varieties of religious views; and to investigate undiscovered powers latent in man. In the first two of these objectives, the Society gave expression to a global outlook, one in which human differences are far less significant than what is held in common. In the third objective, however, the Society endorsed a complex mythology derived from Blavatsky's syncretic blend of religious symbols, occult traditions, and her own fertile imagination.

In 1877, Blavatsky published a thirteen-hundred-page manuscript titled *Isis Unveiled*. Isis is the Egyptian goddess of magic or enchantment; she is the divine power who controls entrée to a world of creatures and energies that lie beyond the veil of material appearances. The large-scale agenda of *Isis Unveiled* was to show that science and religion have a common root. Blavatsky's interpretation of both, however, was so idiosyncratic as to be all but unrecognizable to most observers. Somewhat characteristic was her assertion that the first race of humans arrived on Earth from Venus six and a half million years ago.

The grand sweep of *Isis Unveiled* represented a tour de force of occult speculation. Blavatsky adapted the evolutionary doctrines of Darwin to her own purposes by extending them to the psychological realm. She held that mankind had evolved over the course of several million years through a series of "root races," each one representing a particular temperament and intellectual type. Each of the root races constituted a degree of progress over its predecessors. At present, mankind was advancing through the stages of the fifth root race, and the overarching purpose of the Theosophical Society was to prepare for the inauguration of a sixth.

Among the institutions concealed behind the veil of Isis was a brotherhood of men advanced beyond the material dimension. These Masters of Wisdom inhabit human bodies for convenience, but are not tied to them; they can manifest at will anywhere on the earthly plane. The Masters serve a celestial hierarchy of even more advanced individuals, culminating in the Lord of the World. Blavatsky described the appearance and personalities of several Masters whom she had met personally, as well as the nature of their functions in the bureaucracy of the occult. A first printing of a thousand copies of *Isis Unveiled* sold out in ten days.

During their tenure as leaders of the Theosophical Society, Colonel Olcott and Madame Blavatsky arrived at a broad division of administrative labor. He was President of the TS, responsible for outward, organizational affairs. She looked after the "inner work"; her function was reflected in an Esoteric Section she formed for this purpose. Reserved for a select few, the Esoteric Section offered exclusive access to her private stock of parables, illustrative of avatars, astral planes, and the ancient wisdom of the East.

By the mid-1880s, the TS had attracted followers on three continents, including Thomas Edison in the United States and William Butler Yeats in England. The Society's greatest convert, however, was won in 1889, upon the appearance of Blavatsky's magnum opus, *The Secret Doctrine*. The editor of a London newspaper asked for a review of the book from one of his contributors, Annie Besant. She was considered by many to be the foremost orator and social agitator of her day. When the Theosophical Society won her over, an engine was attached to Blavatsky's speculative sails; and the entire subsequent course of events bore the distinctive stamp of Annie Besant's vision and character.

In her childhood, Annie's devotion to the symbols and literature of Christianity was intense. Her disillusionment was rapid, however, when she married Frank Besant, an English priest, at the age of eighteen. Not only was he dictatorial and insensitive, while she was proud and independent; but, in addition, she discovered through her own investigations that the four Gospels do not agree in their chronologies of the life of Christ. If the Bible did not agree with itself, how could it be the authentic word of a perfect Being? Her experiences among the poor in her husband's parish, moreover, made her doubt that a merciful God could tolerate so much privation and suffering.

The dual crisis of religious conscience and an unhappy marriage resulted in feverish illness and thoughts of suicide. Annie's struggles with Church of England theology were expressed in a series of articles too controversial to be published under her own name. Characteristic of her earliest essays was *An Enquiry into the Nature of Jesus*, in which she advanced the heretical view that the Gospels told the tale, not of a God on earth, but rather of "a struggling, suffering, serving, praying man."

The crisis reached the boiling point when Annie found she could no longer accept Communion from her husband in church: her sense of decency recoiled from participating in such an act when inwardly it held no meaning for her. When the critical moment in the services arrived, she felt in the end compelled to get up from her front-row pew and leave the church.

Frank Besant was not inclined to tolerate the visible repudiation of his role by his wife. He issued an ultimatum: either accept the proper function of her position, or depart his domicile. Because she could not bring herself to "live a lie," Annie chose the latter course. After six years of marriage, she set out for London with her three-year-old daughter Mabel. Nineteenth-century English law made no provision for divorce, but Annie marked her new life with a change in the pronunciation of her name. Instead of Annie Be*sant*, after the fashion of Frank, henceforth she would be known to the world as Annie *Be*sant.

Within a year of her separation from her husband, Besant had met and made common cause with Charles Bradlaugh. Tall and robust, with a broad forehead and noble bearing, Bradlaugh was the son of a laborer, born and raised in a working-class suburb of London. Within a month of their acquaintance, he hired her as a contributor to his journal of ideas, *The National Reformer.* Her columns appeared under the pen name of Ajax, the warrior in the *Iliad* who pleaded for light, even though it was sure to expose him to his enemies.

Bradlaugh had formed the National Secular Society (NSS) in 1868 in an effort to give sinew and muscle to the loose amalgamation of views known as free-thought. The principles of popular free-thought in Britain were never set forth in any systematic fashion, but the movement claimed as its primary heritage Thomas Paine's *The Rights of Man.* The NSS was designed to give voice to points of view that orthodox society sought to suppress from consideration altogether.

Besant chose as the subject of her first public address, "The Political Status of Women." She began by holding up for inspection the arguments that served to deny women the right to vote. The spirit of Thomas Paine slept well the night Annie, at age twenty-six, took those arguments as her adversaries:

> It can scarcely be necessary for me to clear my way by proving to you that there are such things as rights....These rights do not rest on the charter of a higher authority; they are not privileges held at the favour of a superior; they have their root in the nature of man.

Besant burst upon the consciousness of England in 1876, after a bookseller in Bristol was arrested for the sale of obscene literature. The volume in question was the first authoritative source of information for a general audience on the subject of birth control. It was a pamphlet of some forty pages, composed in 1830 by Thomas Knowlton, a physician practicing in Massachusetts.

Knowlton had framed his topic from a broad perspective: he said that human health depends upon the exercise of a philosophical intelligence. He called his work *Fruits of Philosophy*; it was subtitled *The Private Companion of Young Married Couples*. Knowlton described the anatomy and physiology of the reproductive organs before turning to the available techniques for preventing conception. He concluded that the reproductive instinct "cannot be mortified with impunity.... A temperate gratification promotes the secretions, and the appetite for food; calms the restless passions; induces pleasant sleep; awakens social feeling, and adds a zest to life which makes one conscious that life is worth preserving."

Fruits of Philosophy surfaced in England when a bookseller named Henry Cook interwove among its pages some illustrations and advertisements. Cook was arrested on charges that the volume was obscene. He was convicted and sentenced to prison with hard labor for two years.

Bradlaugh and Besant regarded this event as an important violation of the freedom of the press. They brought out Knowlton's pamphlet under a new imprint, The Freethought Press. They delivered a copy of the fresh edition of *Fruits of Philosophy* to the local police, along with a letter announcing their intention to make it available for sale at a specified time and place. A warrant for their arrest followed in short order.

The Solicitor-General for the Tory Government presented the case for the prosecution in a two-hour opening address. He said that *Fruits of Philosophy* contained "a series of paragraphs, one following upon another, each involving some impure practice, some of them of the most filthy and disgusting and unnatural description it is possible to imagine." The passages in question turned out to be those that Knowlton had devoted to methods for preventing pregnancy. The recommended techniques included "withdrawal immediately before emission," and "the baudruche, which consists in a covering used by the male, made of very delicate skin."

Bradlaugh deferred to Besant to speak in their defense. At twenty-nine years of age, she was the first woman to act in that capacity in English jurisprudence. She began by acknowledging the powers that had been assembled against her; and she added, "I might feel less hopeful of success did I pretend to rival the learned solicitor-general in legal knowledge, in force of tongue, or in skill of dialectic. But, gentlemen, I do not rely on these: I rely on a far mightier power; I trust to the goodness of my cause."

Besant began by asserting that she was acting as "counsel for the poor… and it is they for whom I defend this case. My clients are scattered up and down through the length and breadth of the land…." She then turned to the circumstances that made information on birth control so vital. She explained the reasoning of Malthus, who demonstrated that population tends to increase exponentially unless and until its expansion is "checked" by one means or another. She described in graphic terms the effects of overcrowding in the poorest districts of London, where the mortality rate for young children was ten percent, and she wove these statistics into a detailed rebuttal of the prosecution.

Besant presented her case for two and a half days. Most of her listeners considered her arguments eloquently expressed and unerringly accurate in exposing the flaws in the solicitor-general's case. Nevertheless, the jury returned with a finding that "the book in question is calculated to deprave public morals."

The Chief Justice sentenced the defendants to six months in

prison and to fourteen hundred pounds in fines, but he allowed them to defer serving their sentence pending the outcome of their appeal. The appeals court held that the indictment had not been drawn up to form, and on that basis the conviction was overturned. Bradlaugh and Besant resumed publication and sale of *Fruits of Philosophy*, but the prosecution against them was not renewed.

Annie Besant was the first woman on any continent to speak out publicly on behalf of birth control. In the three-month interval between her arrest and her trial, *Fruits of Philosophy* sold 125,000 copies. The case of the Queen vs. Bradlaugh and Besant was followed closely by newspapers throughout the land, and a subject that had been all but forbidden to public discussion was suddenly accessible for consideration. In the aftermath of the trial, the birth rate in England fell by twelve percent.

Besant's assumption of the platform for the National Secular Society coincided with a sustained growth in its membership. From a scattered few hundred in 1874, its rolls exceeded a thousand by 1876, and rose to six thousand by 1880. Her topics were not confined to women's issues, but formed a virtual catalog of free-thought interests. Among the issues she tackled were "Labor and Land," a series of lectures on economic policies and their impact on the poor. British colonial policies also caught her attention: she spoke on "Why the Tory Government Gags the Indian Press" and "Coercion in Ireland and its Results."

Besant's oratory was distinguished not only by the range of her topics and the depth of her perceptions, but by the power of her speech itself. She could hold forth in Queen's Hall, packed with three thousand listeners, and make herself heard by all without amplification. Beatrice Webb described the quality of Annie's voice as neither feminine nor masculine; it was rather, she said, "the voice of a beautiful soul." George Bernard Shaw's estimate of her stature in 1885 was not qualified by references to her gender:

"She was at that time the greatest orator in England, and possibly in Europe."

Throughout the phases of her career, Besant's outlook was animated by a common theme: the drive to secure a firm foundation for a new social order. Such a foundation had to couple a convincing worldview with some practical program for man's regeneration. When Christianity could not meet these standards, she turned to free-thought, to the growing achievements of science, and to materialistic philosophy. In 1889, at the age of forty-two, she had exhausted every available vein of theory, knowledge, and philosophical outlook, and none of them satisfied her craving for something comprehensive and profound. At that moment, perhaps one of vulnerability, a complex and contradictory seed was planted in her mind. The seed was Theosophy, and it took root and flourished there like no other ever had or would.

When the editor of a London newspaper asked Annie to review *The Secret Doctrine,* she was already somewhat familiar with theosophical ideas. Nevertheless, the effect of the work upon her was electric. Fantastic and bizarre, *The Secret Doctrine* was of a piece with everything else in Blavatsky's life and career. The book consists of a series of commentaries on a volume not known to Western civilization, *The Stanzas of Dzyan,* composed in the unknown language of Senzar. The commentaries unfold through two volumes. *Cosmogenesis* presents an account of the basic constituents of the universe and of its development through eons of time. *Anthropogenesis* describes the elements of human nature and how they have emerged through the stages of evolution. Besant's review of the book was favorable, and she requested an audience with the author, then residing in London.

If Besant was impressed with the book, there was something in the personality of Helena Blavatsky that she found even more captivating. Blavatsky warned Annie about her own tarnished reputation. She gave her a copy of a recent report on the Coulomb affair, an exposé of phony "phenomena" Blavatsky had exhibited at her offices in Madras. Besant weighed the evidence described in the report against the person of Madame Blavatsky and found the author far more compelling and convincing.

Besant's transition from the NSS to the Theosophical Society marked the end of her career as an agent of change on a relatively local stage. Henceforth the audience she addressed would not be confined to the English. The object of her attention would be the whole of humanity; and the Theosophical Society, whatever its original intention, became the vehicle for the message she uniquely fashioned.

Chapter Three

THE ORDER OF THE STAR

Among the major rivers of the south of India, the Adyar flows to the east. It empties into the Bay of Bengal just below Madras, some two hundred miles north of the tip of the subcontinent. Adjacent to Madras on its southern side lies the suburb of Adyar, which marks the point where the fresh water meets the sea. There, in 1882, Helena Blavatsky and Henry Olcott purchased Huddlestone's Gardens, twenty-seven acres of beachfront land, and declared it the international headquarters of the Theosophical Society.

In 1884, Blavatsky brought to Adyar an English priest named Charles Webster Leadbeater. Then thirty years of age, Leadbeater had abandoned his parish in London on three days' notice in order to pursue his fascination with the occult world. But Madame Blavatsky, who held the keys to that world, left him behind in Adyar to do work of a more mundane nature. Leadbeater had a gift for answering the correspondence that arrived from all parts of the globe. Inquiries ranged from the personal to the paranormal to advanced points of theosophical doctrine. To answer them appropriately was an art that required a skilled pen, familiarity with theosophical literature, and an ear for the right tone and individual touch. Leadbeater coupled these qualities with a driving energy that enabled him to work long hours for slender rewards.

Leadbeater's apprenticeship lasted four years. When he returned to London, he was engaged as a tutor for the sons of two prominent theosophical families. After a time he began to divulge that while in India he had come into personal contact with the Masters of Wisdom; in fact, one of the Masters had given him detailed guidance in the exercise of occult powers of investigation. The recommended procedure bore a marked resemblance to allowing the imagination to run free; but Leadbeater claimed he had been instructed in how to distinguish extrasensory data from ordinary fantasy, preconceived ideas, and dreams.

Leadbeater's detached attitude and detailed observations lent an air of authenticity to his occult discoveries. His publications in this field were prodigious, and his topics ranged from the structure of the atom to the fate of the cosmos. Among the most popular of his works was a treatise on psychology, *Man: Visible and Invisible*. The book included color plates illustrating the astral body, a cocoon of subtle energy that surrounds the individual and changes color according to the person's emotional state.

Helena Blavatsky, overweight and a heavy smoker, died of the flu in 1891 at the age of sixty. After her death, Annie Besant and Charles Leadbeater assumed responsibility for the Esoteric Section, the all-important occult core of the Theosophical Society, and they each wrote and lectured extensively in Europe and America on theosophical themes. While not of Annie's caliber as an orator, Leadbeater was cogent, charismatic, and tireless. By virtue of their combined efforts, sustained year after year, enrollment in the Society began to swell. Branches of the TS were formed throughout the world, and the internationalist principles of the organization assumed a growing measure of concrete reality.

Besant and Leadbeater's collaboration had matured for over a decade when a charge surfaced that shook the Society to its foundations. Two American teenage boys independently leveled similar accusations: they claimed that while traveling under Leadbeater's care, he had introduced them to the practice of masturbation. The scandal convulsed the TS. President Olcott, now seventy-five years old, conducted an investigation, quasi-judicial in form. Under examination, Leadbeater admitted that he advocated recourse to masturbation for adolescent boys. He understood that his views in the matter were not consistent with theosophical tenets, much less with those of society at large. Nevertheless, he maintained, boys who had no access to this outlet were often consumed with impure desires. As one responsible for the boys and clairvoyantly sensitive to their thoughts, Leadbeater felt it was better to allow them the occasional discharge of energies.

In a letter to Besant, Leadbeater defended himself and described more fully his point of view:

> There is a natural function in the man, not in itself shameful (unless indulged at another person's expense) any more than eating or drinking…. The accumulation takes place, and discharges itself at intervals—usually a fortnight or so, but in some cases much oftener, the mind in the latter part of each interval being constantly oppressed by the matter.
>
> The idea was to set the habit of the regular, but smaller, artificial discharges, with no thoughts at all in between. The recommendation was always to lengthen the interval so far as was compatible with the avoidance of thoughts or desire on the subject.
>
> So when boys came under my care I mentioned this matter to them among other things, always trying to avoid all sorts of false shame, and to make the whole appear as natural and simple as possible, though, of course, not a matter to be spoken of to others.

As a result of the scandal, the investigation, and the embarrassing publicity, Leadbeater resigned from the TS; in so doing, he spared Colonel Olcott the unpleasant duty of having to expel him. A year later, however, Olcott died in his home at the theosophical compound in India; his ashes were scattered in the Adyar River. At his request, Besant assumed the presidency of the Theosophical Society in 1907. Among her early acts in that capacity was to reinstate Charles Leadbeater. Her action had to be ratified by a governing board, but she succeeded in securing the necessary votes. Eighteen months after Besant became president, Leadbeater assumed a position under her direction at the Society's beachfront compound in Adyar.

Besant's loyalty to Leadbeater may have been based in part upon a certain inadequacy she perceived in herself. She claimed little facility for what she called "occult science." She maintained that expertise in this area was much like that in any other: it required natural aptitude as well as long hours of practice. On occasion she did acknowledge receiving instructions from the Masters in her dreams, but she relied upon others for reports of most events in non-physical realms. In the years following the death of Blavatsky, the person to whom she turned increasingly for this purpose was Charles Leadbeater.

Besant's own topics on the theosophical platform were rooted in present actualities. She described the existing state of affairs in science, religion, and in civilization as a whole. Her analysis proceeded from an historical perspective in which the successive epochs of man were seen as a unified development, tending toward a more advanced form of society.

Not until she became the acknowledged leader of the TS, however, did Besant unveil the centerpiece of her theosophical outlook. She took the esoteric vision of Blavatsky and adapted it to more worldly purposes. She introduced into the heart of Theosophy the idea that one of the members of the spiritual hierarchy periodically manifests on Earth in human form. Borrowing from the Buddhists, the theosophists called this individual the Lord Maitreya.

In his earthly episodes, Maitreya was designated the World Teacher. The appearances of the teacher, Besant explained, were governed in part by events in world history: when mankind was entering a period of crisis, the teacher came to offer guidance and stability. Since just such a period was approaching, she said, another visit of Maitreya was at hand. To prepare the world for this event, in fact, was the underlying purpose of the Theosophical Society. More-over, she maintained, the TS would facilitate the process by finding and preparing a suitable "vehicle"—a body and spirit sufficiently refined for Maitreya to enter into and adopt as his own.

Besant's reconstruction of Theosophy catapulted the organiza-tion out of a passive posture and made it the instrument of her activ-ist agenda. Her radical change of course was not achieved without a price: Rudolph Steiner broke with the Society over this issue and took with him many of the German members of the TS; these became the nucleus of his Anthroposophical Society. Even a figure of Steiner's dimensions, however, was no match for Annie's resourcefulness and determination. She and Leadbeater began scouting for a vehicle for Maitreya from the moment of her assumption of the presidency.

On assuming his post at Adyar, Leadbeater had at his disposal the services of a young amanuensis, Ernest Wood. An entrepreneurial success in England at an early age, Wood later became an author and educator in his own right, and he brought a somewhat independent eye to events at Adyar. His attitude toward Leadbeater was at once sympathetic and skeptical. According to Wood, Leadbeater's work day began every morning at six-thirty and continued until late at night. His correspondence was voluminous, as were his publications of his occult observations. He often gave dictation while walking barefoot around the room, and he became so absorbed in his work that he scarcely paused or noticed when he stubbed his toe to the point of drawing blood. So exacting was he in his attitude toward the written word that he corrected the punctuation in the popular novels that he read for relaxation.

In the late afternoons, Leadbeater, Wood and two other assistants often took an hour off to go for a swim in the Bay of Bengal. There they encountered some of the children of the residents of the TS compound, playing on the beach. One day early in 1909, Leadbeater told Wood that one of the boys on the beach had "a remarkable aura," with no trace of self-centeredness.

Wood published an account of this conversation half a century later, based upon a mixture of notes and recollection. The boy whom Leadbeater singled out for attention was fourteen-year-old Krishnamurti, the son of Narianiah, who was employed in a secretarial capacity by the TS. Wood was familiar with Krishna: he was among several boys whom Wood helped with their homework in the evenings. He conveyed these facts to Leadbeater; and he added that he considered Krishna "not one of the bright students."

Leadbeater's interest was undimmed. He declared that one day Krishnamurti would become a spiritual teacher and "a great speaker."

Wood was accustomed to Leadbeater's gift for remarkable assertions, but the idea that Krishna would be a great speaker was so unlikely that he could not let it pass uncontested. He challenged it by invoking an impossible standard for comparison. "How great?" he inquired. And he added, rather mischievously, "As great as Mrs. Besant?"

According to Wood's account, Leadbeater replied, "Much more."

When Leadbeater made his prediction about the boy on the beach, there was little in Krishna's behavior that could have recommended him for special attention. He was known for an expression that others interpreted as vacant or dreamy. At the school that he and his younger brother attended in Madras, Krishna was subjected to corporal punishment, administered with a cane, for inattention. He was not allowed to carry money, as he tended to give it away to anyone he encountered less fortunate than himself.

From his earliest childhood, academic studies held no particular interest for Krishna. According to his father, he much preferred to spend his time in observation of the natural world. He refused to attend school one day when he became absorbed in the workings of a clock he had taken apart. So fascinated was he that he would not eat throughout the day until he had succeeded in putting it back together again. When he was older, he liked to climb each evening to the top of a rocky hill some two miles distant from his house. There he could command the finest view of the surrounding countryside. From an intricate inner mechanism to a broad panorama, there was from the beginning the passion to observe things directly, to see for oneself.

In later life, Krishnamurti described one of his very few memories from his childhood:

> As a young boy, he used to sit by himself under a large tree near a pond in which lotuses grew; they were pink and had a strong smell. From the shade of that spacious tree, he would watch the thin green snakes and the chameleons, the frogs and the watersnakes. His brother, with others, would come to take him home.
>
> To the pond would come snakes and occasionally people; it had stone steps leading down to the water where grew the lotus. The long, thin, green snake was there that morning; it was delicate and almost hidden among the green leaves; it would be there, motionless, waiting and watching.

When Besant arrived in Adyar in November 1909, Krishna and Nitya were with the party who met her at the train station. Krishna had a garland of roses to place around her neck, and later that afternoon the two brothers were formally introduced to her by Leadbeater. She remained in Adyar until mid-December, and the boys visited with her every day.

Almost at once, Besant assumed the role of mother to the two boys, who had lost their own four years earlier. She did so by means of sustained attention and an enveloping atmosphere of care. Her commitments entailed a great deal of travel, but she arranged for the boys to accompany her whenever possible. During long journeys she often sat with them, told them stories, and held their hands. Krishna's first letter to her, a few weeks after they met, opens with, "My Dear Mother, Will you let me call you Mother when I write to you?" In all their subsequent correspondence, he addressed her as Amma, the Tamil term for mother.

On January 12, 1910, Besant wrote to Leadbeater her recollections of the previous night's activities on the astral plane: it was now "definitely fixed" that Krishna was to become the vehicle for the next manifestation of the Lord Maitreya. Available evidence does not permit any objective assessment of what factors or observations persuaded Besant that Krishna was the appropriate choice. The salient qualities were presumably not intellectual but spiritual in nature. Other adolescents were considered candidates for the role, including Hubert van Hook from Chicago, in whom considerable confidence had been invested. The nomination of Krishna originated with Leadbeater's intuitive or clairvoyant perception of the absence of self-centeredness, but Besant could not have relied exclusively upon Leadbeater or any occult sources for so crucial a decision. All we can say with confidence is that she visited with Krishna daily for three weeks before she settled upon her choice, and she must have assessed him closely and with great care. Whatever she observed evidently impressed her with a profound conviction of the correct course of action.

The ramifications that followed, like ripples in a pond, extended in every direction. The vehicle had to be prepared to receive the charged and refined energy of supreme intelligence. Two companions or guardians had to accompany Krishna to protect him wherever he went. The right education and careful exposure to culture and society were essential, and the body had to undergo its own preparation. A vegetarian diet and plentiful exercise were prerequisites. Leadbeater believed that physical objects can absorb and communicate emotional energies, so no one was allowed even to touch Krishna's bicycle or tennis racket.

When the brothers were not traveling with Annie, she left them in Leadbeater's care. He concerned himself with their academic achievement, emotional development, physical prowess, manners, and health. He employed a reverse psychology with regard to expressions of desire: if the boys admitted a preference for porridge, then porridge is what they would have—every morning. If one of them said he would like to ride a bicycle, then both boys would have bikes and would ride them ten miles a day. One afternoon at the beach, Krishna shied away from a place where a hole in the ocean floor created a pocket of turbulence. Leadbeater led him back to the spot later that day and insisted that he swim in it until he had mastered it.

Leadbeater considered that Krishna's pierced earlobes were unsuited to Maitreya and must be sewn up. The face in particular was held to be of crucial significance. If his development proceeded along the right lines, it would be reflected in the beauty and symmetry of Krishna's features.

In March 1910, Narianiah signed over to Besant legal custody of the two brothers. Whether he was fully apprised of her intentions for Krishna subsequently became a matter of dispute. Of the force and effect of the documents he signed, however, there was no disagreement. She was now the boys' guardian by the lights of the law as well as by those of the heart.

Both before and after her assumption of the TS presidency, Besant's theosophical interests dovetailed with her ongoing involvement in practical affairs. In spite of her dissociation from the National Secular Society, her commitment to the principles of free-thought remained intact. After she left the NSS, however, her activities in this area focused on a single cause: nationhood for India.

In 1895, Besant published *The Means of India's Regeneration*, her blueprint for the development of India as a nation. Her strategy consisted of awakening a sense of national consciousness and later addressing the practical politics of the matter. Following her first visit in 1893, Besant spent half of every year for twenty years in India. Her aim was to recall to the Indian mind the depth and beauty of the Hindu culture. Public talks and the print media, as always, were her metier.

After two decades spent cultivating the consciousness of the nation, Besant judged that India was ready for a shift of gears. A new emphasis appeared in her public pronouncements regarding nationhood. Her publications in 1913 included *Wake Up, India; India and the Empire;* and *The Future of Young India.* These were followed the next year by *India: A Nation; The Birth of New India;* and *The Case for India.* Her final volume in this series was *India's Hour of Destiny.*

When she inaugurated The National Home Rule League in 1915, Besant found the point at which she pushed too far. Since 1885 the colonial government had tolerated an annual convention called the Indian National Congress, but it survived only because it was unwilling to rock the British boat. The organization Besant founded was far more provocative in its concept and intention. The British government was sufficiently alarmed to warn that she risked internment if she did not cease and desist in her efforts on behalf of Indian "home rule."

Although she took steps to comply with the government's demands, Besant was apprehended in April 1917 and held in confinement at a remote mountain location south of Madras. The cold and isolation caused her health to deteriorate, and the internment inflamed public sympathies throughout India. A letter addressed to President Woodrow Wilson, signed by a prominent Indian intellectual, described some of the worst characteristics of British rule in

India, including the confinement of Besant. The letter called upon Wilson to make inquiries and prevail upon the government of Lloyd George. Shortly thereafter, Annie was released and a marked liberalization of policies (the Montagu-Chelmsford Reforms) issued forth from London.

In the year following her internment, Besant was elected President of the Indian National Congress—an extraordinary honor for any woman, much less a citizen of Great Britain.

Besant's efforts on behalf of nationhood for India were ultimately eclipsed by those of Indians. She did not subscribe to Gandhi's call for nonviolent confrontation; she saw within it the seeds of violence, in spite of its professed ideal. Nevertheless, she and Gandhi regarded one another with respect and admiration. It was she who bestowed upon him the title Mahatma (Great Soul) that now seems inseparable from his name.

As early as 1911, Besant had foreseen the need for an organizational structure designed to facilitate the introduction of the World Teacher to the world. Membership would be for those who wished to prepare themselves to receive his message. In that year she inaugurated the Order of the Star in the East for this purpose. A star in the east is not yet overhead and so expresses the intention to look forward to the teacher's impending arrival.

The Order was initiated along with a journal, the *Herald of the Star*. Besant named herself and Leadbeater the Protectors of the Order, and designated Krishna as its Head. Throughout the war years, the international membership enjoyed a steady growth. Two years after its inauguration, the Order included fifteen thousand members; by the end of the war, that number had doubled and now rivaled the rolls of the Theosophical Society itself.

Krishna's formal education consisted largely of tutorial instruction in the homes of wealthy theosophists in England. In 1921, Besant determined that his period of academic preparation was over, and the time had come for him to take a more active part in the affairs of the Order of the Star in the East. As a first step in this process, he began to compose monthly editorial columns for the *Herald of the Star*. With his first article, readers might have discerned the distant rumble of the storm of inward revolution. In his opening words, Krishna asked bluntly what the Order had accomplished in its ten years of existence. In his own view, "We have done extraordinarily little." He said the Order had been for years in "a state of coma," notwithstanding an abundance of members and enthusiasm. The time had come, he said, to begin to wake up:

> Let us assume that many of us have shaken off our lethargy and are willing to look at facts in all their nakedness. One great difficulty is that we are personal in every thought and in every action. Our body and soul are so saturated with our personal desires and dislikes that at last we see every object that surrounds us with eyes that are scarcely worthy of being called eyes. We are so blind that we cannot see ourselves, and through the veil which we have created, the healing sunshine can never pierce.

In 1924, the Baron Philip von Pallandt donated to The Order of the Star in the East a five thousand-acre tract of wooded land in Holland. The property featured a well-preserved eighteenth-century manor known as Castle Eerde. This became the international headquarters for the Order and the site of the annual Star Camps, at which members gathered from around the world.

Krishnamurti's talks at the successive Star Camps offer the surest insight into the development of his point of view. The contrast between his outlook and the established doctrines of Theosophy became increasingly apparent from one year to the next. The third annual Star Camp in July 1926 was attended by some two thousand members from all parts of the world. It was the first camp to occur after the death of Nitya. The highlight of each day was a huge bonfire in the evenings at which Krishnamurti gave short talks. That year the theme of his talks revolved around what he called "the kingdom of happiness." He said that this state of mind could be reached only through the intelligent understanding of oneself.

This perspective represented a deep departure from theosophical orthodoxy. Advancement along the Path, rather than happiness, was the aim of Theosophy; and finding favor with the Masters, rather than self-understanding, was the means. Not content to let the matter rest at that, Krishnamurti chided his audience for its attachment to symbols, and he challenged his listeners to show any actual effect of all their spiritual efforts. This challenge must have been disturbing to many theosophists, especially those in the Esoteric Section whose position, prestige, and authority were being called into question.

During one of these talks, a prominent member of the Esoteric Section was observed whispering into Besant's ear. Later that evening she confronted Krishnamurti in his room. She said she had been told that a false and evil magician had been speaking through him at the campfire. Krishnamurti knew what some of the theosophists were capable of, but he had not expected this from her. He met the accusation point-blank: he said if she truly believed that a magician with evil intent had been speaking through him, he would never speak in public again.

When faced in this manner with the full implication of what she had been saying, Besant backed away from her claim. A crisis of moral authority, however, was now spinning out of control. She had to make a choice that went well beyond the individuals involved: at stake were two increasingly incompatible world views. On one hand stood the whole edifice of Theosophy; on the other hand, there was the strangely disturbing message Krishnamurti was beginning to articulate. After the evil magician episode, it was no longer possible for her to pretend that she could subscribe fully to both.

Besant's first impulse, as she proposed in a letter to Leadbeater, was to resign from the Theosophical Society. But upon further reflection, she obeyed another urge: she would cancel all her engagements and accompany Krishnamurti wherever he went. His destination after the Star Camp was Ojai, so she decided she would go there as well. A lecture tour of America was arranged in which she would visit thirty cities in as many days. Her topics were the current state of affairs in India and the imminent advent of the World Teacher.

A throng of photographers was waiting at the dock in August 1926 when Besant, accompanied by Krishnamurti, arrived in New York City for the first time in twenty years. The next morning he took questions from a roomful of reporters at the Waldorf-Astoria Hotel. The *New York Times* wrote that many of those present "tried to trip him up with shrewdly worded questions; he skillfully avoided all these pitfalls and earned their admiration."

At the conclusion of her lecture tour, Besant arrived in Ojai in early October. It soon became apparent to her that Ojai represented a special opportunity, a place in which to plant the last important seed in her life's work. She had no funds to draw upon for the purpose, but she undertook to acquire two large parcels of land in and near the Ojai Valley. One was in the Upper Ojai, adjacent to the valley proper, where she acquired options on four hundred fifty undeveloped acres. The second piece was in the heart of the valley itself. There Besant staked her claim on two hundred acres of level land and gently rolling hills, with open fields alternating with groves of stately, gnarled oaks.

To complete the transactions, Besant needed to raise an amount on the order of eight million dollars in modern figures. She established an organization called The Happy Valley Foundation, designed to receive funds and administer them for her purposes. The property in the Upper Ojai was designated for a school, intended to run from kindergarten through college. The property in the valley itself was set aside for the work of the World Teacher. There he would give talks and hold annual gatherings, somewhat along the lines of the Star Camps at the Castle Eerde in Holland.

Besant's first appeal for funds appeared in the December issue of the *Herald of the Star*. This was followed by a long article and another appeal in the January 1927 issue of the *Theosophist*. The *Herald* issued a third appeal in March, and the *Theosophist* a fourth one in April. In her final request for donations, Besant wrote,

> I am risking on this new venture a reputation based on nearly fifty-three years of public work and all my financial future when I might, without discredit, at nearly eighty years of age, have had what the world would call an easy and pleasant life. And I do it joyfully.

Ultimately, the Happy Valley Foundation received sufficient funds to effect the acquisition of both pieces of property, albeit with a mortgage that stretched ahead for twenty years. But that time frame dwindled in significance in the context of a vision that encompassed laying the cornerstone for a new civilization.

During the course of seven months in Ojai, Besant had the opportunity to observe Krishnamurti at close quarters for extended periods of time. As she did so, she began to modify her conception of the relationship between Maitreya and the vehicle. She wrote to a friend, "J.K. is changing all the time, but it does not seem as though he stepped out and the Lord stepped in, more like the blending of consciousness."

Whatever her idea of the underlying process, Besant's assessment of the authenticity of the outcome grew more and more confirmed. By April 1927, she was ready to render an irreversible verdict. To underscore the clarity of her conviction, she took the step of issuing a statement to the Associated Press. Her message was broadcast around the world. "The Divine Spirit has once again descended upon a man, Krishnamurti," she declared. "The World Teacher is here."

If Besant had resolved for herself any lingering uncertainties regarding Krishnamurti, her statement to the Associated Press only fanned the flames of controversy within the Order of the Star in the East. By the time of the fourth annual Star Camp in 1927, curiosity, speculation, and a sense of free-floating expectancy had reached the boiling point. Everybody wanted to know once and for all the truth of the matter. Was Krishnamurti *really* the World Teacher? How could one know for sure?

Krishnamurti met the issue in a statement memorable for its directness. In the opening sentence of his first talk at the Star Camp that year, he put himself at arm's length from the cradle that had brought him to the platform from which he spoke:

> When I began to think for myself, which has been now for some years past, I found myself in revolt. I was not satisfied by any teachings, by any authority. I wanted to find out for myself what the World Teacher meant to me and what the truth was behind the form of the World Teacher.

He rephrased the issue in terms even more pointed for his audience. He suggested that the World Teacher was just a picture in their minds, an image they had created for themselves. He brought into sharp relief his listeners' preoccupation with that image by contrasting it with the attitude and perspective of the world at large. Implicit in this comparison was a description of the audience he intended to address in the future:

> The people of the world are not concerned with whether it is a manifestation, or an in-dwelling, or a visitation into the tabernacle prepared for many years, or Krishnamurti himself. What they are going to say is: "I am suffering, I have my

passing pleasures and changing sorrows—have you anything lasting to give?"

Krishnamurti was penetrating the question, going into its meaning, opening it up for inspection. In the process, the question began to lose its significance; but that served as no excuse to avoid a direct response. In language that had not been heard from him before—and would not be heard again—he made a clear affirmation.

> I could not have said last year, as I can say now, that I am the teacher; for had I said it then it would have been insincere, it would have been untrue. Because I had not then united the Source and the Goal, I was not able to say that I was the teacher. But now I can say it. I have become one with the Beloved. I have been made simple.

Although his answer was direct, Krishnamurti refused to allow his listeners any easy interpretation of what his affirmation might mean:

> You want Krishnamurti to be labelled, and in a definite manner, so that you can say, "Now I understand"—and then you think there will be peace within you. I am afraid it is not going to be that way. Can you bind the waters of the sea? I am not going to be bound by anyone. I am going on my way, because that is the only way.

Ultimately, therefore, after the years of preparation and the inevitable doubts, Krishnamurti assumed the office Besant had carved out for him. He did so, however, on terms so radical and austere as to threaten the very ground on which they stood. For the time being it was sufficient to mark the event by abbreviating the Order of the Star in the East to the Order of the Star; but the signs of the impending storm were now unmistakable.

Besant was prevented by illness from attending the fifth annual

Star Camp in the summer of 1928. Some observers believed her illness was psychological in origin; a few even suggested she had suffered a nervous breakdown. According to these rumors, her symptoms were precipitated by news of even more radical pronouncements expected from Krishnamurti. Whether her illness was in fact psychological can no longer be ascertained, but the evidence indicates otherwise. She had already faced and resolved this crisis. In any possible conflict between Krishnamurti and the Theosophical Society, she had chosen to stand with him.

Krishnamurti in fact spoke a language at the 1928 Star Camp even more hostile to religious authority than he had in the past. He emphasized that there was no room in his teaching for disciples or followers of any kind. He even held up for inspection the possibility of the dissolution of the Order of the Star. He said he had been urged by some friends to consider this course of action and that he had examined it with care. He said that whether the Order should continue depended on the uses to which it was put. If it could confine itself to mundane details of organizing talks and managing publications, it might continue to serve a useful function. But if it remained, as it had in the past, a focus for spiritual status, for advancing along the Path, then it had no place in his work.

Besant might indeed have swallowed with difficulty any talk of this kind, but the inference that it broke her health or affected her mental stability is not warranted by the facts. On the contrary, after hearing the account of what Krishnamurti actually said, she did all in her power to cooperate with his outlook. She took the decisive step that was the ultimate acknowledgment of the validity of his message: she shut down the entire structure—international in scope, transcendental in purpose—of the Esoteric Section of the Theosophical Society. In October 1928, Annie in Adyar wrote to Krishnamurti in Ojai to inform him of her action. "Beloved," she wrote, "I have done everything in my power to make a clear field for you. You are the only Teacher."

Even this act of renunciation, however, was not sufficient to still the storm of revolution brewing in Krishnamurti. It had been seven years since his experience under the pepper tree, and whatever dynamic was set in motion at that time had still not unfolded all its consequences. He had begun to articulate a message that was wholly original, and the primary test of any action or decision was whether it served to advance or to impede the clarity with which that message was received.

The same standard had to be applied even to the institution of the Order of the Star. After careful deliberation, it was evident to Krishnamurti that the effect of the Order on his listeners' ability to understand what he was saying was negative. Against that realization, the fact that the Order was the foundation of his work—an international network of support, stable financing, the very land from which he spoke—counted for little.

At the sixth international Star Camp in August 1929, Krishnamurti gave formal notice of the dissolution of the Order of the Star. His closest associates had been forewarned, and his audience of three thousand must have sensed what was coming. All that remained was to hear the manner of his explanation, the reasons he would offer, and any indication of the course of action he intended to pursue in the future.

His opening remarks could almost qualify as a biblical parable if they were not so wry and ironic.

> You may remember the story of how the devil and a friend of his were walking down the street, when they saw ahead of them a man stoop down and pick up something from the ground, look at it, and put it away in his pocket.
>
> The friend said to the devil, "What did that man pick up?"

"He picked up a piece of Truth," said the devil.

"That is a very bad business for you, then," said his friend.

"Oh, not at all," the devil replied. "I am going to let him organise it."

Perhaps this story originated with Krishnamurti himself. He followed it directly with the seminal statement of his point of view. When he said that truth is a pathless land, not only did he offer a diamond metaphor; but, in addition, he drove a stake through the heart of Theosophy, whose esoteric core consisted of nothing if not the Path.

> I maintain that Truth is a pathless land, and you cannot approach it by any path whatsoever, by any religion, by any sect. This is my point of view, and I adhere to that absolutely and unconditionally. Truth, being limitless, unconditioned, unapproachable by any path whatsoever, cannot be organised; nor should any organisation be formed to lead or to coerce people along any particular path... So that is the first reason, from my point of view, why the Order of the Star should be dissolved.

In no way, however, did this act entail any abdication of his work. To the contrary:

> I want to do a certain thing in the world and I am going to do it with unwavering concentration. I am concerning myself with only one essential thing: to set man free. I desire to free him from all cages, from all fears, and not to found religions, new sects, nor to establish new theories and new philosophies.

But he reserved the burden of his remarks for the indictment of every form of religious institution:

Organisations cannot make you free. No man from outside can make you free; nor can organised worship, nor the immolation of yourselves for a cause, make you free.... So why have an organisation?

You are accustomed to being told how far you have advanced, what is your spiritual status. How childish! Who but yourself can tell you if you are beautiful or ugly within? Who but yourself can tell you if you are incorruptible? You are not serious in these things.

So why have an organisation?

In his concluding remarks, he described the sense of deliberation with which he had arrived at the irrevocable:

For two years I have been thinking about this slowly, carefully, patiently, and I have now decided to disband the Order, as I happen to be its Head. You can form other organisations and expect someone else. With that I am not concerned, nor with creating new cages, new decorations for those cages. My only concern is to set men absolutely, unconditionally free.

The most immediate effect of the dissolution of the Order was the loss of the annual dues of its forty-five thousand members. In addition, many properties and trust funds had to be returned to their original owners. Except for the immediate area on which the annual camps were held, the Castle Eerde and the five thousand acres were returned to the Baron von Pallandt. Future talks on the land that remained would be open to the public at large. However, the trusts Besant had created for the properties in Ojai were designed to ensure that they could be retained for the continuation of Krishnamurti's work.

Beyond the financial ramifications, the deeper effects of the dissolution were psychological in nature. Many members of the TS could not reconcile to it. One leader of the Society told Emily Lutyens that Annie Besant must be "non compos" if she still believed that Krishnamurti was the World Teacher. At the annual TS convention in Adyar in December 1929, Charles Leadbeater would have little to do with Krishnamurti. Although outwardly friendly, he was letting it be known privately that the coming of the World Teacher had "gone wrong."

Annie Besant remained unperturbed by Krishnamurti's radical action. Far from feeling crushed or bereft, she worried instead for his welfare. Who would look after him now? How would he manage? What if all his audience disappeared? Only the depth of her love and respect for him gave her confidence for the future.

As for herself, she would have preferred to go where he went, to sit with his audience, and to absorb his evolving, maturing message. In the few years that remained to her, however, her activities were increasingly confined to the theosophical compound at Adyar. There her powers of perception gradually dimmed. After the dissolution of the Order of the Star, she was persuaded by the elders of the TS to reopen the Esoteric Section. This was, in a sense, a logical outcome of the fact that Krishnamurti no longer spoke for the TS in any capacity. In any case, there is little evidence that her final years were clouded by an awareness of the utter contradiction between the doctrines of Theosophy and the message of the one she called the World Teacher.

❧

Krishnamurti visited Besant for the last time at Adyar in May 1933. She lived by then in a land of deep shadow, but she did recognize him. He sat with her for a while and held her hand. "I brought you up," she said fondly, "didn't I?"

Annie ceased breathing in her sleep at four in the afternoon on September 20, 1933. The signs of her impending end were sufficiently clear that Charles Leadbeater had had time to sail in from Sydney. Next morning as the sun arose across the Indian Ocean, he lit the flame of her funeral pyre; it stood on the sands by the banks of the Adyar, where the waters of the river return to the limitless sea.

No one present thought or bothered to inform Krishnamurti of her death. The only notice he received occurred the following day, when he ran across the report that appeared in the pages of the *New York Times*.

Chapter Four

THE SEED OF AWARENESS

Annie Besant inaugurated The Order of the Star in the East for a single purpose: to facilitate the emergence and manifestation of the World Teacher. Krishnamurti was appointed Head of the Order, with plenary authority to determine its policies and the direction he intended to pursue. His dissolution of the Order was not without risk for him personally and for his mission in life, and it brought into focus a penetrating question: did he have the capacity to carry out anything like the task he had set for himself?

Reduced to its essential core, the mission of the World Teacher consisted of nothing less than the transformation of human consciousness. There was nothing partial or provisional about it. The act of dissolving the Order of the Star could easily have entailed or justified a corresponding abdication of the mission. Yet precisely the opposite occurred. Far from abandoning his role, Krishnamurti embraced it, although he did not describe it in those terms. Indeed, with the benefit of hindsight, one can see that the dissolution of the Order was in fact part and parcel of the role of the World Teacher. It marked not the end of his work, but the commencement of it.

The fact that Krishnamurti was assuming his mission, not abdicating it, is apparent by the whole of his subsequent career. It is also clear by the terms in which he described his action at the time. His stated intention was unequivocal: "My only concern is to set men absolutely, unconditionally free." This was not an assumption of the label or concept or outward form of the World Teacher; rather, it was a declaration of the essential substance of the work by which the teacher would be defined.

The nature and magnitude of the task Krishnamurti had embraced is not easy to bring into focus and perspective. The sheer audacity of the concept of World Teacher was somewhat astonishing in its own right. The fact that Annie Besant had seized upon this notion and elevated it to the pinnacle of her own career represented in itself a remarkable agenda. For any individual to move into such a role with graceful acquiescence was beyond any normal set of expectations.

But Krishnamurti's dissolution of the Order of the Star exceeded even these improbabilities. He entered into his role while simultaneously ending the very structure designed to enable him to achieve his mission. Given these circumstances as the point of departure for his work, a certain set of questions must arise. To what extent did he succeed in his herculean task? What resources did he draw upon, now that he had renounced or returned most of the assets that had been placed at his disposal? What form did his efforts take? Perhaps above all, what was the substantive content of his effort to transform consciousness? These are among the questions that must be considered and addressed.

Prior to the dissolution of the Order of the Star, Krishnamurti had at his disposal a wide network of individuals available and willing to assist him in any capacity. The necessary tasks included arranging his travel and accommodations, scheduling his public appearances, editing his talks for publication, raising funds, and writing for and publishing the journals supporting his work. After the Order was disbanded, these administrative tasks and functions devolved upon a single individual. Desikacharya Rajagopal was the son of a judge who was a devout member of the Theosophical Society. The father brought young Rajagopal to a theosophical convention where Leadbeater met him and declared him to be "one of our own." According to Leadbeater, Rajagopal had enjoyed an illustrious series of past lives and had an even more auspicious future, including a lofty position in the spiritual hierarchy on the planet Mercury.

In 1920, Rajagopal was sent by the elders of the TS to Cambridge, where he shared rooms with Nitya while he studied constitutional law and English history. His intellectual skills were considerable, and he obtained his degree without difficulty. He was sent to Ojai in 1924 to help look after Nitya and to assume some of the functions that he was unable to fulfill due to his illness. After Nitya's death, Rajagopal moved into an increasingly responsible role with the title of Organizer in Chief for the Order of the Star.

When he arrived in Ojai, Rajagopal befriended Rosalind Williams, who had been present from the first days that the brothers arrived in Ojai. He was twenty-four when they met and she was twenty-one. Her sister was a theosophist and a friend of the woman who had provided the property where Krishna and Nitya were staying. Rosalind was attractive and cheerful, and she moved into a supportive role in the care of Nitya right from the beginning. She was a witness to the events surrounding Krishna's experience under the pepper tree, and she became an integral part of the network of individuals associated with him.

Rosalind's presence in Ojai proved to be propitious for Rajagopal. In 1927, in a union blessed by Annie Besant, they married and commenced a relationship that defined, to some extent, the outward parameters of Krishnamurti's life for many years. Theirs was not a marriage by any normal or conventional standard, but it evidently served a vital economic and psychological function for them both;

and, in any event, it was widely regarded as a significant and enduring social reality.

Rosalind and Rajagopal established their home at Arya Vihara, the old ranch house on the eleven-acre property that included Pine Cottage. Besant had secured this property for Krishnamurti's work independently of the Order of the Star, and it became the terrestrial foundation for his career in America. Krishnamurti spent several months each year in Europe and India, and Rajagopal often traveled with him, but Rosalind maintained the domestic fires in Ojai for the three of them.

Rosalind gave birth to a daughter, Radha, in 1931. Rajagopal was traveling in Europe at the time and considered his obligations there more important than to be present at Radha's birth; and he expressed little interest in her when he returned to Ojai several weeks later. In fact, he announced to Rosalind that their conjugal relationship was now fulfilled and need not continue. Henceforth, he informed her, he would make his residence near his editorial offices in Los Angeles, although he would continue to visit Ojai on weekends. This turned out to be not a casual or impulsive pronouncement, but accurately predicted his subsequent behavior.

Rajagopal's decision regarding his living circumstances was consistent with other characteristics of his personality. He was fastidious to a fault and exacting in his expectations for others to conform to his standards for punctuality, cleanliness, and adherence to his rules and regulations. The crying at odd hours, changing of diapers, and other needs and behavior of a newborn were not at all compatible with his habits and preferences. His unusual temperament may also have contributed to his reluctance to engage in a sexual relationship. In any case, his abdication of the role of husband and father was unequivocal, notwithstanding the social fiction of a marriage.

Krishnamurti himself was not exempt from Rajagopal's

demands for close adherence to his schedules, logistical arrangements, and reporting requirements. One might imagine that Rajagopal would have adopted an attitude of deference and appreciation for the opportunity to serve the World Teacher. On the contrary, however, any deviation from his standards for performance was met with sharp criticism and assertions of authority that bordered on bullying. These patterns of behavior were established early on and continued, with increasing severity, for many years.

In 1933, two years after her daughter was born, Rosalind was thirty years old. Krishnamurti was sharing with her the property that had been his home for a decade. He had assumed substantial responsibility for the daily care and nurturing of Radha, especially in the absence of Rajagopal, who was rarely on the scene. These were the circumstances in which Krishnamurti, at age thirty-eight, entered into his first sexual relationship. His affair with Rosalind lasted for a decade and a half. The meaning of this relationship and the motivations of those involved were subsequently a matter of controversy; and what may have been beautiful in the beginning was later made ugly and used for corrupt purposes. But in 1933, all of that lay in the far distant future.

⌒

According to legend, Archimedes declared, "Give me a place to stand and a lever long enough, and I will move the world." Krishnamurti's home in Ojai and the support of the Rajagopals represented his place to stand with regard to his intention to move the consciousness of mankind. It was a slender platform for so lofty a goal, but it was sufficient for his purpose.

Of greater significance was the lever, the element in this analogy that Archimedes meant to highlight. In Krishnamurti's case, the lever consisted solely of his message. There would be no organization to speak of, no select body of followers, no ritual, ceremony, or hierarchical structure—nothing whatsoever beyond the content of the message he delivered from a public platform. That was the lever and nothing more, and everything depended upon the sum and substance of what he had to say.

During the decade of the 1930s, Krishnamurti took his message to almost every corner of the globe. He spoke in twenty-two nations, from Scotland to Scandinavia, in India and Pakistan, Australia and New Zealand, the United States and Canada, and several countries in South America. He spoke in London, Berlin, Athens, Buenos Aires, Sydney, Melbourne, Auckland, Rome, and Rio de Janeiro. In the United States alone he delivered talks four times in New York, twice each in Chicago and Seattle, as well as in San Francisco, Oakland, Minneapolis, St. Paul, Kansas City, Cleveland, Philadelphia, Rochester, Atlanta, Birmingham, and San Antonio. Including five series of talks in Ojai, he gave over six hundred public talks in all.

These talks were delivered with an absolute minimum of any element extraneous to the spoken word. There was no charge for admission; no one introduced him; nothing was for sale. All that occurred was a low platform on which was placed a single, simple, straight-backed chair, from which he delivered extemporaneous remarks for an hour or an hour and a half. The absence of any other element served to highlight the significance of the message itself.

Krishnamurti has often been called a spiritual teacher or a religious philosopher, but these designations fail to convey the actual content of his message. What he offered instead was a panoramic exposition of the psychological structure of the individual in his relationship with society at large. If his views could be translated into conventional disciplines of inquiry, they would fall largely within the parameters of psychology and sociology. One reason those disciplines cannot accommodate his message lies in their inherent tendency to divide and subdivide their subject matter, to categorize and qualify, to elevate differences over commonalities. Krishnamurti's perspective, by contrast, applied equally to all individuals in every culture or corner of the world.

The following description is drawn from a series of twelve talks given in Ojai in 1934, representing fifteen or twenty hours of discourse in all. The point of departure for Krishnamurti's exposition was the individual, considered without regard for his or her nationality, religion, status, or profession. The individual cannot be understood, however, in isolation from what he called "environment," the vast network of social, political, and economic forces that shape each human being. The environment represents a prison within which the individual struggles to conform, to find security, to succeed. To do so, however, represents little more than to decorate the walls of the prison, to yield to endless conflict, rather than to find a life of freedom, harmony, and creative action.

To this extent, Krishnamurti's message might have been expressed by a sociologist or political philosopher, although his language is more colorful than academic: Environment is "wealth, poverty, exploitation, oppression, nationalities, religions, and all the inanities of social life in modern existence." It continually molds the individual, and, as a result, "Life becomes a school, a frame, a steel frame, in which the individual is beaten into shape." Social organizations are based fundamentally on efforts to meet human needs, but

> ...our needs for shelter, food, and sex, which are simple, natural, and clean, have become complicated and made hideous, cruel, appalling by this colossal and ever-crumbling structure which we call society, and which man has created.

The plot thickens at the point where he looks more closely into the nature of the individual. He or she is little more than a reflection of the values and standards embedded in the environment.

The individual is merely the collection of "the various hopes, fears, longings, prejudices, likes, personal views which we glorify as our temperament," but which are in fact all reactions to the environment.

With these observations we are getting closer to the most characteristic features of Krishnamurti's philosophy. The essential nature of the individual includes what he called the "I-process," or "I-consciousness," the sense of identity or self. According to Krishnamurti, the individual's sense of identity is not in fact a living reality, but rather something constructed from memory. Identity, he maintained, is nothing but a "long scroll of memory," consisting of all the accumulated incidents that collectively represent the story of one's life.

Assigning the whole structure of identity to the province of memory is part of a larger and deeper distinction he drew between memory and what he called mind. Mind itself, unclouded by memory, is intelligence. It is undistorted perception, capable of seeing the true significance of the environment. Indeed, the keynote of the entire series of talks consists of the conditions that enable the full operation of intelligence. "So liberation or truth or God is the release of the mind, which is itself intelligence, from the burden of memory."

Such intelligence is the means by which the individual becomes free—not by resisting or escaping or overcoming the prison of the environment, but rather by "piercing," "penetrating," discovering for oneself its actual meaning and value.

> By questioning the environment and trying to understand its significance, we shall find out its true worth. Most of us are enmeshed, caught up in the process of trying to overcome, to run away from circumstances, environment; we are not trying to find out what it means, what is its cause, its significance, its value. When you see the significance, it means drastic action, a tremendous upheaval in your life....
>
> There is the family, the neighbor and the state, and by

questioning their significance you will see that intelligence is spontaneous, not to be acquired, cultivated. You have sown the seed of awareness and that produces the flower of intelligence.

Krishnamurti advocated what he called an experimental approach to the understanding of his message. In a more modern idiom, what he had in mind might better be described as empirical: the direct observation of events, an understanding rooted in facts, not theories or speculative ideas. In particular, he rejected any form of authority in the process of self-discovery. He reserved special scorn for "guides, Masters, systems.... They are the tricksters who become priests, exploiters, mediators, swamis, and yogis." The admonition against authority in the psychological field applied equally to what he had to say. Nothing was to be accepted on the basis of his role or reputation; only the individual's own understanding had any value whatsoever.

Nothing in these talks remotely resembled the principles and premises of the Theosophical Society. Rather than any focus on Masters of Wisdom or the Path of spirituality, Krishnamurti's point of view is secular, oriented toward the factual realities of the daily life of the individual and the structure of society. To be sure, he does acknowledge an unusual kind of god, one that is synonymous with truth, beauty, and creative intelligence. To that extent he merits the designation of religious philosopher; otherwise, his point of view is grounded in the here and now.

As the 1930s came to a close, it would have been reasonable to ask whether Krishnamurti had made good on his intention to set human beings free. A decade had elapsed since the dissolution of the Order of the Star, and sufficient time had passed to discern his strategy and prospects for achieving so audacious an aim. It would seem uncharitable to expect the full realization of his intention, but some degree of progress would not have been too much to expect.

Perhaps the best that can be said is that Krishnamurti had made a modest down payment on the promissory note he signed in 1929. He had demonstrated a dedicated willingness to pursue his aim, as well as the practical means to begin to carry it out. He had articulated a radical and original message, one that, if taken seriously, might well have eradicated some of the impediments to cooperation on a global scale.

On the other hand, it is doubtful that his efforts had actually produced any appreciable dent in the consciousness of the world. The impending outbreak of world war was hardly an auspicious indication of the fruit of his labors. Were it not for his evident passion to continue his endeavors, one might conclude that his efforts to date were in vain. But his passion to continue was in fact inextinguishable; and the only remaining questions were what form his efforts would take in the future, and with what effect.

Chapter Five

ALDOUS HUXLEY

From the age of fourteen until the end of his life, Krishnamurti rarely remained in one place for more than a few months at a time. By a rough calculation, his cumulative lifetime travel equaled fifty circumnavigations of the globe. The decade that followed the dissolution of The Order of the Star was no different in this respect than the decade that preceded it. With the advent of World War II, however, all of this travel came to a sudden stop. The global crisis required that he remain in one locale for an extended period, including four consecutive years during which he gave no public talks. As an exercise in controlled experimentation, this interval offers a unique opportunity to ascertain what Krishnamurti would do, and with what effects upon him, when deprived for several years of his primary mode of occupation.

Among the questions we might consider are whether Krishnamuri would suffer, or exhibit signs of dysfunction or depression, without the stimulation of an attentive audience. Alternatively, did he welcome the opportunity and greet these years of relative silence and solitude with a sense of relief? Perhaps of greater significance would be to explore what impact these years of lying fallow had upon the substance of his teaching. When he returned to the public platform, were there changes in his manner of expression, or any significant shift of emphasis, or even an entirely new set of insights? These are among the issues that this episode illuminates.

Our primary source of first-hand observations of this period is the memoir of Radha Sloss, the daughter of Rosalind and Rajagopal. Much of her book, published after Krishnamurti's death, served as an effort to communicate her parents' grievances, and she missed no opportunity to insert disparaging comments and innuendo about him. In spite of herself, however, her more direct and factual observations paint a portrait decidedly different than the negative caricature her parents preferred to convey.

The eleven-acre property in the east end of the Ojai Valley is not quite correctly described as a ranch, or a farm, or an estate, or a community, although it had elements of all of these. For lack of a better name, we can refer to it simply as the east end residence. Its structures included Pine Cottage and an office building, as well as the aged, elongated ranch house called Arya Vihara, and it was populated during the war years by a lively blend of helpers, visitors, animals, gardens, and groves. There were two cows and a goat, a coop for some seventy chickens, a set of beehives, a large and diversified vegetable garden, and a dozen varieties of fruit trees. At one time or another, Radha looked after geese, ducks, possums, two dogs, a cat, a tanager, and a flock of turkeys. Rosalind was the dominant personality on the premises, the one who managed daily operations, bonded with the guests, cultivated the gardens, and contributed a sense of domesticity to the enterprise.

Among the various adults in her life, Radha reports that Krishnamurti was "definitely the most fun." He never failed to exhibit the desired expressions of shock and surprise when she played pranks on him, from frogs in his bed to pails of water dropped on his head while he passed underneath the tree where she was hiding. He walked with her to and from the school bus stop each day, but he did so from behind a wall that ran parallel to the street so that she would not feel monitored or embarrassed by his presence. He looked after her in every respect and filled the role of father that Rajagopal had abdicated.

Krishnamurti participated without reservation in the daily chores, manual labor, and menial tasks required to keep the residence running smoothly. He had no compunctions about washing dishes, cleaning out the chicken coop, or collecting cow patties for the compost heap. He joined in games of hide and seek with the children and Monopoly or poker with the adults after dinner. He maintained a regular schedule—rising early, afternoon walks, bedtime at nine o'clock—and kept his Patek Philippe pocket watch accurate to the second. Radha remembers him as the one who laughed most often and easily, rarely quarreled, and tended to fade into the background at social events. He blended so thoroughly into the affairs of daily life that those around him were able to forget his reputation and his mission. Rosalind in particular, according to Radha, never regarded him in the role of World Teacher, no matter how many of his public talks she attended.

Krishnamurti's regular round of activities included long walks alone into the foothills adjacent to the east end residence. A path behind the property led up into Horn Canyon, where it crossed a stream several times as it ascended through sagebrush and ceanothus to an elevation of five thousand feet. There it reached the peak of Topa Topa Bluff. By setting out early in the morning, one could attain the summit by midday, admire the view of the valley below, and return home by nightfall. Vivid recollections of scenes from these walks, including encounters with bobcats and rattlesnakes, are scattered throughout Krishnamurti's nature writing. He later remarked that he sometimes completed walks of this kind without a single thought arising through the entire journey.

In spite of his unassuming demeanor, Krishnamurti's presence was the magnet that drew a steady stream of visitors and guests. Some of these had prominent or colorful reputations of their own.

Beatrice Wood, the celebrated ceramicist, moved to Ojai and settled into a home and workshop near the east end residence. Her bohemian personality and lifestyle and her innovative artwork earned her the title Mama of Dada, and she became a close and lifelong friend of Rosalind. Iris Tree was an English poet, artists' model and actress who also relocated to Ojai during the war and became a familiar member of the company around Krishnamurti. At the age of nineteen, she served as the model for a naturalistic nude portrait by Modigliani, leaning against a sofa with her delicate face, eyes closed, resting demurely on her shoulder. Tree acted for many years in a repertory theater company she established in Ojai that featured plays by Shakespeare and Chekhov. She had roles in several motion pictures, including an appearance as herself in Fellini's *La Dolce Vita*.

Among others who sought out Krishnamurti during these years were Bertrand Russell, Alan Watts, Greta Garbo, and Igor Stravinsky. Perhaps the most illustrious of those whose presence Krishnamurti attracted, and the one with whom he formed the strongest bond, was Aldous Huxley. Huxley and his wife Maria had immigrated to Southern California in 1937 in advance of the gathering war clouds in Europe. The friendship he formed with Krishnamurti was deep and enduring, and it earned him a place of honor among those most instrumental in the unfolding course of his career.

With the heritage of Thomas Henry Huxley and Matthew Arnold in his veins, Aldous was cut from cloth of an unusual texture. His intellectual gifts were a given, and what complemented these most admirably were his personal qualities. He seemed to radiate an air of generosity; quarrelling was not in his repertoire. Coupled with his congeniality, however, was the attitude of the detached observer of human affairs.

When Aldous was fifteen, his family determined that his vocation lay in the field of medical research. His studies at Eton were interrupted when an inflammation of both corneas persisted for weeks without effective diagnosis or treatment. When the illness reached its peak, Aldous could see nothing at all; and when the infection faded away, patches of opacity remained. He was able to make out the printed page only with his right eye.

One effect of the loss of vision was to end all thought of medicine as a career. Huxley graduated from Oxford, where he was drawn inexorably to literary pursuits. During his twenties he published three volumes of poetry and two novels, sophisticated parodies of the aristocratic echelons in which he moved. He enjoyed his first big success at the age of thirty-four with *Point Counter Point*, a dramatization of the intellectual life of 1920s London.

By his mid-thirties, Huxley had exhausted the resources of English society as a subject for his observations, and a sea change occurred in his outlook. He turned his attention away from acidic sketches of his contemporaries and toward the tendencies inherent in civilization as a whole. Partially deprived of sight, Huxley became a seer; and the result, composed in four months in 1931, was *Brave New World*.

In Huxley's nightmare vision of the future, children are trained by electric shock to despise flowers in order to prepare them to work their entire lives underground. Intelligence is a carefully regulated commodity, parceled out to embryos in test tubes. The resulting classes of individuals, from intellectual Alphas to lowly Epsilons, are all the better adapted to their work. The very calendar has been reconstructed to celebrate the virtues of a mechanistic society: the events described take place in the Year of Our Ford 632.

In Huxley's portrait of tomorrow, communism and capitalism are eviscerated with equal thoroughness and dispatch. Thrown into the mix is a conception of science as a kind of evil genie, all-powerful and entirely in the service of totalitarian impulses. With worldwide sales measured in the millions, *Brave New World* is considered among the most controversial and influential novels of the century;

and Huxley, author of forty-eight books, was nominated seven times for the Nobel Prize in literature.

Within a few months of arriving in Southern California, Huxley sent a hand-written letter to "The Secretary, Star Publishing Trust." "I should greatly appreciate an opportunity of seeing Mr. Krishnamurti," he wrote, and he asked "whether it would be possible for him to receive us" the following week. Krishnamurti himself replied several days later. He said he was away until the following month, but "it would give me great pleasure to meet you."

In a letter to Emily Lutyens, Krishnamurti described their first meeting: "Of course Huxley is what is called an intellectual but I don't think he is merely that. We talked about almost everything," and he added that Huxley and his wife would be coming to spend the day in Ojai the following week. And so began what may have been the closest friendship Krishnamurti ever formed. Born just a year apart, the two men both came of age in England; both were vegetarian and outspoken pacifists; and both were dedicated walkers, keenly sensitive to nature, with unconventional views and interests that encompassed global affairs and all of humanity.

The Huxleys' lives were intertwined throughout the war with those of Krishnamurti and Rosalind. They spent days at a time together, in Ojai or at the Huxleys' second home in nearby Wrightwood. The quality of relationship that developed between the two men is conveyed by three surviving letters from Huxley. One is dated March 1945 and addressed to "My dear Krishnaji," the form of affectionate regard employed by many of his friends. There is no way to prepare for the opening paragraph, and Huxley plunges in without hesitation:

> I think I ought to tell you that I have just received a letter from Miss Helen Boardman, accompanied by what she calls a 'psychiatric report', in which she sets out to prove that you are suffering from an advanced form of dementia praecox. I have returned the report to her address in Los Angeles with

an attached visiting card, on which I have said that it is of no interest to me.... But it is deplorable that the wretched woman should be bothering to send out such a thing to perfect strangers.

Having disposed of the immediate occasion for the letter, Huxley continues with casual familiarity:

I have finished my book [*The Perennial Philosophy*] and got the MS off to the publishers.... Maria's sister writes from France begging us on no account to throw anything away, when we think it is worn out. In a country where there is literally nothing and where there is little prospect of there being anything in substantial amounts for years to come, the most despised odds and ends will come in useful.

So tell Rosalind to keep Radha's outgrown garments and the household's outworn rags; when communications become easier, they may be a great boon for somebody who has nothing to wear out or grow out of.

Our best love to you all.
Ever yours,
Aldous.

Huxley wrote again a few months later from Wrightwood to extend an offer and invitation:

My dear Krishnaji,

We bought a cabin here some weeks ago and have come and gone at intervals since. But meanwhile another house has come up for sale, much better situated and with a finer view; so we have decided to acquire that instead.... which means that our present house will be available until such time as we sell it. So if you would like to make use of it during that period, you know very well how very happy we should be.

For those who, unlike the Americans, can still make

use of their legs, there are beautiful walks in the immediate neighbourhood; and by driving four or five miles one can get up to the Blue Ridge, at eight thousand feet or so, where there are splendid panoramas.... So do come, if you have nothing better to do.

> Ever yours affectionately,
> Aldous H.

The third letter, also from Wrightwood, was sent in January 1948, when Krishnamurti had been in India for three months. It covers four handwritten pages, with the last several lines entered perpendicularly into the left-hand margin.

My dear Krishnaji,

We got back here in November and have been very busy ever since. I hope to have my book [*Ape and Essence*] finished in another couple of months....

Meanwhile what a world we live in! Rosalind tells us you find India very sad—which I can well imagine. It has gone a stage further along the road of starvation than the rest of the world—but it will be caught up with pretty soon by the others. I was sent a book recently by Fairchild Osborne, the biologist—a study of the way man has abused and destroyed the natural resources of the world in which he lives....

How strange that we should be so much more conscious (once we have reached civilization) of the artificial problems we ourselves have fabricated than of the cosmic problems presented by the Nature of Things—more conscious of political and social relations than of the relations between man and Nature, material and spiritual....

> Maria joins me in sending best love.
> Yours affectionately,
> Aldous.

Krishnamurti's career as a writer originated in response to a suggestion put forth by Huxley. He experimented with some words on paper, and he showed Huxley the result. "Marvellous and unique" was the critical assessment: Krishnamurti had coupled luminous observations of nature with recollections of individuals who had come to seek his counsel. The result was the collection of pieces, eighty-eight in all, that appeared in the first of three volumes under the title *Commentaries on Living*.

In 1954, Huxley contributed a closely reasoned, ten-page foreword to *The First and Last Freedom*, Krishnamurti's second book brought out by a mainstream publisher, Harper & Brothers. In it, he locates Krishnamurti's philosophy within a broad framework of human endeavor. "Man is an amphibian," he begins, "who lives simultaneously in two worlds—the given and the home-made, the world of matter, life and consciousness and the world of symbols." He develops the role of symbols throughout history before turning to the meaning and significance of words and thought in Krishnamurti's philosophy. His exposition deftly explores many of the major avenues of the teachings and reveals his familiarity with their themes and terminology:

> Through choiceless awareness, as it penetrates the successive layers of the ego and its associated sub-conscious, will come love and understanding, but of another order than that with which we are ordinarily familiar. This choiceless awareness— at every moment and in all the circumstances of life—is the only effective meditation.

Huxley attended Krishnamurti's talks in Switzerland in 1961, and he called them "among the most impressive things I have ever heard. It was like listening to a discourse of the Buddha—such power, such intrinsic authority." The two men met again in Rome the following year. Huxley confided that he was suffering from cancer of the tongue, although he had not told anyone, not even his wife. He died several months later, on the day of the assassination of President Kennedy.

Many years later, Krishnamurti remembered Huxley in sharp detail, and he found an opportunity to reflect upon the nature of their relationship. In the passage that follows, he has assumed the persona of a third-party observer, someone who had once been friends with both Huxley and himself. What he calls "a strange relationship" is in fact a fair description of the essential qualities of friendship—affectionate, considerate, and nonverbal.

> Aldous Huxley... was a very serious man. I had met him several times with Krishnamurti in California, when his first wife was living, and often in London and Rome. He was an extraordinary man. He could talk about music, the modern and the classical; he could explain in great detail science and its effect on modern civilisation, and of course he was quite familiar with the philosophies, Zen, Vedanta and naturally Buddhism.
>
> To go for a walk with him was a delight. He would discourse on the wayside flowers and, though he couldn't see properly, whenever we passed in the hills of California an animal fairly close by, he would name it and develop the destructive nature of modern civilisation and its violence.
>
> We used to go for walks with Krishnamurti, who would help him to cross a stream or a pothole. These two had a strange relationship with each other, affectionate, considerate and, it seemed, a non-verbal communication. They would often be sitting together without saying a word.

The early evolution of Krishnamurti's philosophy can be understood by examining three series of public talks: those he gave in Ojai in

1934, 1940, and 1944. As we have seen, the 1934 talks revolved around the relationship between the individual and his or her social, cultural, and economic environment. The value structure embedded in the environment functions as a prison, within which the person struggles to survive and to succeed. Those values are fundamentally false and designed to exploit, rather than to bring about freedom and harmonious living. The intelligent response to the prison is to "pierce through" or "penetrate" the false values, to see their true significance, and so to enable the individual to find a more authentic and meaningful life.

In this exposition, the person and the environment receive roughly equal attention, but by 1940, that balance has shifted in the direction of the individual. Now the discussion examines in detail the kind of relationships in which each one is engaged. These consist of relationships with things, with people, and with ideas. "To be is to be related," and understanding oneself requires understanding the actual motivations that shape the quality of these interactions.

Most relationships are driven at bottom by "craving," which takes the form of greed for material things, possessiveness of people, and seeking security through ideas and beliefs. Craving generates the psychological self, the active agent always engaged in partial and contradictory motives and desires. No system or method can free consciousness from the trap it has created for itself, for any method would function in the service of the same set of impulses. The only lasting solution, said Krishnamurti, is "kindly, tolerant, dispassionate" observation of the actual process of thought and feeling in daily life.

After 1940, Krishnamurti did not speak in public for four consecutive years. The talks he gave in Ojai in 1944, 1945, and 1946 made clear that the period of lying fallow had a major effect upon the substance of his philosophy. Many of the themes and language remained familiar, including self-awareness, the problems of greed, fear, and possessive love, and the role of memory in constructing the sense of identity or self. But the central spotlight has undergone a further inward shift, beyond what had occurred in 1940. Now the activity of thought is no longer just another player in the drama of consciousness; it has become the primary focus of attention. This shift represents a refinement in the deep structure of Krishnamurti's work, and it prefigures the central concerns of his teaching in its maturity.

Throughout his career, Krishnamurti maintained that no method or systematic practice can precipitate significant psychological change, but in 1944 he described one activity designed to facilitate awareness in a non-mechanical way. Key to his philosophy was attention to the processes of thought, but one difficulty is that thought moves too fast; like the blades of a whirling fan, its separate components are lost in the speed of activity. In order to slow thought down and observe it more closely, Krishnmurti suggested writing down each thought as it arises. It might not be possible to commit every thought to paper, but the effort to do so begins to slow the process, and it provides a record for future study and reflection.

Krishnamurti urged his listeners not to turn this activity into a mechanical routine: "Don't make it into a hard and fast system, a tyrannical technique." It was meant to serve as a catalyst to examine the judgments and reactions that would arise when reviewing what one had written. From the questions that arose in his audience, however, it soon became apparent that his listeners were making this proposal into a rigid procedure, without grasping the spirit in which it was intended. As a result, he discontinued making this recommendation. Nevertheless, it stands as a landmark for the nearest he came to prescribing any method or practice, and it serves to highlight the kind of activity he considered crucial: close and careful attention to the process of thought and the corresponding reactions that inevitably arise.

Another development of even greater significance appeared in 1944. The inseparability of the thinker and the thought was introduced almost casually in the seventh of ten talks. It occurred as the third and final step in the understanding of any problem:

> Are not the thinker and the thought an inseparable phenomenon? Just as the qualities cannot be separated from the self, so the thinker cannot be separated from his thought. When such integration takes place there is complete transformation of the thinker. This is an arduous task demanding alert pliability and choiceless awareness.

In 1945, he elaborated on this theme.

> The thinker must not only understand his many contradictory thoughts, but he must understand himself as the creator of these many entities. The I, the thinker, the observer, watches his opposing and conflicting thoughts-feelings as though he were not part of them, as though he were above and beyond them, controlling, guiding, shaping. But is not the I, the thinker, also these conflicts? Has he not created them?
>
> A tree is not just the flower and the fruit but is the total process. Similarly, to understand myself, I must, without identification and choice, be aware of the total process that is the me.

In 1946, this idea reappeared several times, now in company with a corresponding comment about the observer. At this time he introduced the more succinct formulation that "the observer is the observed." This became in due course his signature epigrammatic statement. This basic principle was now on record, and it bears testimony to the ongoing inner activity that lay beneath the surface of Krishnamurti's life during the years of relative silence and solitude.

To experience the thinker and his thought as one is very arduous, for the thinker is ever taking shelter behind his thought.... But if you are aware deeply, you will perceive that the thinker and his thoughts are one; the observer is the observed. To experience this actual integrated fact is extremely difficult, and right meditation is the way to this integration.

By spring of 1946, the day was approaching when Krishnamurti would begin again his annual round of worldwide talks. Rosalind was familiar with the long months when he was away: his travel formed the backdrop of her life from the age of nineteen to thirty-six. Now, at forty-three, she was faced with the resumption of that pattern into the indefinite future, and the time was ripe to consider investing her energies in a new sphere of activity.

Radha was due to enter high school in the fall. Thanks to the contributions of a pair of benefactors, the mortgage on the property set aside for a school had been reduced to manageable proportions. Circumstances seemed favorable for Rosalind to take the initiative and to make the long-awaited school a reality. Krishnamurti appointed her director of the school, and he and Aldous Huxley were among the members of the original school board.

The Happy Valley School opened its doors in the fall of 1946 with nine boarding students lodged at the east end residence. The school was based on principles familiar to Rosalind from several sources. Among these were the teachings of Krishnamurti, although the manner in which his views translated into classroom practices was not always clear. It was evident to Rosalind, however, that the school should be organized on a non-competitive basis: neither on the playing field nor in the classroom would students be asked to battle against one another. A system of letter grades to evaluate performance was avoided in favor of written reports describing the individual progress of each student. The role of the teacher became less formal and distant, and learning was encouraged for its own sake, rather than in order to achieve some future goal.

Happy Valley was predominantly a boarding school, and the added personnel required for that purpose, coupled with the small size of classes, yielded a low ratio of students to staff. Without an endowment to provide a supplementary source of income, the labor-intensive quality of education produced a chronic financial strain. Perhaps for this reason, the school developed a reputation for accommodating difficult students whose families could afford an innovative private boarding school.

⚬

Nothing in the available evidence indicates that the long confinement in Ojai had any appreciable effect, either positive or negative, on Krishnamurti's prevailing moods or state of mind. But when global circumstances made travel possible again, he scheduled an extended series of talks in India, planned to begin in late 1946. On the eve of his departure, however, he developed a kidney infection from which he did not recover for nearly a year. During much of this period he was confined to his bed, although he was able to sit up for a few hours each day; according to Radha, he added a quiet and beneficent presence on the periphery of the school. This illness added another to the years of relative inactivity, and the trip to India was postponed until October 1947.

⚬

Among Radha's recollections of life during the war, the participation of her father is notable for its lack of visibility. For some of that time he kept his office and residence in Hollywood and visited Ojai only on occasional weekends. In 1942, however, Rajagopal gave up his Hollywood quarters and moved back to Ojai. He had built for himself an upstairs apartment over an office building adjacent to Pine Cottage. After that he was available in principle to join in the chores and challenges of maintaining the east end residence during a time of rationing and privation. But he kept himself apart from these activities as well as from much of the community social life.

Rajagopal ostensibly worked late into the night, which purported to explain why he was not up until mid- or late morning. Radha went out of her way to describe him in favorable terms, but even she acknowledged that her father was "very fastidious" and "painfully meticulous about everything." When one of her ducklings ran over his bed, he turned upon her the irritation that he usually reserved for others. Krishnamurti once entered Rajagopal's apartment without sufficiently wiping his shoes; this precipitated such a scene that he never went into the apartment again. Numerous similar episodes came to light many years later.

What these outbursts concealed was in fact a far more insidious set of behaviors involving Rajagopal's financial, property, and archive responsibilities. His malfeasance would take decades to be exposed, but the predicate for his actions was implicit and already apparent within attitudes conspicuous much earlier. Whatever contradictory impulses raged within Rajagopal issued in his superficial commitment to Krishnamurti's work coupled with a long campaign of strategic subterfuge. The consequences of his dual and destructive nature represented the greatest practical challenge Krishnamurti ever faced, and it revealed much about his inner resources and his skill in confronting a mortal threat to his mission.

Chapter Six

NANDINI MEHTA

Nandini Mehta was thirty years old when Krishnamurti arrived in India in October 1947 for the first time in nearly a decade. A woman of delicate beauty and acute sensitivity, she was married to a wealthy and socially prominent industrialist in Bombay. She and her husband had three children under the age of nine.

The father of Nandini's husband was Sir Chunilal Mehta, who served on the council that governed Bombay under British authority. He was raised in a theosophical family, and he had known Krishnamurti for years prior to World War II. He was present at the airport to meet him when he arrived in Bombay, and escorted him to the residence where he would be staying, not far from Sir Chunilal's home. He expressed to his daughter-in-law his delight in seeing Krishnamurti again, and he invited her to accompany him to the morning dialogues Krishnamurti would be conducting in the weeks ahead.

Nandini's description of her first encounter with Krishnamurti is suffused with emotion and suggests something mystical and fore-ordained. She took her seat in the corner of a crowded room, and time stood still, she felt, when he gazed at her for a few seconds. The power of his presence and the atmosphere he generated, coupled with her refined sensibility, caused tears to flow from her eyes. When the meeting concluded, he approached her and was introduced by her father-in-law. She reports that he was laughing with joy, and she claims that he said, "Why have you come? I have been waiting for you for thirty years."

The catalogue of improbable quotations attributed to Krishnamurti would fill a substantial volume, and "waiting for thirty years" should probably be included in it. Nandini's intense emotion no doubt colored what she observed and remembered, and whatever Krishnamurti said was received through the filter of her feelings. If her report of his words may not be reliable, however, the response he evoked in her can be accepted at face value. She felt an immediate, intuitive rapport of paramount significance.

Nandini's sister was Pupul Jayakar, who was destined to become an enduring force in the cultural affairs of India. Jayakar served as the national minister in charge of the development of handcrafted artifacts, including pottery, fabrics, and devotional artworks of every variety. These local, small-scale industries were an essential element of India's growing economy as well as a means of preserving the nation's rich and ancient heritage. According to one observer, Jayakar "strode colossus-like" over the cultural affairs of India for forty years.

Nandini brought her sister to the morning dialogues with Krishnamurti, and Jayakar established herself as one of his foremost interlocutors and collaborators. In due course, she became the pillar of the administration of his work in India. She engaged in dozens of dialogues with him, many of them recorded by shorthand and published. Jayakar was a powerful writer and author of several influential books, including a biography of her close friend Indira Gandhi. After Krishnamurti's death, she wrote a biography of him, steeped in her understanding of Indian religious traditions and her appreciation for Krishnamurti and his philosophy.

After his long confinement in Ojai, Krishnamurti's trip to India in 1947 was unusual in several respects. One significant feature is that he traveled alone. From the time he was adopted by Annie

Besant until he died, he typically traveled in the company of one or two others, not only for assistance in practical matters, but also as a form of protection. To accompany him in this manner was part of Rajagopal's role, and his absence at this time foreshadowed the developing rift between the two men.

The duration of this trip was also unusual. Normally Krishnamurti stayed in India for four to six months at a time, but on this occasion his visit lasted eighteen months. The number of his meetings was increased correspondingly: he conducted well over one hundred talks and dialogues in several major cities.

Above all, this trip was noteworthy for an interlude that occurred about halfway through. In May 1948, Krishnamurti planned a period of rest and relaxation from his schedule of events. He invited several friends, including Nandini Mehta and Pupul Jayakar, to accompany him to a mountainous retreat. His request to have the sisters join him was indicative of the close bond he had already formed with them, and it was fortuitous in view of the role they were destined to play in the series of events that occurred at that time.

One of the characteristics of the colonial occupation of India was the construction of dozens of "hill stations," designed to serve as comfortable enclaves for the members of the occupying elite. Located at significant elevations, the hill stations offered relief from sea-level temperatures, as well as lush gardens, verdant groves, and well-appointed cottages and luxury hotels. One of these was located at Ootacamund, or Ooty, in the Nilgiri Mountains in the south of India. Known for its sylvan setting and pristine environment, Ooty was acknowledged as the "queen" of all the hill stations.

Krishnamurti had settled into a house in Ooty called Sedgemoor when Nandini arrived with her three children and Sir Chunilal, and Jayakar arrived with her daughter. Jayakar took contemporaneous notes of what occurred after they arrived, and later she supplemented the notes with her recollections.

The events in question took place on a daily basis over a period of two or three weeks, and they followed a characteristic pattern. Krishnamurti typically went for a walk in the late afternoon, often accompanied by Pupul and Nandini. On one of these occasions, he began to feel unwell while they were out. When asked if he needed a doctor he said no, but he wanted to return to his room at Sedgemoor. He asked the two sisters to stay with him, and he told another friend at the house that he should not be disturbed.

Krishnamurti gave the sisters precise instructions before he lay down on his bed. They should remain calm and quiet, without fear, and not speak to him. If he fainted or lost consciousness, they should not call a doctor or attempt to revive him. Above all, they should not leave him alone. A few minutes later, he began to exhibit symptoms reminiscent of the "process" and the three-day episode in Ojai in 1922. He complained of pain in the head, neck, spine, and stomach. The pain varied in degree and moved from one place to another, and, when it reached a peak of intensity, he fainted.

Much of the time, his normal personality was absent and was replaced, as it had been at Ojai, by the voice and manner of a child four or five years of age. The child would call out for his mother or beg for Krishna to return, only to reprimand himself and say he was not supposed to do that. He said that "only a bit of me" was functioning.

Most peculiar and perplexing were Krishnamurti's repeated references to an unknown "they" who were conducting operations upon him. They were "burning" him, he said, but he "knew what they were up to." They knew how much pain he could tolerate. One evening he went for his walk alone, and while he was out, something unexpected occurred. He said he nearly did not return, and he felt as though his body had been scattered in pieces by the side of the road. However, "they rushed back," he reported, and repaired whatever damage had been done.

These events did not culminate, as they had at Ojai, with an experience of mystical union or a transcendental vision of life. Nevertheless, at the end of the process one evening, Krishnamurti said he had been "polished" and "soaked with gasoline. The tank is full." He referred to a state of mind of emptiness that permitted the cells of his brain to expand or to see how much energy they could absorb. "Tomorrow," he said, "I will be like a raindrop—spotless."

Jayakar's factual descriptions were interspersed with more subjective comments. Among these were references to a pulsating but unseen presence and moments when Krishnamurti's face and posture changed, suddenly filled with energy and a beatific demeanor. It is difficult to know whether these descriptions tell us more about Krishnamurti or about Pupul's projection of her image of an Indian sage.

Her notes are not always easy to interpret, in part because she sometimes neglected to distinguish between the voice of the mature Krishnamurti and that of the child. However, she spoke to him some days after these events and tried to probe their meaning. His replies were not very illuminating, but he tended to minimize any mysterious element or mystical explanation. There were not two distinct personalities within him, he maintained, but when the pain was intense his normal consciousness simply vanished, and the voice that remained was that of the body alone. He offered no explanations of or references to "they." He acknowledged that some form of energy was flowing into his brain, and this produced the pain in his head and body. Beyond that, he himself could not explain what was happening, and he felt for some reason that it was not even appropriate for him to ask.

Jayakar elicited one remark, however, that shines another, possibly more objective, light upon Krishnamurti's odd behavior. She asked whether the sequence of events represented a symptom or byproduct of a mind or brain that was functioning fully, as if it were opening up and flowering to the maximum extent. "Possibly," he acknowledged; and he reinforced that explanation by suggesting that his schools existed to bring about a similar result.

The events at Ooty clearly represented the recurrence of an acute form of the process that had made its first appearance in 1922. Available evidence does not permit any comprehensive account of the frequency, duration, or intensity of the process for extended periods of Krishnamurti's life. Numerous indications, however, suggest that in a more brief and muted form it was a regular if not daily reality for him much of the time. Letters he wrote years later to Pupul and Nandini, for example, refer to the "wheels of Ooty" continuing to function and operate upon him.

None of the existing evidence, however, offers any convincing explanation of the meaning, origin, or cause of Krishnamurti's process. Only the effect of it has any possibility of plausible interpretation. For reasons outside the scope of rational analysis, the process evidently had a salutary effect on Krishnamurti's sense of clarity and inner well-being. This conclusion follows not only from the events at Ooty but also from subsequent indications that will be examined later. The beneficial consequences of the process, however, do little to ameliorate the mystery associated with it. Indeed, it may well be that the favorable outcome only serves to magnify the mystery, rather than to mitigate it.

Even while these events were occurring in the evenings, Krishnamurti maintained his normal schedule of activities during the day. Among these was a ninety-minute conversation with Prime Minister Jawaharlal Nehru. He happened to be staying at Ooty, and he inquired through Jayakar whether he could speak with Krishnamurti. The meeting was arranged and she accompanied him and was present for the conversation at Nehru's residence.

India had achieved independence from Great Britain in August 1947, two months before Krishnamurti arrived in Bombay, and the partition between India and Pakistan had convulsed both nations with deadly animosity between Hindus and Muslims. In parts of both countries, riots, looting, rapes, and massacres were the order of the day. Mahatma Gandhi, Nehru's close friend and mentor, was assassinated in January 1948, and India's first prime minister was profoundly troubled by the pervasive brutality that independence had unleashed.

This was Nehru's state of mind when he asked to see Krishnamurti. The two men met in his oak-paneled private quarters, seated before dancing flames in a massive fireplace. Jayakar remarked upon the quality of their faces: "… sculptured, sensitive, with fine translucent skin that accentuated the bones and heightened mobility—the eyes of the seer encompassing vast distances, emanating compassion and silence; the other with the swift, nervous energy of an arrow."

Nehru perceived the chaos in which India was engulfed in broad and fundamental terms. He saw it as a form of evil, and he inquired how such a force could be contained and transformed: What was right action in the face of pervasive conflict and violence? Krishnamurti replied in a manner reminiscent of the message he conveyed from the public platform. Regeneration, meaningful change, could only begin within the individual, he said; but if a few people could free themselves from the factors of destruction, something new could arise. Only alert awareness within each individual could initiate such a change and serve as a bulwark against the forces of evil.

In a passage published several years later, Krishnamurti described Nehru as "intensely sincere and ardently patriotic. Neither narrow-minded nor self-seeking, his ambition was not for himself but for an idea and for his people." The two men parted on warm and cordial terms and agreed to meet again at the next opportunity.

Krishnamurti returned to Ojai in March 1949 and remained there for six months before setting off for India once again. When he returned to the United States in the spring of 1950, he delivered his first public talks in America in more than three years—five talks in New York City and another series of five in Seattle. These talks offer the opportunity to see whether his philosophy had evolved due to the extended stay in India, or to the events at Ooty, or simply due to the passage of time and increased maturity.

While the precise sources of any changes are difficult to discern, his message in these talks displayed a refinement in both substance and language, in its content as well as the manner of expression. One conspicuous change was the elimination of references to "craving." Perhaps the word itself now seemed somewhat dated. Desire, a close cousin of craving, still occupied a leading role in Krishnamurti's drama of consciousness, but it took its place among other elements, rather than functioning as the driving factor.

Certain features of the teachings remained consistent with what had gone before. Life is relationship; to be is to be related. The individual and society cannot be understood in isolation from one another; society is the projection of the individual. The key to the problems of life is self-understanding, which comes about through moment-to-moment awareness of each thought and feeling as it arises. There is no method for the process of such awareness, because any method shapes what is being observed and therefore prevents understanding of the actuality. These themes and principles appear and reappear, woven into the exposition and elaborated on at length.

In reply to a question from his audience, Krishnamurti offered some observations about the nature and origins of creativity. Research conducted in recent years examines creativity from neurological, genetic, and demographic perspectives and explores the tendency for creative individuals to suffer from bipolar illness and other forms of mental dysfunction. (See, for example, the work of Kay Redfield Jamison.) In Krishnamurti's view, creativity is not associated with mental disorder; it is not an achievement, nor the product of any effort or technique; it does not even require expression. Rather, it is a condition that comes into being when the mind is not caught in any form of conflict or contradiction. Such a state of mind is not brought about by the desire to achieve a result, but rather through awareness and understanding of conflict in daily life.

Most noteworthy in these talks was an extended series of reflections on the thinker and the thought. These remarks occurred in the first of the five talks in New York and were accompanied by comments intended to emphasize their significance. Our feeling or impression that the thinker is separate from our thoughts is the conflict "in which most of us are caught—it is our whole problem." The thinker and the thought

> ... are not two different processes, but a single, unitary process. Thought divides itself and creates the thinker for its own convenience.... Now, when you really see the falseness of that process, you will discover that there is no thinker, but only thoughts—which is quite a revolution. This is the fundamental revolution which is essential in order to understand the whole process of thinking.

In the opening words of his last talk in Seattle, Krishnamurti introduced the phrase "radical transformation," which was to become a hallmark of his message for many years:

> Most of us are very easily satisfied with explanations, theories, and words, and our superficial interest will obviously never bring about a fundamental revolution. What is necessary, surely, is to have a radical transformation in oneself, and this transformation affects not only our personal relationships, but also our relationship to society. Without this deep inner revolution, there can be no lasting happiness, no final solution to any of our problems.

Two years after she met Krishnamurti, Nandini Mehta informed her husband that she would no longer engage in any physical intimacy with him. If he were to insist, she told him, she would feel compelled to leave his house and file for divorce. Her husband might have attempted to understand and reach some accommodation with his beautiful, sensitive wife and the mother of his three children. Instead, he chose to fight. Due to the social prominence of Sir Chunilal and his family, the court case that followed was widely publicized in Bombay and beyond.

Central to the divorce proceedings, brought by Nandini on grounds of cruelty, was the claim by her husband that she had been influenced by the teachings of Krishnamurti. Entered into evidence were extensive excerpts from his public talks, in which he had chastised Indian men for their domineering, patriarchal attitude toward their wives. Implicit in the publicity surrounding the case was the suggestion that Krishnamurti's relationship with Nandini might have been improper to some unspecified degree.

The English judge in the High Court of Bombay held that Nandini failed to prove cruelty on the part of her husband, and her petition for divorce was denied. The practical effect of the finding of the court was that if she separated from her husband, she would be denied any form of support as well as custody of her children. Her decision to leave in spite of these consequences revealed the depth of her resolve not to continue in a marriage that no longer held any meaning for her.

In March 1950, *Time* magazine published a sensationalized account of the court case under the title "Revolt of the Doormat." In one of his public talks, Krishnamurti had used the word "doormat" to describe the attitude of Indian men toward their wives, and *Time* wove a snarky and misleading story around that image. The article viewed Krishnamurti through a theosophical lens and compared the interest in Theosophy to the 1920s enthusiasm for the game of mah-jongg; Annie Besant was reduced to the role of rejected lover of George Bernard Shaw. The article highlighted the idea that Krishnamurti was pursuing Nandini under the guise of a spiritual guru, and it all but exulted that the judge declared her petition for divorce unfounded. In *Time* magazine's account, justice was served by denying the impetuous revolt of the doormat.

When Rosalind read the article in *Time*, the metaphorical feces hit the proverbial fan. Her suspicion and jealousy exploded beyond all bounds. She castigated Krishnamurti and grilled him relentlessly. According to Radha, he acknowledged at one point that Nandini might have caused his heart to "flutter" momentarily, but nothing was ever established beyond deep friendship and innocent love.

In Rosalind's rendition of events, the article in *Time* is what precipitated her confession to Rajagopal of her long-standing affair with Krishnamurti. The idea that her admission was the first he knew about it is implausible at best. To people who observed Krishnamurti and Rosalind more than casually or lived with them for any length of time, the nature of their relationship was evident. The idea that Rajagopal, of all people—inquisitive and suspicious by nature, and intimately involved in both of their lives—could have been blind for so many years strains credulity beyond the breaking point. Yet this is the narrative that Rosalind promulgated through her daughter.

Equally bizarre was Rajagopal's purported response to his wife's confession of her infidelity. He held her blameless, as if she had no agency or responsibility for her actions. Krishnamurti alone, in his view, was the active party in the relationship, the one who deceived and betrayed him. This was no temporary or superficial response, but rather one that Rajagopal nursed, cultivated, and employed as a bludgeon to blackmail Krishnamurti in the years ahead.

After the talks in New York and Seattle, Krishnamurti returned to Ojai and discontinued traveling and public speaking for sixteen months. Even this extended stay was not sufficient to quell Rosalind's jealous antagonism, and she continued to pester and berate him about Nandini for years to come.

One of the central mysteries of Krishnamurti's life revolves around his continued allegiance to Rosalind and Rajagopal in spite of the accumulating evidence of their indifference to his work and his personal welfare. Rajagopal's belligerent attitude and behavior were apparent early on, and after Rosalind's jealousy was provoked, she adopted a similar disposition. Krishnamurti tolerated them with passive acquiescence, even though the consequences for his mission in America were severe. Only with the passage of many years did he find the wherewithal and the resources to confront the damage that the two of them had done to his work. He himself remained puzzled to the end of his life why he put up with them for so long; and so at the level of practical action, a mystery exists almost on a par with the enigma of his inner life.

In the years immediately following the war, Krishnamurti's career in America depended upon a platform that continued to deteriorate. The extent of Rosalind and Rajagopal's program of undermining his mission had not yet fully materialized, and it would take even longer for their behavior to be exposed. Nothing they did, however, seemed to affect his clarity of mind or the quality of the teachings.

On the contrary, Krishnamurti's understanding continued to flower and to find expression in ever more original ways. Evidently something within was impervious to external influences, no matter how misguided or malicious they might be. The impregnability of the teachings, in spite of all impediments, represents a testimony to the depth of his commitment to them.

Chapter Seven

THE EMPTINESS OF EXILE

His confinement in Ojai during the war led Krishnamurti to initiate a new form of expression for his work. He began at that time to commit words to paper in a more sustained and systematic manner than he had done in the past, and his efforts bore fruit for the following decade and beyond. His first book-length composition, as distinct from a transcript of his talks, was *Education and the Significance of Life*, published by Harper & Row in 1953. In 125 pages, Krishnamurti expressed some of the original and far-reaching principles of his educational philosophy. The following excerpt illustrates the scope of his reflections.

> In our present civilization we have divided life into so many departments that education has very little meaning, except in learning a particular technique or profession. Instead of awakening the integrated intelligence of the individual, education is encouraging him to conform to a pattern and so is hindering his comprehension of himself as a total process. To attempt to solve the many problems of existence at their respective levels, separated as they are into various categories, indicates an utter lack of comprehension.

The first of three volumes titled *Commentaries on Living* appeared in 1956. These books recount private interviews with people who had come to seek Krishnamurti's counsel on personal or psychological issues. His outward life was dominated by public talks and dialogues, but he was also accessible to individuals seeking answers or relief from various problems. The *Commentaries* represented his written recollections of these interviews, detailed case studies that illustrate the meaning of his talks.

In the *Commentaries*, each conversation is preceded by a scene from nature, vividly recalled and serving as a counterpoint to the stories of human travail. The scenes tend to evoke a heightened awareness and receptivity to the psychological observations that follow. The coupling of these two kinds of experience represents an original literary form, one unique to Krishnamurti and an expression of his philosophy. One cannot have a right relationship with human beings, he maintained, unless one has a relationship with nature. The meaning of that proposition receives a demonstration on the printed page in the juxtaposition of the two forms of experience.

The *Commentaries* are highly significant for another reason as well. Krishnamurti's philosophy represents a wellspring of psychological insight coupled with a comprehensive understanding of the nature and operation of consciousness. Such a perspective provides a fertile resource for the field of clinical psychology. The *Commentaries* demonstrate the application of his philosophy for the purpose of individual healing, and the day may come when a new form of therapy emerges, one rooted in the teachings as they illuminate specific problems and issues.

The copyright for these publications was vested in Krishnamurti Writings, Inc., or KWInc, a legal entity formed by Rajagopal during the war. In 1946, Krishnamurti signed a document that made KWInc the "central Foundation throughout the world" for the publication of his work. The document provided that KWInc would be governed by a board of trustees consisting of five members. As the two founding members of the board, he and Rajagopal were empowered to appoint the other three.

In the years following the formation of KWInc, a sequence of events occurred that illustrated the depth of Krishnamurti's trust in Rajagopal. First and foremost, he resigned from its governing board. As if to underscore his indifference to this and all other administrative matters, Krishnamurti retained no memory of this event. Even with this degree of disinterest, the laws governing copyright did not permit him to forsake the rights to his own work unless and until he did so explicitly.

In November 1958, Rajagopal composed and presented to Krishnamurti a legal instrument that formally transferred to KWInc all responsibility for copyright of his writings, including everything composed before as well as subsequent to that date. The Madras document, as it was called, invested in Rajagopal personally, as president of KWInc, the authority to execute all contracts pertaining to the publication of Krishnamurti's work. With no discernible resistance, Krishnamurti signed his name to this unequivocal release of his copyright. His blind trust in Rajagopal would prove to carry painful and momentous consequences far into the unforeseeable future.

❦

Late in 1955, some five years after the article in *Time* had appeared, Rosalind resolved to accompany Krishnamurti on his annual visit to India. According to Radha, her primary motivation in undertaking this journey revolved around her deep and unresolved suspicion regarding Krishnamurti's relationship with Nandini. There was no question of actual infidelity; Rosalind simply could not contain her jealous resentment that he might hold feelings of affection for another woman.

Some measure of Rosalind's understanding of Krishnamurti can be gleaned from her response to the publication of *Education and the Significance of Life*. She read the lucid, cogent prose with surprise bordering on incredulity: she considered Krishnamurti incapable of composing such a book. It could only have been written, she concluded, by Rajagopal.

In India, Krishnamurti was consumed by the demands of daily dialogues and public talks and rarely had the occasion even to see Nandini. Rosalind took no interest in attending his events but demanded that he accompany her on sight-seeing expeditions. Pupul Jayakar marveled at her domineering demeanor and Krishnamurti's willingness to tolerate it, and she noted that his refusal to reciprocate Rosalind's argumentative attitude had the effect of infuriating her all the more.

Rosalind found nothing in India to nourish her insatiable suspicion, but the trip did not resolve her sense of grievance. She traveled to Europe after five months in India and met there with Rajagopal. She informed him that she had determined to free herself of her involvement with Krishnamurti—and, as a result, that he should no longer return to Ojai for any purpose. She would continue to live at Arya Vihara and direct the Happy Valley School, but Krishnamurti, she had concluded, could just as well live anywhere else.

At the age of fifty-three, Rosalind may have been suffering from midlife challenges, but even by the most generous interpretation of her state of mind, it is difficult to fathom her proposal. Her home and her work were entirely derivative of Krishnamurti's benevolence and generosity to her. If he were to abide by her decision, he would not only allow her to usurp his home, but he would also abdicate his work in America. Radha reports that even Rosalind later admitted, in an unwitting understatement, that her demand was "somewhat outrageous."

The first line of defense against her proposal consisted of the exercise of some restraint by Rajagopal. He was the individual in whom Krishnamurti had vested all administrative responsibility, encompassing not only publications and travel arrangements, but also financial and property management. Both men were solicitous of Rosalind's concerns, generous to her and inclined to accommodate her whenever possible, but when push came to shove—as it clearly had—Rajagopal had the authority to curtail her more egregious suggestions. Nothing in his portfolio was more elementary than securing Krishnamurti's right and access to his Ojai home.

But Rajagopal did nothing of the kind. He not only tolerated Rosalind's demand but may have encouraged it. In any case, he did nothing to stop it, and he served as her emissary to communicate her decision to Krishnamurti.

The only remaining question was what action Krishnamurti would take to confront an impossible situation. He would have been within his rights to remove Rosalind from the east end residence altogether. More characteristic might have been to pay her proposal little regard, return to Ojai, and make the best of whatever discord might arise at that time. He might even have accepted her demand for a few months, as a gesture of conciliation, until she had time to reconsider.

But Krishnamurti's actual response fell far outside the bounds of any reasonable expectation. He responded with a degree of passivity beyond comprehension. He simply acquiesced to Rosalind's intemperate demand, not only for the short term, but for the indefinite future. He left Ojai for India in November 1955 and did not return to his home for more than four years; and even then his visit was only a temporary respite from a much longer period of exile.

For two decades, Rajagopal and Rosalind supported Krishnamurti's work, facilitated his travels, and contributed to his endeavors. All that time, they were securing their own niche within the world he had offered to them; and, in the end, the tenants evicted the landlord and left him to fend for himself. The only thing more incomprehensible than their behavior was Krishnamurti's inordinate passivity and acceptance of it. The meaning of his lack of action defies easy explanation, but the magnitude of the mystery compels some effort to understand it.

If Krishnamurti were merely sacrificing his personal convenience for the sake of Rosalind's preference and peace of mind, we might attribute his deference to her wishes as an outsized act of generosity or a misplaced sense of gallantry. But the implications of his lack of action go much deeper than his personal discomfort. There can be no doubt how seriously he took his mission to convey his understanding of consciousness and a new approach to life. To give up his home in Ojai for an indefinite period of time was tantamount to abandoning that mission with respect to an entire continent. To be sure, he could and did continue to speak throughout those years in India and Europe, but the expression of his philosophy in America suffered immeasurable damage.

Certain features of Krishnamurti's philosophy suggest some possible clues to account for his behavior. He called for a transformation in consciousness, especially with respect to psychological conflict. His teaching can be construed, in fact, as a diagnosis and remedy for all forms of conflict, both inwardly and in relationship. In any case, it stands to reason that we should seek clues to Krishnamurti's behavior in his teaching, especially when his actions are most difficult to comprehend. For this purpose, we can consult a series of talks he gave when he returned to Ojai in the summer of 1960 and see what light they may shed on this issue.

Early in the series of talks, Krishnamurti declares that the world is in a state of crisis, but not one of an economic, social, or political nature; it is a crisis in consciousness. The situation can be addressed and transformed, but not through any kind of mystical or sentimental approach. What is required is an alert and pliable state of mind, earnest about self-understanding, and willing to face facts rather than escape into theories or speculation. Among the threats to self-understanding are submitting to authority in psychological matters and the accumulation of images and ideas about oneself.

From this somewhat familiar point of departure, the talks explore an original set of observations about time and knowledge and show how they are related to psychological freedom and creativity. Krishnamurti maintains that knowledge is pervasive throughout the field of consciousness, and he explores at length what that implies. Knowledge, thought, and time, in his view, are intimately interconnected, because thought comes from knowledge, which comes from the past. In his exposition, these concepts appear, not as airy abstractions, remote from everyday life, but rather as constituents of quotidian reality, the daily lot of every human being.

Krishnamurti presents this state of affairs as a crisis in consciousness. When time, thought, and knowledge are so dominant, psychological freedom is no longer possible. He proposes that the operation of thought is mechanical, always functioning within the framework of cause and effect; such action, he says, is the denial of freedom. He brought out the meaning of action based on cause and effect by contrasting it with two phenomena that are not mechanical: energy and life itself.

This series of talks included no reflections on conflict in relationship, although that was an important feature of the teachings in other years. Nevertheless, the difficulties associated with Krishnamurti's life at home found expression

in a more emphatic way. Eight talks were originally scheduled, typical of his normal pattern, but he began the third talk by announcing that the number this year would have to be limited to four. He apologized to the people who had come from a distance to hear him, but he said he was physically unable to complete the series.

According to Mary Lutyens, the difficulty had its source in tensions boiling over at the east end residence. The issue consisted of a bitter dispute between Rosalind and Rajagopal. He had found another woman whom he wanted to marry, and he was seeking a divorce that she refused to grant. Evidently their arguments were numerous and loud, and the open hostility interfered with the energy and focus that Krishnamurti required in order to complete the series of talks.

Here lies a clue as to why he agreed to stay away from Ojai for four years and continued to do so after 1960. Unless he were prepared to remove Rosalind and Rajagopal from the property altogether, the atmosphere they generated made it impossible for him to function normally. Their antagonism was no longer directed only at him, but they found another outlet for chronic disharmony. However damaging it was to his work to abandon his home in Ojai, remaining there now made things even worse.

The clarity and originality of the four talks he gave provides evidence that discretion was the better part of valor. Had he continued to live within the orbit of Rosalind and Rajagopal, the fresh set of insights that he expressed might never have been realized. By remaining in exile from America, he evidently nourished and preserved his philosophy. Such a result may seem counterintuitive, but if anyone knew what was required to generate his teachings, no doubt it was Krishnamurti. In the large scheme of things, in spite of everything, it appears that his action may have been correct.

In 1961, Krishnamurti initiated a new venue for an annual, comprehensive series of talks in the Western Hemisphere. Ojai had served this purpose for many years, but after the aborted series in 1960, he clearly needed to find a new location. The place he selected was Saanen, Switzerland, in a region of rolling hills and open pastures, held in the embrace of accessible mountains, forests, and lakes.

Saanen is located a few miles away from the better known village of Gstaad, a tourist attraction and upscale ski resort.

The catalyst for the connection to Saanen was Vanda Scaravelli, a woman who had supported Krishnamurti's work for many years. Scaravelli's family moved among the cultural elite in Florentine society and served as patrons to artistic and other progressive causes; her husband was professor of philosophy at the University of Rome. She was a pianist of high caliber and an ardent practitioner of yoga. She inherited from her parents a house near Florence called Il Leccio, named for the spreading ilex tree, a species of oak, that graced its parklike grounds. Il Leccio served as a place of refuge for Krishnamurti for weeks at a time in his travels to and from India.

Scaravelli often rented a two-story summer cottage in Gstaad called Chalet Tannegg, and she invited Krishnamurti to stay there with her and a few friends in 1961. This invitation precipitated a gathering of his audience and led to leasing the land in Saanen that served as the venue for his talks. The selection of Saanen as the setting for the annual series was therefore as fortuitous as it was farsighted.

The first series of ten talks occurred in July 1961. In spite of its somewhat remote location, Saanen attracted listeners from all parts of Europe and beyond. In subsequent years, the talks were held in a huge, tent-like structure that accommodated an audience of a thousand, with loudspeakers set up for the overflow crowd outside. The annual series provided a new form of predictability for Krishnamurti's audience and continued to do so for the next twenty-five years.

⸎

During his years of exile from Ojai, Krishnamurti composed a set of written reflections of outstanding significance, a diary recounting his innermost experiences and states of mind. This was not a record of personal problems, interactions with individuals, or external events. Among other elements, the diary contained descriptions, as factual and objective as possible, of encounters with some ineffable presence or quality of energy outside the parameters of normal daily life.

Krishnamurti referred to this energy or entity as an immensity, a benediction, or simply as "the other." His diary encompassed a nine-month period beginning in June 1961, 265 entries in all, and "the other" makes an appearance in roughly half of these. Because it is invisible to ordinary perception and too elusive for language, "the other" elicits only spare and suggestive words of description. Its defining characteristics include power coupled with purity and a silence or stillness that is deep and intense. How it makes itself known is not entirely apparent but evidently includes a sense of throbbing, pulsating energy, a palpable reality. Krishnamurti insists "the other" is not illusory or a product of the imagination. He regards it as something sacred, unknown and unknowable.

Encounters with "the other" occurred intermittently and unexpectedly, almost at random intervals. Crucially, this presence or energy was uninvited, not the result of any cause, intention, or desire to bring it about. Although its essential nature was almost impossible to characterize, the diary appears to have been written in part for the purpose of testifying to its presence in his life.

These episodes are presented not as isolated incidents, but rather embedded in a larger context. Foremost among the other elements are scenes from nature, reminiscent of those that appeared in *Commentaries on Living*—vivid, moving, and recorded with precision and clarity. Also included are reflections on the issues of relationship, conflict, thought, illusion, and other topics familiar from the public talks. Finally, the diary describes what Krishnamurti characterized as meditation, a unique state of mind unlike what is normally associated with that concept.

Among the first few dozen entries are references to the

intermittent pain in his head and neck known as the "process." For the first and only time, Krishnamurti offered a window into the frequency, intensity, and duration of the process, as well as clues regarding its meaning. Words used to describe it include "pressure," "pain," "strain," and "ache," sometimes accompanied by qualifiers such as "peculiar," "deep," "acute," "intense," and "heavy." When the pain is at its worst, he adds remarks such as, "How much can the body stand!"; "… it was almost unbearable so that one was forced to lie down"; and, "There is a limit beyond which the body will crack."

The diary also offers evidence regarding the effects of the process: it is unmistakably coupled with numinous, expansive, and blissful states of mind. It occurs in association, for example, with a "feeling of immense vastness," or "great and unutterable beauty." At one point, a "strange, sacred blessing was there."

The process appears in sixty of the first sixty-seven daily entries, and the diary includes additional clues regarding its more objective characteristics. "One has only to be quiet for it to begin." "It isn't something recent." "It's strange how this process adjusts itself to circumstance." And finally, the last time it is mentioned: "The process has been acute the last few days; and one need not write about it every day."

From this evidence, it seems reasonable to infer that the process was woven into Krishnamurti's life in an ongoing manner, varying in intensity, and paradoxically integral with positive, even blissful experiences. At one point he acknowledged that, "There is an unknown energy involved in all this." Krishnamurti himself cannot account for the process, but he yields to it without resistance, as if it were an inevitability. The unknown energy evidently defies not only description but investigation; yet somehow implicit within it lies an imperative to tolerate and accept it without question or concern. It seems to be simply a given for him, a fact of life like gravity or the weather.

This diary, published in 1976 as *Krishnamurti's Notebook*, represents a unique contribution to the corpus of his lifetime endeavors. The vast majority of the remarks he delivered from a public platform focus upon factual descriptions of the consciousness of normal individuals. The diary, by contrast, represents a movement into another dimension. Here alone, among all his talks and writings, he opens a window into the quality of spirituality as it existed in his own life and states of mind.

Two of the briefest entries may serve to represent the diary's most characteristic features. The first was written in Rome on September 27, 1961.

> Walking along the pavement overlooking the biggest basilica and down the famous steps to a fountain and many picked flowers of so many colors, crossing the crowded square, we went along a narrow one-way street, quiet, with not too many cars; there, in that dimly lit street, with few unfashionable shops, suddenly and most unexpectedly, that otherness came with such intense tenderness and beauty that one's body and brain became motionless.
>
> For some days now, it had not made its immense presence felt; it was there vaguely, in the distance, a whisper, but there the immense was manifesting itself, sharply and with waiting patience. Thought and speech were gone and there was peculiar joy and clarity. It followed down the long, narrow street till the roar of traffic and the over-crowded pavement swallowed us all. It was a benediction that was beyond all image and thoughts.

The second entry was written October 8, eleven days later, when he was staying at Il Leccio.

> It had been raining all day; the roads were slushy, and there was more brown water in the river, and the slight fall of the

river was making more noise. It was a still night, an invitation to the rains which never stopped till early this morning. And the sun suddenly came out, and towards the west the sky was blue, rain washed and clean, with those enormous clouds full of light and splendor. It was a beautiful morning, and, looking to the west, with the sky so intensely blue, all thought and emotion disappeared, and the seeing was from emptiness.

Before dawn, meditation was the immense opening into the unknown. Nothing can open the door save the complete destruction of the known. Meditation is explosion in understanding. There is no understanding without self-knowing; learning about the self is not accumulating knowledge about it; gathering of knowledge prevents learning; learning is not an additive process; learning is from moment to moment, as is understanding. This total process of learning is explosion in meditation.

In his public talks, Krishnamurti very occasionally refers to God as something synonymous with truth, reality, and timelessness. Little more can be said because this is the realm of the unknown, that which lies beyond knowledge, time, or limitation. It appears to consist of a form of awareness in which there is no distinction between the mind and what it is aware of. Other than these references, the talks avoid anything that might be called mystical or spiritual.

In his diary, however, Krishnamurti earns the designation of religious philosopher. Each of the elements included in it—"the other," the scenes from nature, the reflections on consciousness, the process, the moments of meditation—is imbued with a religious quality, something ineffable that pervades the fabric of his life. Krishnamurti's teaching emphasizes the irrelevance of his personal characteristics to the truth or meaning of his message. He never says anything about himself that might be interpreted to suggest that he should be regarded as special or any kind or source of authority. His diary represents a singular counterpoint to his standard reluctance to divulge any information about his private experiences or states of mind.

The long period of exile from Ojai cannot be understood or evaluated apart from what happened precisely because he was deprived of his home and his base of operational support. The insights expressed in the Ojai talks in 1960, the commencement of the annual talks at Saanen, and the composition of his diary might never have occurred had he remained within the field of Rosalind and Rajagopal. We cannot know this for certain, but the evidence suggests that the emptiness of exile opened up the space for something new and creative to occur.

Krishnamurti's willingness to tolerate Rosalind's eviction of him can hardly be attributed to any expectation that something better would ensue. But it may have reflected a wisdom of a more subtle nature; and, in any case, whatever damage the exile did to his work in America received a measure of compensation in other, unexpected forms. His extreme passivity was not a calculated gamble; but, in the final analysis, the benefits may have outweighed the very considerable costs.

Chapter Eight

MARY ZIMBALIST

Among the personal qualities that distinguished Mary Zimbalist were a fine aesthetic sensibility and good taste. She presented herself with unassuming modesty and grace, which might have allowed those in her company to overlook her discerning eye and cool appraisal of people, circumstances, and events. She moved through social situations with a gentle, reserved manner, attentive and available when called upon, but otherwise serene and self-contained. Just beneath her slightly remote exterior, however, lay deep dedication and a warm and sensitive heart.

She was born Mary Taylor in 1915 and raised in New York City. Her family was wealthy and socially prominent—her father was president of the New York Stock Exchange—and she attended the exclusive boarding school Bryn Mawr. Her career as a model and actress began in her teens and led to a contract with *Vogue* as well as several portraits by the distinguished photographer Cecil Beaton.

At the age of sixteen, Mary was diagnosed with cancer of the bone in one leg, and the ensuing radiation treatment left her with chronic pain for the rest of her life. Her career was unimpeded, however, and led to roles in a series of films, including *Lady of the Tropics*, produced by legendary impresario Sam Zimbalist. In 1952, when she was thirty-seven and he was fifty-one, they married.

Zimbalist was on the set in Rome in 1958, finishing *Ben Hur*, when he suffered a fatal heart attack. After six years of marriage, the shock of his premature death left Mary devastated. *Ben Hur* won the Academy Award for Best Picture the following year. Mary accepted the Oscar on her husband's behalf, and the video of her acceptance speech (accessible on YouTube) displays her grace, beauty, and grief in equal measure.

Mary had undergone psychoanalysis in her twenties, and she discussed her treatment with a friend who recommended that she attend Krishnamurti's talks in Ojai. She did so for the first time in 1944. She also met him that year for a private interview and was struck by his quality of attention and penetrating insight. In the years that followed, she continued to attend occasional talks and said she was impressed with his "sweeping iconoclasm" and fresh outlook on fundamental issues of living.

The sudden loss of her husband propelled Mary into a vortex of grief. Two years later, in 1960, she attended the talks in Ojai and arranged another private interview. Krishnamurti spoke with her in a way she found clear and meaningful as well as unexpected and original. He said that death was psychological as well as physical and that one could "die to the past" each day; in so doing, living becomes free and creative. In his words and his manner, Krishnamurti communicated something that Mary found true and moving, and it helped to release the burden of her sorrow.

Mary's involvement in Krishnamurti's life began in Saanen in 1965, when she was fifty years old and he was seventy. The conduit for her introduction to his circle of associates was her friend, the fellow actress Iris Tree, who was part of the Ojai community during the war. Tree introduced Mary to Vanda Scaravelli, Krishnamurti's hostess at Chalet Tannegg in Gstaad. She invited Mary to lunch at Chalet Tannegg, and there occurred the kindling of her connection with Krishnamurti.

The sequence of events that brought her more closely into his orbit had its roots several years in the past. Krishnamurti suffered a kidney ailment in 1957 that left him weak and unable to continue with a planned series of talks in Europe. Rajagopal was incensed that he would have to cancel events that he had already arranged, and he declared his refusal to serve any longer in that capacity. Any future travel or speaking plans, he said, could be arranged by Doris Pratt, the secretary for KWInc in England, and paid for with funds she managed.

This remained the state of affairs until the summer of 1964, when Alain Naudé (Nah-DAY) arrived on the scene. A classical pianist of French descent, Naudé was born in South Africa and trained and performed in Europe, where he met Krishnamurti at the age of thirty-five. He gave up his career as a pianist and professor of music in order to travel with Krishnamurti and serve as his secretary. Naudé was cultured, multilingual, and congenial, and he moved effortlessly into Krishnamurti's network of friends and associates. Doris Pratt requested Rajagopal to provide a salary for Naudé with funds from KWInc in Ojai, and he agreed.

Not long after his appointment as Krishnamurti's aide-de-camp, Naudé served as a catalyst for Mary Zimbalist's entrée into Krishnamurti's world. He and Mary enjoyed one another's company, and they began spending increasing amounts of time together with Krishnamurti. Drives through the countryside, afternoon walks, movies, and meals formed the matrix for a developing set of relationships. By 1966, their triangle had settled into an ongoing arrangement for purposes of travel, public talks, and all the associated affairs of daily life.

Mary's entrance into Krishnamurti's life was a blessing to him beyond calculation. For the first time since the death of Nitya, he had a companion who was attuned to his needs and preferences, his moods and sense of humor, someone fully appreciative of his personal qualities as well as his mission. Their compatibility encompassed every dimension, from diet and travel to nature, social issues, and the study of consciousness. Their attraction may or may not have included a romantic current, but it was magnetic and unmistakable.

In his travels between England and Ojai, Krishnamurti sometimes stopped and stayed in New York at the home of a friend of many years. Frederick Pinter was a donor who was familiar with others who had contributed to Krishnamurti's work. On one such visit in 1960, Pinter conveyed to Krishnamurti some disturbing reports regarding Rajagopal's management of funds donated to KWInc. Rumors were circulating to the effect that donations intended to support Krishnamurti's work were being used by Rajagopal for personal purposes. Pinter warned that Krishnamurti had better assume some responsibility for the affairs of KWInc and find out for himself whether the finances were being managed properly. The first order of business would be for him to become reinstated to KWInc's board of trustees.

Krishnamurti took Pinter's warning to heart. During the course of his stay at Ojai, he requested for the first time to have access to the financial records of KWInc, and he informed Rajagopal that he wished to resume his place on the board. Rajagopal flatly denied both requests. Radha notes that for three decades Krishnamurti had raised no question or challenge regarding Rajagopal's administrative behavior or management of funds. Accordingly, he reacted now as if he were insulted and not at all inclined to agree to Krishnamurti's request.

The situation had been reduced to terms as spare and sharply defined as they were ominous. The organization that existed for the sole purpose of supporting Krishnamurti's work had refused to grant him access to its financial records or admission to its governing body. Not only was this circumstance preposterous on its face; in addition,

Rajagopal had the effrontery to act offended, to feel and behave as if he were the victim of Krishnamurti's impetuous interference with his authority.

After Rosalind evicted Krishnamurti from the east end residence, he was unwilling to return to Ojai unless he was invited by both her and Rajagopal. That occurred in 1960 and again for three weeks in 1961. When he returned in the summer of 1961, he repeated his request to be reinstated to the board. Rajagopal refused again. Later that year, Krishnamurti put his request in writing in the form of a letter addressed to Rajagopal and all the members of the board. Rajagopal neither responded to this letter nor shared it with the board.

After 1961, the invitations to Krishnamurti to return to Ojai ceased until 1966, when he was asked to conduct another series of talks in the Oak Grove. During that five-year interval, nothing occurred to ameliorate his concerns about the management of KWInc. The long interval in which his presence in Ojai remained unwelcome was no doubt due in part to his repeated requests for information and participation in the affairs of KWInc.

The Rajagopals had effectively propelled a wrecking ball through Krishnamurti's work in America, notwithstanding that their role was precisely to facilitate his activity. He was complicit by virtue of his passivity, but nothing can mitigate the magnitude of the damage they did. The facilitators became the barriers to his work, and in so doing they betrayed their deepest responsibility.

⌒

After the four talks he gave in Ojai in 1960, Krishnamurti did not speak again in the United States until the fall of 1966. During that interval, his talks and dialogues were confined to several venues in India and four locations in Europe: London, Paris, Rome, and Saanen. When he finally returned to America, it was due to Rajagopal's invitation to give a series of talks in Ojai. These were preceded by six talks in September at the New School for Social Research in New York. As these were his first talks in America in six years, they provided an opportunity to ascertain what changes may have occurred in the substance and the manner of expression of his philosophy.

With the talks in New York, Krishnamurti's teaching had arrived at a state of maturity. Here we can see the full development of his point of view, expressed in a modern idiom, with all the elements in their proper place and proportion. Much of the content is familiar from previous years, but here it is expressed with a new clarity and focus. It bears the relationship to the previous material that a man in middle age bears to himself as a teenager or young adult.

Much of the exposition consists of the negation of all familiar methods and techniques for self-understanding. He castigates every form of authority in the psychological field—the priest, the professor, the psychoanalyst. Self-understanding requires inward freedom, and submission to or acceptance of authority in psychological matters is the very denial of such freedom. More deeply, any image of the individual who is writing or speaking prevents observation, including any image of Krishnamurti. "If you say, 'Well, he's an Indian from India with all his mystical ideas, or romantic ideas,' and so on, you're not actually seeing."

Krishnamurti maintained that the fundamental problems of life cannot be solved piecemeal, one at a time, because they are interrelated. Life can only be understood as a whole. What is required, therefore, is a complete revolution in consciousness, a radical transformation. Any desire to fulfill or motive to achieve such a change, however, can only exert a distorting influence upon clear observation. Therefore, what will precipitate transformation? "To put that question, we must be tremendously earnest because if we put the question with a motive, because we want certain results, the motive dictates the answer. Therefore we must put the question without motive, without any profit; and that's an extraordinarily difficult thing to do."

What is required to resolve the issues of daily life is a mind that is attentive without being forced to attend. Such a mind is capable of "observing the total movement of our own selves inwardly, every movement of thought, feeling, word, gesture, and what lies behind the word, behind the thought—this whole structure of the psyche." Observation itself, in Krishnamurti's view, is the catalyst for change. "This is a problem of great awareness, not of some spiritual, absurd, mystical state." In the sheer act of observation, the content of consciousness undergoes a deep transformation.

Several other elements in the panorama of the mind require examination and penetrating insight. Foremost among these are fear and pleasure. Fear is anathema to undistorted exploration, but it cannot be eradicated by any act of will or deliberation. Only deep understanding of the manner in which the mind produces fear can eliminate it. Fear and pleasure are products of time and thought, and so these elements too must find their right place. Thought and time are inseparable, and together they form the matrix in which most mental activity occurs.

> When you have understood fear, authority, and the putting away of all demands for experience—which is really the highest form of maturity—then the mind becomes completely silent. It is only in that silence, which is very active, that you will see, if you have gone that far, that there is a total revolution in the psyche. Only such a mind can create a new society.

The foregoing inquiry represents a process designed to remove the impediments to an even more fundamental insight. The culmination of the inquiry revolves around Krishnamurti's signature statement that the observer is the observed. The observer is the ego, the self, the psychological entity at the center of consciousness, the one that observes not only outward events but inward desires, motivations, and emotions. Because the center considers itself separate from phenomena such as fear or anger, it attempts to monitor, control, and regulate what it observes. According to Krishnamurti, that sense of separation is false and the source of pervasive, chronic conflict. To see factually, directly, the inseparability of the observer and the observed represents the key to psychological harmony and freedom.

> When the mind realizes, understands the nature of the observer and the observed, conflict comes to an end; and the cessation of conflict is essential because then the mind becomes completely peaceful. Then we can find out what the significance of existence is—not before, not when we are ambitious, greedy, envious, acquisitive, seeking more and more and more experience.
>
> All that immature stuff ceases when the observer realizes that what he observes is the observer; the seeker is the sought. If one sees that, then there is a totally different kind of action—not this restless, meaningless activity.
>
> The mind has examined, has understood the whole meaning of seeking, and also it is rid of fear. Therefore there is complete quietness, stillness, silence of the mind—which hasn't come into being through drill, through mesmerism, through self-hypnosis. It comes because we have understood all this.

The evolution of this defining principle in Krishnamurti's teaching is a point of major biographical interest. As we have noted, it was not until after World War II that he first articulated this idea, and, when he did so, it was in a brief, incidental manner. Twenty years later, it has assumed pride of place as the pivotal, overarching insight at the core of his philosophy. And there it would remain for the rest of his life.

Numerous additional topics were addressed in the course of the six talks, including love, death, the unconscious, instincts, LSD, and whether experience forms a valid basis for self-understanding. This is quintessential Krishnamurti, at or near the peak of his powers. The beauty, coherence, and sweep of the talks underscore the magnitude of the loss to America as a result of his ten-year period of exile.

Krishnamurti's exile coincided with a dearth of reliable information regarding his activities and relationships. This situation underwent a complete reversal with the advent of Mary Zimbalist as his companion. Among the changes she initiated was a flood of recorded observations about his daily behavior, states of mind, physical health, interactions with people, and incidental comments and reflections. She wrote with precision, clarity, and sensitivity to the meaning and implications of his relationships with myriad individuals. From an historical and biographical perspective, it was as if his life had emerged from a long, dark tunnel into a fully illuminated landscape.

Among the fortuitous features of Mary's involvement in Krishnamurti's life was access to the house she owned in Malibu, an hour's drive from Ojai. Situated on a bluff directly overlooking the ocean, the home had been her residence with her husband Sam, and, beginning in 1966, it served for many years to accommodate her and Krishnamurti whenever they were in the United States.

The availability of Mary's house represented a somewhat remarkable turn of events. A decade after his eviction from his Ojai home, Krishnamurti found another residence located near Ojai and equally if not more attractive than the providential appeal of Pine Cottage. Mary's home was spacious, quiet, and private, and furnished with her exquisite taste and considerable wealth. It had a magnificent view of the ocean as well as easy access to the beach below. Ojai would always retain a special hold upon his affections, for emotional, historical, and spiritual reasons, but Malibu represented a surpassingly suitable substitute.

These accommodations enabled Krishnamurti to gather the focus and energy required to deliver another series of talks in Ojai. The proximity to Ojai, however, was not without complications. The matter of Krishnamurti's access to information and responsibility for the affairs of KWInc had not been resolved to any degree since it had first been broached in 1960. These issues as well as arrangements for the talks required Krishnamurti to engage in a series of phone calls with Rajagopal. Mary was present during these calls, and, as a result, a window opened into the tone and texture of the quality of interaction between the two men.

Krishnamurti and Alain Naudé arrived in New York in September 1966 and met Mary at the apartment of her brother where they would be staying for the next month. The afternoon of their arrival, Rajagopal called and spoke with Krishnamurti for the first time in more than a year. The primary purpose of his call was to berate Krishnamurti for scheduling talks in New York without his knowledge or approval. Why this would be a source of contention was not at all clear to Mary.

The most salient characteristic of the conversation, from her point of view, was the tense and strident quality of Rajagopal's remonstrances, which she could overhear from the other side of the room. For the first time, she witnessed the aggressive, demanding attitude that he projected and Krishnamurti's curious passivity in response. He was not insensitive to or untouched by it; on the contrary, he emerged from the phone call shaken and disturbed. Yet neither in his attitude to Rajagopal, nor in his explanations to Mary, did he display any effort to stand up for himself or take steps to rectify the situation. The interaction exhibited in microcosm the inexplicable acquiescence that characterized his toleration of Rosalind's eviction of him from the east end residence.

Mary, Naudé, and Krishnamurti arrived in Malibu in mid-October and spent a few weeks there prior to the talks. During this interval, Rajagopal called Krishnamurti on three occasions, and each call repeated the belligerent pattern Mary had observed in New York. Two of the calls ended with Rajagopal hanging up on Krishnamurti.

On November 4, the party of three drove up to Ojai where they planned to stay at the east end residence throughout the period of the talks. Krishnamurti had his rooms in Pine Cottage, while Mary and Naudé stayed in separate apartments located nearby. When Krishnamurti showed Mary around the property, he pointed to an outdoor closet attached to his cottage containing a water heater. He mentioned that one night, many years earlier, he had come home from a long walk in the hills without his keys to the cottage. It was long after dark, and he was so afraid of disturbing the Rajagopals that he spent the entire night standing in the closet to stay warm. This incident suggested that the pattern of hostility on one hand, and passivity bordering on self-destructive negligence on the other hand, was deep and long established.

At one point Mary asked whether the aggressive attitude she witnessed had led to the cancellation of the talks in 1960. Krishnamurti acknowledged that it was a contributing factor. He added, however, that it would not happen again because now he had Mary and Naudé with him, whereas in 1960 he had "no one to talk to" about it.

Several additional conversations between Krishnamurti and Rajagopal occurred during the two-month stay in Malibu and Ojai. Some of these exhibited Rajagopal's vituperative and threatening attitude that was now familiar to Mary, but toward the end she observed Krishnamurti begin to display some spine and a sense of resolve. In consultation with her and Naudé, he wrote up a proposal for a revitalization of KWInc that included expanding the board of trustees and having no one person play a dominant role. At first Rajagopal seemed to respond favorably, but a few days later, he roundly rejected the proposal. Krishnamurti finally found the wherewithal to confront him and inform him that he was considering withdrawing from any further association with KWInc. Rajagopal interpreted this as a threat and responded by cursing Krishnamurti and redoubling his belligerence.

By the time Krishnamurti left California with Naudé in early December, his relationship with Rajagopal and with KWInc had gelled into a new and different configuration. He had asked Rajagopal for copies of the recordings of the talks he had given and was refused. His diary manuscript was now in Rajagopal's possession, and his request for that to be returned was also refused. He had not yet considered taking legal action, but the general direction of his future behavior was now unmistakable. He stated both privately to Mary and directly to Rajagopal that henceforth he was "out," in the sense that he would have nothing further to do with KWInc. Psychologically and in essence, if not yet by law, a parting of the ways was now at hand.

Not for another year were more concrete steps taken to address and resolve the contradictions in the administration of Krishnamurti's work. Gerard Blitz was a friend of Krishnamurti's with long experience in the administration of business affairs. He was the founder and chief executive of the Club Méditeraneé, an enterprise offering vacation packages featuring long cruises and luxury resort destinations. Blitz offered to serve as an intermediary and to meet with Rajagopal personally in an effort to review the legal landscape and, if possible, effect a reconciliation. Krishnamurti accepted the offer, and Blitz met Rajagopal in Ojai and discussed the situation for several hours.

Blitz came away from this meeting with a more precise

understanding of the legal background that now governed the affairs of KWInc. Since the 1920s, two organizations had existed for the purpose of receiving donations and preserving Krishnamurti's talks, letters, and other expressions of his teachings. The Star Publishing Trust, formed in 1922, named Krishnamurti as its primary governing officer; The Star Institute, formed in 1929, gave Rajagopal exclusive control over its affairs. KWInc was originally organized to encompass both organizations, but in 1956, Rajagopal secured Krishnamurti's signature on a legal instrument transferring the authority over both organizations to him. This was yet another instance of Rajagopal's legerdemain and Krishnamurti's blind willingness to sign whatever document he put before him.

Blitz conveyed to Krishnamurti these basic legal realities, as well as the meaning of the Madras document he had signed in 1958. Krishnamurti later described what he learned at that time in these terms:

> Now as I was not interested in the administrative details of KWInc, and as Rajagopal was extremely secretive about administrative matters, I always naturally signed everything he asked me to sign. I had complete confidence in his integrity. That is how I signed a paper apparently, transferring all the assets of [Star Publishing Trust] to the Star Institute, over which Rajagopal had complete control. This happened in 1956. Of course I had no idea that I was doing this, as Rajagopal did not explain to me what I was signing.
>
> So he is now in complete control of all the assets of KWInc, which are considerable, which run into millions of dollars. Also I have signed away to this body which he now controls completely the copyright of everything published under my name. This is what had been revealed to Mr. Blitz in his investigations and subsequent conversations with Rajagopal.

Spurred on by these revelations, Krishnamurti consulted an attorney to ascertain what options, if any, might be available to recover the rights to his work. Michael Rubinstein, based in London, was an expert in copyright law, and he began to investigate whether the Madras document could survive legal scrutiny. After consulting with attorneys in India, he determined that it could not.

Over the course of several months in early 1968, a flurry of correspondence occurred between Krishnamurti's representatives and the board of trustees of KWInc. None of these communications were successful in restoring Krishnamurti to the board and giving him access to the financial records of KWInc. Krishnamurti went so far as to inform the board by letter that he would have nothing more to do with that organization so long as Rajagopal remained its head. In April, he met with Mima Porter, one of the KWInc trustees, and told her he was determined to formally disassociate from it unless Rajagopal agreed to meet his requests in the very near future.

Even while these events were unfolding, Krishnamurti was making preparations for new and more constructive expressions of his work. He had for years wanted to start a school in Europe, just as he had created schools in India and in Ojai. Now, with the support of Mary Zimbalist, Alain Naudé, and other friends, the opportunity was at hand for the new school to materialize. He found an experienced educator, Dorothy Simmons, who was able and willing to direct the school, and he began to consider the administrative structure necessary to receive funds and guide its development.

In view of the impending separation from KWInc, Krishnamurti consulted with Rubinstein about creating an organization that would never become vulnerable to the kinds of behaviors perpetrated by Rajagopal. The distribution of responsibilities among members of the board would prohibit any single individual from assuming exclusive authority, and respect for Krishnamurti's intentions would be built into the founding documents. The new organization would be based in London, and its proposed membership included Mary Zimbalist, Alain Naudé, Gerard Blitz, and Mary Lutyens. In the event that his relationship with KWInc was not somehow restored, the chrysalis of a new administrative structure was now already in place.

The April ultimatum conveyed to Mima Porter was met with silence until June 29, on the eve of the commencement of the annual talks in Saanen. At that time, Krishnamurti received from her a letter that agreed to nothing, but merely stated that Rajagopal would be willing to discuss the unresolved issues next time Krishnamurti was in Ojai. After eight years of requesting to be reinstated to the board of KWInc, Krishnamurti had finally had enough. He wrote to Rajagopal and the trustees of KWInc and revoked his grant of authority over his copyright and formally declared his decision to have no further relationship with KWInc of any kind.

On July 9, before the second talk at Saanen, Rubinstein read the following statement to the audience that had gathered from all parts of the world.

> Krishnamurti wishes it to be known that he has completely disassociated himself from Krishnamurti Writings Incorporated of Ojai, California. He hopes that, as a result of this public announcement, those who wish to be associated with his work and teachings will give support to the new, international, Krishnamurti Foundation of London, England, whose activities will include a school. The Deed which establishes the Foundation ensures that Krishnamurti's intentions will be respected.

Krishnamurti may have been slow to act, but when he did so, it was decisively. When he dissolved the Order of the Star in August 1929, his address to the audience made clear that he had been considering it for a period of years. Now, some 39 years later, the separation from KWInc represented an act of almost equal significance. It had been twelve years since his eviction from the east end residence and eight years since he had first requested to resume his place on the board of KWInc. His patience may have been naïve, misplaced, and excessive, but it was not unlimited; and the manner of his action, once its aim was clarified, was categorical.

But Rajagopal was a determined and resourceful adversary, and the divorce from KWInc would not be as straightforward as the dissolution of the Order of the Star. On the contrary: what had occurred so far was not the finale but merely the prelude to a larger drama. In fact, the battle had only just been joined.

Helena Blavatsky

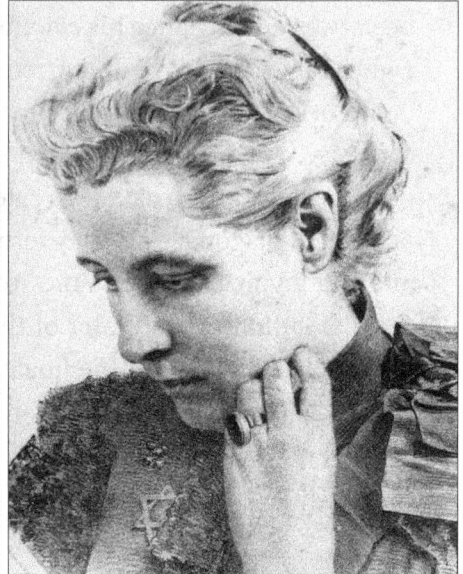

Annie Besant

Krishnamurti at age fifteen with Charles
Leadbeater and Annie Besant

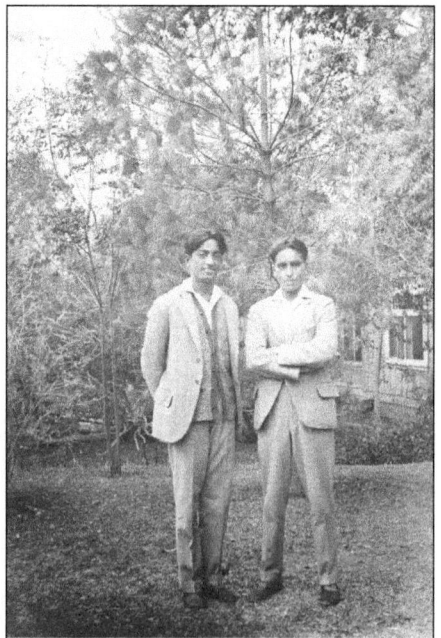

Krishnamurti and Nitya in Ojai
circa 1922

Krishnamurti at age twenty-seven with Rosalind, Nitya, and Mr. Warrington, president of the American chapter of the Theosophical Society

Nitya and Krishnamurti circa 1918

Rajagopal and Krishnamurti
circa 1925

Annie Besant and Krishnamurti
circa 1927

Pepper tree and Pine Cottage circa 1922

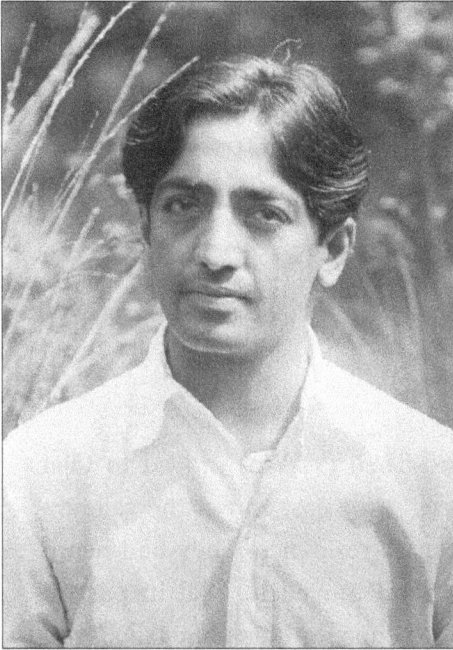

Krishnamurti at approximately
age thirty-eight

Krishnamurti at approximately
age forty-nine

Krishnamurti at approximately age sixty

Chapter Nine

ERNA LILLIEFELT
AND THE KFA

Erna Lilliefelt and her husband Theo (TAY-o) moved to Ojai in 1968 and purchased a house in the east end of the valley, a quarter mile away from Krishnamurti's residence. They had heard him speak many years earlier and had moved to Ojai in part to spend their retirement years near the venue for his public talks. And so they were alarmed to discover, shortly after their arrival, that Krishnamurti had announced his disassociation from KWInc. At the time, this seemed to suggest that he might sever his ties with Ojai altogether.

Erna and Theo were in their late fifties. He had enjoyed a distinguished career as a diplomat in the United Nations, with postings in Lebanon and other locations in the Middle East. Born in Sweden, he had performed in his youth as a concert pianist in cities all over Europe. Theo was handsome, stocky, fluent in several languages, and well schooled in manners and behavior appropriate under all circumstances. He was congenial but reserved, and he carried himself with the air of a somewhat authoritarian personality.

In spite of Theo's Old World disposition and masculine characteristics, Erna was the dominant personality of the two. Her appearance was presentable, but she kept her gray hair cut short, and she wore a minimum of makeup. Her dress tended to be formal and devoid of color or flair. She was capable of showing warmth, animation, and moments of kindness, but her standard mode of interaction was brisk, businesslike, and to the point.

Erna had started work as a secretary in a Texas corporation and had risen through the ranks to become its chief executive. Such a career prior to the age of feminism, especially in Texas, was almost without parallel, but Erna excelled in every attribute required for corporate leadership. She had the determination of a bulldog, a sharp if narrow intelligence, and the absolute conviction of her own rectitude. However distinguished was Theo's career as a diplomat, in their retirement he was essentially Erna's accessory.

She understood at once that something must be amiss within the governing structure of KWInc if Krishnamurti had separated himself from the organization and its assets. Funds donated in support of his work would no longer be available for that purpose. To allow that to happen would be not only unjust, in her view, but unethical. She smelled an unmistakable rat, and she had the acumen and diligence to pursue it where it lived. That was in the record of property transactions available for inspection in the offices of the Ventura County Recorder. There she devoted weeks of research into an intricate network of sales conducted by Rajagopal over the course of decades on behalf of KWInc and related organizations. The evidence she found of malfeasance and misappropriation of funds was incontrovertible.

A little over a month after his disassociation from KWInc, Krishnamurti received a letter from Erna outlining the results of her investigations. She urged him not to forsake his responsibility to those who had donated on behalf of his work. This letter evidently made an immediate impact. At the first opportunity, he, Mary, and Rosenstein met with Erna and Theo in New York to review her findings and consider a course of action. A few months later, in February 1969, the Krishnamurti Foundation of America (KFA) was formed, with Erna, Mary, Alain Naudé, and Krishnamurti constituting the initial board of trustees. The first order of business of the nascent organization was to recover the assets and archives that by all rights belonged to Krishnamurti and his work.

Over the course of the next three years, the KFA and KWInc engaged in a dizzying blur of meetings, letters, phone calls, proposals, and memoranda. The efforts to find some accommodation with Rajagopal were as extensive as they were futile. His attitude alternated between pathos and insolence, with a persistent theme of victimhood coupled with vindictiveness. His behavior was marked by meetings scheduled, postponed, and re-scheduled, only to result in hours of inconclusive conversation. Throughout it all, he refused to permit any audit of the financial books of KWInc.

Another current of events revolved around the participation of Laurence Tapper, the Deputy Attorney General for the state of California. At the suggestion of Sidney Field, a lifelong friend of Krishnamurti, the KFA solicited the involvement of the attorney general in the hope that the case against KWInc was sufficiently strong to bring the state into the proceedings on KFA's behalf. Presented with some of the evidence unearthed by Erna, Tapper agreed to look into the matter, but he was doubtful that a lawsuit could succeed against Rajagopal. His opinion was based not only on the apparent legitimacy of the governing documents of KWInc, but also on his personal friendship with Rajagopal's attorney, Jim Loebl. Tapper was convinced that Loebl would never have allowed Rajagopal to misappropriate any charitable assets or funds.

Within a year, Tapper began to see things differently. Rajagopal's pattern of procrastination, his resistance to suggestions for reconciliation, and his refusal to allow an audit gradually brought Tapper around to the view that the attorney general might intervene on behalf of the KFA. After another year, this possibility had crystallized into a firm conclusion. Tapper stated outright in a letter to the KWInc attorneys that any further proposals could proceed only if predicated on the recognition that Rajagopal had misappropriated over a million dollars in charitable assets.

Rajagopal's obstinate attitude was based only in part on his venal attachment to the charitable empire he had designed and cultivated. He also feared the personal humiliation that would follow if it were acknowledged that he had embezzled massive amounts of donations. The trustees of the KFA were sensitive to his possible mortification, and they did their utmost to give him a way to save face. They offered him a seat on the boards of both the American and English foundations, provided that KWInc could be dissolved and its archives and assets transferred to the new organizations. Even this proposal was insufficient for Rajagopal, and he declined the offer.

In November 1971, after three years of fruitless negotiations, the Attorney General for the state of California filed suit in the County of Ventura on behalf of the KFA against the organization and the trustees of KWInc. The complaint listed five causes of action: self-dealing by trustees of KWInc; dissipation of trust assets; failure of defendants to carry out the charitable purposes of the trust; antagonism between the defendants of the trust and its beneficiaries; and "injunctive relief," legalese for recovery of property and other charitable assets.

And so, in a maelstrom of attorneys and legalities, the KFA arose to correct the mismanagement of decades of donations on behalf of Krishnamurti's work. In this thicket of documents and discussions, Erna Lilliefelt was the instrumental, driving force guiding every step in the unfolding sequence of events. She and Mary Zimbalist, along with a handful of other supporters, rescued Krishnamurti's work in America and enabled him to fulfill his mission there for the final two decades of his life.

Mary recorded her impressions and memories of life with Krishnamurti at his request. He suggested she keep a record of what it was
like to be with "the man from Madanapalle," the town of his birth,
and she did so faithfully for twenty years. The memoir she composed,
In the Presence of Krishnamurti, adheres closely to her diary notes
and therefore follows events in a strictly chronological manner. As a
result, several themes recur at odd intervals, woven into the fabric of
events as they happened at the time. The net effect is chronological
coherence achieved at the expense of a certain degree of thematic
disorganization. Some of the threads are more meaningful and illuminating when drawn together into a single strand.

One set of interactions that Mary records revolved around the
tone and quality of her involvement in Krishnamurti's life. He was
somewhat formal in his manners and not inclined to familiarity or
public displays of affection. Mary moved into the orbit of his daily
routine rather quickly, and it must have taken some time for them
both to sense that the partnership would endure.

A little more than a year after she began to travel with him, he
sat down with her and Naudé one evening for a conversation that she
described as "bewildering." His immediate concern was whether she
was spending too much money on his behalf and if her family would
object. She assured him that he had nothing to worry about in that
regard, but he hardly listened and insisted that she not extend herself
too much financially.

A little later, this conversation shifted gears and took a turn that
Mary described as whimsical and "wild." Krishnamurti playfully
suggested that he might consider getting married; Naudé chimed
in that he might get married too. Mary cheerfully volunteered to
arrange both of their weddings, and the three of them enjoyed a
good laugh.

Krishnamurti's fantasy, however, reflected a certain underlying reality. Mary evidently discerned the implicit seriousness of the conversation, for after Naudé left the room, she took the opportunity to make it clear that her relationship with him was platonic. Krishnamurti covered her mouth with his hand and said he needed no confessions; but she stood her ground and said she thought he should know. The conversation ended with him kissing her hand.

Another episode along similar lines occurred about three weeks later. Krishnamurti and Mary were riding in the back seat of a car with a friend, with some bags of groceries in the space behind the seat. Mary put her arm back to steady one of the packages, and Krishnamurti joked, "A lady is putting her arm around me"; and he added, "She might kiss me!" Mary laughed and said she might, but she would have to work up to that slowly. "Yes, slowly," he agreed, and that was apparently the end of the moment of flirtatiousness. And yet that evening, she went into his bedroom to say goodnight before leaving in the morning to catch a plane. He had a poultice of some kind on his stomach under the covers. It created a mound on his abdomen, and he joked that he was pregnant. And so the merry fantasies arrived at their semi-logical conclusion.

After these events, Mary records no more incidents of a similar kind. She never suggests nor gives any hint that their relationship proceeded according to the laws of nature and normal intimacy. And yet they clearly shared a strong and human love, and they slept under the same roof for many years. For all intents and purposes, they were married in every way except by the lights of the law. Mary Lutyens later wrote that Mary "knew and loved" Krishnamurti at "every level of his being." On a casual reading, that phrasing might seem somewhat vague with respect to physical intimacy; but a little reflection suggests that it may be taken at face value.

Krishnamurti commented several times in a more serious way on the meaning of Mary's involvement in his life. Some two years after she had started living and traveling with him, he cautioned that she was now responsible not only to herself but to "something else," and therefore must take extra care. He said he was part of some "other thing," and that she must "never leave that other." He described a "seeming protective providence" that he had felt all his life. At times, Mary also felt that her actions were infused with a heightened awareness, as if "something was taking charge." She said she began to feel "responsible to something other—some purpose behind his life."

On another occasion, Krishnamurti elaborated on these suggestions and made them more explicit. He told Mary that she must outlive him because her presence in his life was "part of a plan." Vanda Scaravelli was not available for that purpose, he said, and therefore Mary "had been appointed." A few days later, he returned to this theme. If Mary's husband had not died, he said, she would not have been able to help him; but since she was free, "the decision was made" to have her be "the guardian."

Mary appeared to accept without question the authenticity of Krishnamurti's sense of a protective providence. She evidently never asked whether any objective evidence could support his feeling. She did, however, address the conspicuous incongruity between his sense of protection and his treatment at the hands of the Rajagopals.

She questioned him in the context of a conversation that occurred one afternoon in August 1971, a few months before the lawsuit was filed. Krishnamurti confided in Erna, Theo, and Mary at length regarding "what went wrong with Rajagopal." He said the young Rajagopal had been brought into the work of the Theosophical Society because he was capable and intelligent, although neither Leadbeater nor Annie Besant were close to or fond of him. As the son of a district judge, he had an air of entitlement, unwilling to do the dishes or anything with his hands. He and Rosalind had provoked quarrels with Krishnamurti that were so vehement "it was surprising they had not shot" him. Rosalind hit him on the head with a wrench on one occasion, and she tried to hit him with a bottle on another. She kneed him in the groin so hard that he was unable to walk for a day. She urged him once to jump onto the tracks before an oncoming train.

Mary asked Krishnamurti why he had tolerated such egregious behavior. He said he did not know and could not understand it himself; but he added that he would never have allowed the Rajago-pals to influence the manner or content of his talks. If they had tried, he said, "I would have left." Mary concluded that a personal attack was somehow insignificant to him so long as the teachings were kept inviolable.

Krishnamurti's sense that his life was unfolding according to a plan is highly compatible with the theosophical idea of the World Teacher. He seemed to acknowledge as much when he explained to Mary what the theosophists believed, including the participation of a pantheon of Masters and of the Lord Maitreya. Nevertheless, he said he did not endorse that account. He made it clear that he was merely recounting what they said and that he neither accepted nor rejected their point of view.

In a related conversation, Krishnamurti described the sequence of events that had occurred in 1922, when he was semiconscious at times and suffered intense pain for three days. He seemed to attribute significance to this strange episode, but he maintained that even the theosophists were at a loss to interpret what it was all about. More-over, decades later, he had no independent sense of the meaning of what had occurred. He acknowledged nothing more than to say, "It would be interesting to know."

At the time the lawsuit was filed, Mary had been with Krish-namurti for nearly seven years. Her memoir for that period of time is meticulous and detailed. She mentioned restaurants they visited for lunch, appointments with the tailor, dentist, or homeopathic doctor, and innumerable incidents or comments that were noteworthy for one reason or another. And yet she records not a single quarrel or conflict except for her disappointment that he did not respond more forcefully to the Rajagopals. Her affection and admiration were unwavering, and it is clear how much he appreciated all she had done for him.

Mary wrote with a distinctive voice and sensitivity to words. She described the Taj Mahal as a "strange, snowy apparition that seemed more a thing imagined than a building, legendary but far beyond any preconception. It floated in the moonlight, a disembodied eloquence of beauty." The city of Benares was

> ... a torrent of people, swarming bicycles, buses with impatient horns, wandering cows, ponderous buffaloes, sometimes a camel, and even an elephant. On foot, rounding a corner, I barely missed a collision with a thin, cloth-wrapped corpse across the back of a bicycle being taken to the ghats. There the smoking pyres fed that ancient destination of the pious.

Eating lunch at a hotel in Paris, Krishnamurti was "the embodiment of every aristocracy the past had ever produced.... also as innocent as a beautifully mannered child." She described a scene at the airport where "K was all elegance and simplicity. He went off with the grace, exquisite manners, and face lit with affection that only he had."

Mary's role in Krishnamurti's life was so important and sustained that it overshadowed the significance of Alain Naudé. He preceded her involvement by several months, and his friendship with her facilitated her entrance into the daily round of Krishnamurti's activities. Of almost equal significance was his gift for arranging venues where

Krishnamurti's message could reach a wider audience. It was he who had the insight—obvious in retrospect, but not at the time—that Krishnamurti's talks were well suited for a younger demographic of people entering adulthood with questioning, open minds. College campuses were fertile territory for Krishnamurti's views, especially during a period of upheaval within the culture of those who were coming of age in America.

As a former college professor, Naudé coupled this insight with the system awareness necessary to navigate university bureaucracies. With Naudé serving as his advance man, Krishnamurti embarked on a flurry of appearances on campuses on both coasts. These talks were emblematic of the new trajectory of his engagement with an American audience.

Over the course of six months, Krishnamurti gave thirty-seven talks and dialogues to students at nine American universities. In September 1968, he gave several talks at the New School for Social Research in New York and at Brandeis University in Massachusetts. Two talks were held at Lowell House at Harvard. In November, he returned to Malibu and gave a series of eight talks at Claremont College in Southern California. In February 1969, he embarked on a month-long trip to the San Francisco Bay Area, where he gave four talks at the University of California at Berkeley, four at U. C. Santa Cruz, and four at Stanford University. The collective impact of these appearances served to catapult him into the awareness of a new generation in America.

Naudé also arranged for Krishnamurti to conduct dialogues with numerous individuals who were receptive to his work. Among these were Allen Ginsberg, Timothy Leary, and Alan Watts, although these conversations failed to produce memorable results. Three professors of religious studies, by contrast, succeeded in conducting meaningful conversations with Krishnamurti. Among these were Huston Smith, author of the best-selling *The World's Religions*, and

Jacob Needleman, another highly regarded and prolific author. Alan Anderson, in the religious studies department of San Diego State College, formed an unusual rapport with Krishnamurti, and the two men conducted an eighteen-part videotaped series of dialogues. U Thant, Christopher Isherwood, and Buckminster Fuller were among those who also met with Krishnamurti during this period.

Naudé himself conducted several recorded conversations with Krishnamurti. This stood in contrast to Rajagopal, with whom Krishnamurti never discussed issues pertaining to the teachings. Two of Naudé's dialogues were of sufficient interest to merit publication. One of these examines the inseparability of the observer and the observed with unusual clarity and attention to subtle detail. The second dialogue addressed whether good and evil are objective qualities that exist in the world or are merely conditioned judgments superimposed by society and tradition. Krishnamurti hesitated to use the word "evil" because it is loaded with Christian preconceptions; but he acknowledged that psychological disorder, which issues in violence and cruelty, warrants that term. He contrasted that with the behavior of a shark, whose killing is not evil because it is for survival and part of the natural order of the biological world.

In a footnote to these dialogues, Naudé described himself as "a musician, for six years closely associated with Krishnamurti as his secretary and assistant, and above all as his student." For most of that time, the triangular arrangement seemed to function flawlessly. At some point, as Mary assumed increasing responsibilities, perhaps Naudé began to feel superfluous. In any case, an extended holiday turned into a parting of the ways, and Naudé settled in San Francisco. He continued to visit from time to time, and he conducted additional dialogues with Krishnamurti. Regrettably, he never recorded his recollections of their years together, and his final assessment of their relationship remains unknown.

The increased frequency and varied location of Krishnamurti's talks resulted in a wave of new publications. His appearances on college campuses were published in 1970 as *Talks to American Students* and in 1973 under the title *You Are the World*. *The Awakening of Intelligence*, published by Harper & Row, included talks given in New York as well as dialogues with Alain Naudé, Jacob Needleman, and theoretical physicist David Bohm. Harper & Row also published *Beyond Violence*, consisting of talks given in Santa Monica and San Diego as well as in London and Brockwood Park.

Krishnamurti delivered his public talks extemporaneously, with an absolute minimum of forethought or planning. He often asked Mary and others, even as he was being driven to the venue where he would speak, what he should talk about. As a result, the talks have a slightly impressionistic quality. In view of the lack of planning, they are remarkably coherent and well organized, but at times they exhibit some overlap of topics or indirection before arriving at a point.

Krishnamurti's written work, by contrast, is more dense, cogent, and direct than the public talks. The *Commentaries on Living*, for example, and *Krishnamurti's Notebook* display little of the extemporaneous quality discernible in the talks. For this reason, two additional publications warrant special attention. *The Only Revolution*, which appeared in 1970, and *The Urgency of Change*, in 1971, consist of pieces dictated by Krishnamurti rather than transcripts of his talks and dialogues. As a result, they have the more focused quality of his written work.

The pieces that appear in these two books consist of dialogues Krishnamurti conducted with a questioner invented for this purpose, someone who is thoughtful, widely read, and fairly familiar with Krishnamurti's work. The imaginary visitor raises issues that reflect an understanding and appreciation of the teachings, and he challenges Krishnamurti in a way that few people in real life were able to do. He is not merely a passive enabler, tossing softball questions that elicit easy answers. His questions are pointed, probing, and designed to expose weaknesses or contradictions in the teachings. These two books represent a unique addition to the teachings and a valuable resource for serious students of Krishnamurti's work.

✑

As 1971 came to a close, the transformation that had occurred in Krishnamurti's life in America was immeasurable. The KFA was firmly established and engaged in a mortal struggle with KWInc, with all of its legal armor and deep financial resources. His talks and dialogues were finding new outlets, and publications were proliferating. He had a companion as close and compatible as anyone had been since Nitya. An auspicious new day had arrived, and his work was finally flowering with unexpected colors and creativity.

Chapter Ten

THE SOURCE OF
THE TEACHINGS

One of the pillars of Krishnamurti's philosophy is that any form of authority in the psychological field acts as an impediment to self-understanding and freedom. This principle was central to the dissolution of the Order of the Star, and he repeated it at every opportunity in all the years since. It followed that Krishnamurti himself was not to be taken as an authority. His teachings were offered for examination entirely on their own merits, without regard for any assessment of the individual who had expressed them.

This was all well and good and required little elaboration were it not for one rather awkward fact. Krishnamurti's early life in the embrace of the Theosophical Society was oriented around a contrary premise. There he was hailed as the next World Teacher, an individual imbued with exceptional authority in the matter of everything pertaining to consciousness and the human condition. Not only that, but his life unfolded in a way that bore an uncanny resemblance to the prophecy that had been made. His actual career represented precisely the kind of behavior that one might expect from an individual attempting to guide humanity on a global scale. He spoke on three continents in a manner designed to effect a fundamental transformation, and he did so with unceasing determination for decade after decade. What was the relationship between Krishnamurti's early life and his present teaching? Did his

philosophy have its origin in some mystical source? If not, what was
its actual source?

With the advent of the KFA and the proliferation of talks and
publications, these questions were becoming a matter of increasing
concern. Someone new to the teachings might not understand the
significance of Krishnamurti's dissolution of the Order of the Star
and his break with Theosophy. The trustees of the foundation began
to realize that they would be responsible, now and after his death, to
address this issue for anyone who asked. As a result, three years after
the KFA was formed, the trustees asked Krishnamurti for his own
understanding of all that these questions entailed.

The trustees' request resulted in two recorded dialogues that
must have far exceeded their expectations. Krishnamurti examined
his relationship with Theosophy and the idea of the World Teacher
with diligence and in depth. The result was his most comprehensive
and definitive statement regarding what contributed to or precipitated his work.

He approached the issue in a tentative, exploratory manner, as
if he were unsure of the answer and investigating with the trustees.
His point of departure was that one can understand the source of
his work only if one understands the teachings themselves. In that
way, one might enter into the state of mind of the teacher. But he
put that aside and proceeded to examine the theosophical milieu in
which he was raised. Little of what he was reporting was the product
of his own memory, he said, but rather had been related to him by
individuals who were present at the time.

After these preliminary considerations, Krishnamurti turned to
the matter at hand. What was the source or origin of his philosophy?
He emphasized the significance of what he called the "strange" or
"peculiar" quality of his mind during childhood and adolescence.
"That boy," he said, was unusually vague, passive, and "vacant"
psychologically. He was steeped in theosophical language and

ideology, but none of it penetrated or affected him more than superficially. The psychological emptiness evidently served to prevent any deep conditioning from taking root. "I was never a theosophist," he maintained.

Prior to his entry into the Theosophical Society, Krishnamurti was raised in an orthodox Brahmin family, one in which no deviation from strict rules and customs was tolerated. Attendance at temple three times a day was mandatory. Any contact with a Westerner was a source of impurity and required washing and a change of clothes. Vegetarianism was essential, and alcohol was anathema. But Krishnamurti insisted that none of this affected him deeply or conditioned his consciousness. He accepted it at the time without resistance, but it did not determine his sense of right and wrong. He did not identify with it. Outwardly he conformed, but inwardly he remained untouched.

In a somewhat similar vein, Krishnamurti described the effect on him of his brother's death. The shock was tremendous, but he never succumbed to bitterness or felt antagonistic toward those who were prominent in the TS and had assured him that Nitya's welfare was protected by the Masters. "What a joke this is," he said at the time; but he was not tempted to act out in any angry or self-destructive behavior. In all these respects—Brahmin upbringing, immersion in Theosophy, the loss of his brother—why did he remain immune from the forces that would have shaped and conditioned most people? If that could be ascertained, it would help explain what enabled him to discover and express his teachings. He made this point repeatedly.

Krishnamurti also described the development of the concept of the World Teacher. Besant, Leadbeater, and others in the TS regarded it with a deeply serious attitude. Annie Besant believed in it with absolute conviction, and she was willing to stake her reputation on the prophecy that Krishnamurti represented the fulfillment of that idea. What was less definitive were the exact relationships among the Lord Maitreya, the World Teacher, and the individual chosen to fulfill that role. Was Krishnamurti some kind of channel or medium, an empty vessel through which another consciousness was speaking? He adamantly rejected that possibility.

> Then are you asking if there is a World Teacher who is using you—K? "Are you aware that you are being used? Do you know the World Teacher and therefore accept this role? Are you a medium?"
>
> Of course, I'm not a medium; that's obvious. That would be too childish, too immature, too illogical. Because if he were a medium, then K would be stupid, trivial, a low kind of bourgeois, and K isn't that.
>
> So he's not a medium; so we've got that. "Is he aware that he is being used?" Right? No. That would be like a petrol station which is being used by others. Impossible.

Another narrative associated with the World Teacher was that the individual selected for that role was the product of many lives and their progress through reincarnation.

> According to the theosophical explanation, this boy was chosen to be a vehicle many, many lives ago. And the body was prepared then, not just now, because that face was created through all those incarnations so that the World Teacher could use it. Bear that in mind also. You may not believe all this; I am just stating what they considered.

Krishnamurti also found this point of view untenable, but he followed it directly with another proposition that he did not reject. That is noteworthy, since he did find fault with all the other hypotheses that he considered.

> Why was he not conditioned? Either you say it was reincarnation, or there was some force, some energy—I don't

call it "entity"—which felt this boy must be kept that way, because that energy was going to operate. Whether you call that energy Lord Maitreya or ... what do you say?

Mary Zimbalist made handwritten notations on the transcript of this dialogue, and, in the margin next to this passage, she drew four small vertical lines. Above the four lines, she wrote, "K's Position."

Regrettably, the trustees did not pursue or explore this suggestion. Instead, they took the conversation in another direction entirely. One of them raised the possibility that Krishnamurti's psychological characteristics could be the product of a unique biological, congenital predisposition. Krishnamurti acknowledged that some kind of physiological characteristic might be a contributing factor, but it could not account for all that needs to be explained. "I think that's partly true, partly; but if we restrict it to only physiological things, it doesn't answer the whole picture. There are other greater factors involved in this." In this context, he alluded to experiences similar to those described in his diary.

> Say, for instance, this morning, last night, I woke up at three-thirty, and there was a tremendous sense of energy, bursting energy, great beauty. All kinds of things happened. This kind of experience is going on all the time, night after night, when the body isn't too tired.

Krishnamurti also mentioned the three-day episode that occurred in 1922 and the somewhat similar experiences in India in 1948. These events required explanation along with the vacant mind in his youth and the lack of deep conditioning. None of the proposals that had been suggested were sufficient to account for all these phenomena.

> You see, sir, I am very careful about all this. I don't want to be caught in some illusion, in some mystification, in some

fanciful hope and all the rest of it. But also, I don't want to be caught in purely physiological facts, because there is something much greater than all this.

Krishnamurti added that he was not sure whether it was necessary or even appropriate for him to investigate these issues.

> You see, I have never asked, "What am I doing? What is all this about?" I might have said it casually, but never questioned: "Do the Masters exist? Does Lord Maitreya exist?" I never said, "Is it true or is it false?" I somehow felt it was not my concern. I never felt it was important, even.

At this point, the outcome of the dialogue was beginning to come into view. None of the available explanations could account for all of the evidence. There seemed to be an element of mystery that no one, including Krishnamurti, was able to penetrate. "You see, I feel—forgive me for saying so—you are coming to it with a very small bucket." The conversation concluded with an amplification of this theme:

> You see, sir, I personally feel it's something so immense that the brain saying, "I am going to find out," can't find out; but the intimation of it is really quite extraordinary for me—not that I'm mystical or deceptive or I want a great experience. I have a horror of that.
>
> But there is something extraordinary which happens, which shows, which occurs, which gives hints, and opens the door. And after that I don't want even to open the door to say what it all is. I don't think the brain can understand it.

Several weeks after this conversation, Krishnamurti and the trustees returned to these issues and reconsidered them from a different point of view. Must anyone who wants to explore and understand Krishnamurti's philosophy undergo a set of experiences similar to what had occurred to him? Krishnamurti examined this question in terms of the theosophical theory of an ego and a body that had been "preparing, preparing," for "lives and lives" to come to this point. "From what I have been able to gather, this is a very, very rare occasion; because the Lord Maitreya, or the World Teacher, comes very rarely to the world; and therefore it is an extraordinary event in the religious field."

Again, he rejected this point of view. If that were the case, his teaching would be implicitly hierarchical, "not for everybody, only for the chosen few—tremendously aristocratic, if you like to put it that way—blue-blooded." For the ordinary man or woman, this idea must be deeply discouraging. "If I, an ordinary man, can't come to this naturally, it would be a disaster in my life." The story of Krishnamurti's life is irrelevant. "Discard all that, forget the past; find out about yourself; be a light to yourself."

Nevertheless, people will be curious about his early life because they are attracted to the mysterious, the occult, and "there is a great deal of fodder for this in that." As a result, it was necessary to address whether the theosophical idea of a World Teacher had any validity at all. Krishnamurti did not reject the theory outright, but he said, "To put it that way is very superficial. I feel that very strongly. I think the thing is much more deep and profound than saying a World Teacher, a body—you follow? It looks so superficial, so mechanical."

What followed was a more complete exposition of the conclusion Krishnamurti had reached in the previous dialogue. (In the passage below, selected excerpts are brought together in order to present a more coherent statement of his point of view.)

> When you look at this quite impartially, then there is a factor which is not the theosophical schematic. I don't feel it is any of that at all. And there is something in it which I don't know if I can describe, discuss, even talk about. There is a factor which has nothing whatever to do with the theosophical

interpretation, which I feel is much more vast and greater than putting it down in black and white.

I feel we are delving into something which the conscious mind can never understand. Which doesn't mean I am making a mystery of it, please. That must be clearly understood. I am not making a mystery of it. That would be a childish and stupid trick. There is a mystery which you have to approach with extraordinary delicacy, hesitancy and tentativeness. And the conscious mind can't do this. The conscious mind can only categorize or schematically bring about a design.

I want to be clear that we are not creating a mystery out of nothing. That would be exploiting people. That's a dirty trick. When you really deeply put that aside, I think there is something much too vast to put into words. There is a tremendous reservoir, as it were, which, if the human mind can touch it, would mean something which no intellectual mythology, invention, supposition, dogma can ever reveal.

Trustee: You used the word "reservoir." That's about as good as any.

K: It is there, all right.

These remarks represent the most complete expression of the central findings of the two dialogues.

One of the trustees persisted in his concern about the relationship between Krishnamurti as an individual and the philosophy he articulated. He raised the question of whether the person and the teaching were entirely consistent with one another. Was the teacher a valid or authentic example of the ideas he expressed? "How do you know?" Krishnamurti replied.

You're conditioned. You say he must not sleep with somebody. "He must not tell a lie." "He must be vegetarian." "He must, etc., etc." That's your conditioning.

When the man says, "Be a light to yourself" from morning 'til night, why do you bother about whether that teacher is this, that, blue-eyed, purple-eyed, or long-haired? When the house is burning, you don't inquire into the color of the man that set it on fire.

But if you say, "Will it stand by itself?" Not, "Who said it?" "Is the thing said, true?" Sir, this is much more vital than the other. The other belongs to all the human structure.

The question also arose whether the Theosophical Society might try in the future to claim that Krishnamurti was an expression of Theosophy.

So you have this problem of a group of people throughout the world, a minor, very small group, saying, "You are part of us; we brought you up; you belong to us. You are saying the truth which we also accept." And he says, "No. Sorry. We part company. We parted company long ago."

In the process of addressing this issue, Krishnamurti provided his most succinct account of his relationship to Theosophy. These comments are revealing and definitive for anyone who wonders whether Krishnamurti was at one time committed to Theosophy or retained some residual allegiance to it. (In the following remarks, Krishnamurti alternates between referring to himself in the first and third person.)

Look, sir, I've said it. It's very clear now. First of all, I never belonged to Theosophy. I've never been a theosophist. I grew up in it. To be exact, grew up in it from 1909 or '10 'til 1914. After that, he was taken to Europe; and there was the Order of the Star in the East, of which he was the head, and he didn't know what it was all about.

He didn't fight it. He didn't say, "Oh my god, what am I doing with this?" Or, "Why am I put in this position, how terrible, what shall I do?" None of those questions arose. There was no battle in myself whether I should be or should not be. And when Dr. Besant died, they pushed me out. And that was the end of that.

One final issue was of concern to the trustees. Krishnamurti had always maintained that his teachings speak for themselves and require no "interpreters" to make their meaning clear. His concern was not only for the present, but for the distant future, long after he was gone, when people might present themselves as his official representatives or spokesmen. The image of a church with priests serving as middlemen was particularly abhorrent to him, and his admonition against interpreters was intended to obviate any possibility of that kind.

On the other hand, this note of caution was not intended to inhibit or suppress active exploration of the meaning of the teachings. And so it was important to distinguish between the two:

> You can interpret according to your logic, your emotions, or your conditioning. Or you can write about it, saying, "This is what I think. I see he is right in this way; he's wrong in this." Discuss, criticize. Go into it. That's not interpretation.
> "I read K's books, and I intellectually tear it to pieces. Or intellectually go with it. Does he mean this, does he mean that?" You follow? Discuss. That's not interpretation.

It was prescient for the trustees to address this issue. The difference between interpretation and meaningful inquiry into the teachings has proven to be elusive since that time. The passage quoted here sharply and effectively distinguishes between the two forms of discussion.

Taking the two dialogues together, a few points emerge most clearly. The teachings are what is important, not the teacher. They are available to be explored, tested, and assessed by each individual listener; but only if he or she is a "light to oneself" can they have any lasting value. Nevertheless, people will inevitably inquire about the person who expressed the teachings, and the theosophical explanation of a World Teacher does not suffice to account for Krishnamurti. It is too superficial, too mechanical; nor can a purely physiological explanation make sense of all the evidence.

To understand fully the source of the teachings, one would have to enter into the state of mind of the teacher. Failing that, an important clue consists of the vagueness or inward vacancy of Krishnamurti in his youth and the absence of conditioning, in spite of all the influences to which he was exposed. In addition, there remains a vital element that is difficult to describe—something ineffable, too vast for the brain or conscious mind to comprehend. Some kind of reservoir of energy exists, a force or quality that facilitated or enabled Krishnamurti to understand and express his philosophy. Words do not suffice to characterize that quality, but its action was evidently unmistakable.

The second conversation came to a close with an elaboration on this theme. Krishnamurti attempted to explain why he had been willing to examine these issues at such length. In addition to the false ideas and extraneous explanations, there was also something valid and significant in this inquiry. The point was not to investigate the teacher, but rather to explore more deeply what he had to say:

> After all, that is seeking truth. Not the mystery, but the capacity of a mind, the quality of a mind that can go into that. And that interests me tremendously—intellectually, morally, ethically, artistically. Not whether there are Masters or not Masters, or all that, which is rather childish, if I may say so. There is no path, no system; but a mind that has really discarded every form of human system or invention or illusion—when you put all that away—and you must, obviously—then you are really out of it.

What, then, is that which they have all talked about? You understand? The real teachers—not the phony, not the middle-class. The real ones have always talked something about it. Not put into words. They say it is there. I know it is there. It is there.

The first deposition in the lawsuit brought by KFA against KWInc revealed some unexpected and highly salient facts. Ernest Biascoechea was a wealthy man from Puerto Rico who had contributed to Krishnamurti's work for many years. In his sworn testimony, Biascoechea confided a secret that he had held for many years. In 1946, he had confronted Rajagopal over irregularities in the way he was handling Biascoechea's contributions. In particular, he questioned the requirement to make out some of his checks paid to the order of Rajagopal personally. Rajagopal responded with a threat: he told Biascoechea about Krishnamurti's affair with Rosalind; and he threatened to expose what he knew if his behavior were questioned too closely.

This testimony demonstrated two remarkable facts. Rajagopal had clearly acknowledged to Biascoechea his recognition of his own financial wrongdoing. In addition, he revealed that it was false when he claimed years later that he first learned of the affair when Rosalind told him about it in 1956.

The deposition of Rajagopal produced two findings that were noteworthy. A discrepancy was exposed in the amount of $378,000 that could not be accounted for in the financial records of KWInc. Rajagopal was forced to reveal that he was maintaining those funds in a non-interest-bearing account located in Switzerland, over which he had exclusive control. The second revelation was that he had never given up his membership in the Theosophical Society and continued to identify himself as a theosophist.

Of these two discoveries, the fact that Rajagopal had remained a theosophist was the most surprising and disturbing to Krishnamurti. He mentioned it repeatedly in the days that followed and said that he found it appalling. How could a man who had edited the talks for so many years continue as a member of the TS? "This is worse than stealing money," he said. If he had known Rajagopal had remained a theosophist, he added, he would never have allowed him to edit the talks.

Four months after the KFA filed suit against KWInc, Krishnamurti was intercepted by a process server at the moment when he was about to walk onstage to address an audience of three thousand people at the civic auditorium in Santa Monica, California. The process server presented him with a summons for his deposition. This was the first notice of a cross-complaint filed by Rajagopal against the KFA for breach of contract, slander, and "fraudulent interference."

Notification of the cross-complaint and service of the summons would normally have been handled by the attorneys for each side, so interrupting Krishnamurti right before his talk served no purpose apart from harassment. He handed the document to Theo Lilliefelt and proceeded to give his talk with no apparent effect from the distraction. After it was over, however, his assessment of this incident was sharply negative: he said to Mary that Judas was not in Rajagopal's league with respect to treachery.

Krishnamurti's deposition occurred three weeks later at Mary's home in Malibu, and it occupied two full days. Rajagopal attended both days, uninvited, with two of his trustees. Mary wrote that Rajagopal had "an ancient, simian look: tense, tight-mouthed, hands clasped and twisting, an air of decay about him."

The deposition lasted from nine-thirty to four-thirty each day. The attorney for KWInc, dressed "in a loud shirt and tie," with gold glasses, circled around the main issues for hours with detailed questions about Theosophy and the early days. On the afternoon of the second day, he began to ask about Krishnamurti's relationship with Rajagopal.

> As the afternoon wore on, K, looking so frail in his jeans, blue shirt, and sweater, seemed to become smaller, and also seemed to gain a different strength. He began to speak on his own level—of trust and friendship in the early days that allowed him to leave everything to Rajagopal, of how that trust was eroded by Rajagopal until it was gone, and he had to break with him.

When it was finally over, "We all felt euphoric." The KFA attorney told Krishnamurti that he had scored one hundred percent, "and K was both shaking and laughing as the strain was beginning to unwind."

The depositions and the acceleration of legal activity had the effect of eliciting some revealing comments from Krishnamurti. He had an abiding sense of some quality or energy that protected him, and he wondered aloud why it had allowed Rajagopal to come into his life. Mary asked if his sense of protection was an acknowledgment of the existence and participation of the Masters. He said no, he did not mean that. "But something has acted, something has looked after things. I don't think, I know that." In spite of the protection, Rajagopal was drawn ineluctably to Krishnamurti because "evil is attracted to good. Its presence is a lure." He added, "I must have been mad to put up with them."

> It was like a prison with them. I never discussed anything serious with them. When in Ojai, we led parallel lives. I lived my own inner life; I liked to look at mountains, trees, birds, to walk, work in the garden raising vegetables, plants.
>
> Rosalind has no more inner life than a chicken. She doesn't know what it means. Though she talks about art and good taste, and all that, she has no idea of it at all.

The depositions were followed by months of legal maneuvering, replete with interrogatories, pre-trial conferences, negotiable and non-negotiable items, and all the other arcana characteristic of a complex civil case. Almost lost amid the flurry of documents and proposals was a key element in the effort to understand the affairs of KWInc. An outside audit of its financial records should have been among the first and most straightforward pieces of the puzzle, but Rajagopal refused to allow it in the absence of an explicit court order. Once that order was obtained, further resistance followed in the form of procrastination, postponements, and insufficient production of documents. In fact, a complete audit was never conducted, and KWInc engaged in settlement negotiations only when the missing financial records were identified and made the focus of scrutiny.

Rajagopal's terms for settlement revolved in part around his wish to maintain his reputation within the worlds of Theosophy and those who had supported Krishnamurti's work. This entailed his right to republish the many years of talks that he had edited and made available previously in the form of dozens of pamphlets. He envisioned publishing the collected works of all of Krishnamurti's talks from 1933 until the advent of the KFA in 1968. He insisted on his right to reproduce this material, including the administrative structure necessary to carry it out.

The KFA was willing to concede to this demand provided all the other elements of a settlement were in place. The collected works were eventually realized in the form of eighteen volumes, all edited by Rajagopal. The publication of this material represented a major achievement, a testament to what he considered the essence of his work. The strange case of Rajagopal revolves around the paradox of his dedication to this work, coupled with his subversion of the purposes of KWInc and the person of Krishnamurti. He must have been a man consumed with inner conflict and therefore impervious to the meaning of the talks he had edited assiduously for so many years.

Eighteen months of legal maneuvering were required before serious proposals for settlement began to be exchanged between the two sides. A major complication involved another organization Rajagopal had created called the K&R Foundation, a nonprofit corporation with purposes that ran parallel to those of KWInc. The terms of the settlement proposals had at their core the complete dissolution of KWInc and turning over most of its assets and archives to KFA. At the same time, the K&R Foundation would continue to function, primarily for the purpose of bringing out the collected works. However, Rajagopal had transferred many of the KWInc archives to K&R, and the disposition of that material subsequently became a matter of controversy and dispute. The terms of the settlement provided that KFA would have access to the K&R archives and ultimately these would also be transferred to KFA. For the time being, that was a compromise KFA was willing to make in order to arrive at a resolution of all the other outstanding issues.

An additional eighteen months and seven versions of the settlement proposal were required in order to bring the negotiations to a close. The terms of the final agreement enabled the KFA to acquire the Oak Grove property, one hundred fifty acres in the heart of the Ojai Valley where Krishnamurti had given his public talks for many years. In addition, KFA recovered the east end residential property, including Pine Cottage and Arya Vihara, as well as four hundred thousand dollars in liquid assets.

The Order and Final Judgment by the Superior Court of the State of California was heard in open court and approved by Judge Richard C. Heaton on December 26, 1974. It had been three years since the lawsuit was filed, and six years since the KFA had initiated efforts to negotiate a resolution with Rajagopal. Mary wrote in her diary, "So ended the year with the sense that Krishnaji had regained outward things that had been taken from him and been freed from the exploitation of those who had betrayed his trust."

Mary's assessment of what had occurred was an exercise in understatement. The lawsuit would have been more than worthwhile if only for the recovery of Pine Cottage, with its historic pepper tree, now a towering expression of beauty and strength. All the other assets—the Oak Grove, the cash, the archives—represented an immense acquisition and a resounding vindication of the legal and ethical correctness of the action of the KFA. At a practical level, this was the most important event in Krishnamurti's life in America; and it was an affirmation of the crucial contribution of Erna Lilliefelt.

Chapter Eleven

THE ADVENT OF OAK GROVE SCHOOL

The acceleration in Krishnamurti's activity in America after he separated from Rajagopal increased exponentially following the settlement of the lawsuit. Central to his new endeavors was to be a school for elementary and secondary students, the fulfillment of a vision that had its roots half a century in the past. Annie Besant had foreseen in 1927 the need for this element in Krishnamurti's work, and she raised funds at that time to purchase land for this purpose. Well before the settlement was finalized, Krishnamurti began conducting meetings with KFA trustees and prospective teachers in order to initiate the momentum necessary to realize this objective.

Krishnamurti made his intention more definite in April 1974 when he appointed thirty-four-year-old Mark Lee to serve as director of the school. Mark was born and raised in Santa Barbara, a coastal city thirty miles north of Ojai. He had worked for seven years as a teacher and assistant principal of the Rishi Valley school, Krishnamurti's three-hundred-acre residential campus in the south of India. He had a large and handsome head with widely spaced, pale blue eyes, and a warm and winning smile. He stood well over six feet tall and carried himself with an innately aristocratic air.

My own involvement in the events described in this book began in 1975, although my participation had its roots in earlier years. I grew up in West Los Angeles and was living there in 1972 when

Krishnamurti spoke at the Santa Monica Civic Auditorium. I was enrolled at that time in a graduate program in political theory at UCLA. I had been reading Krishnamurti's books for several months and found them far more interesting than my doctoral coursework. I attended the talks in Santa Monica, and that summer I joined a group expedition to Saanen. I began driving up to Ojai each spring for the annual series of talks in Ojai, and, by 1975, my interest in Krishnamurti's philosophy had become a central feature of my inner life.

Mark announced to the audience assembled for the Ojai talks in April 1975 that the KFA intended to open a school in the fall. He said candidates for teaching positions should introduce themselves after the talk and schedule an appointment to be interviewed. I did so without hesitation, and, a few months later, I was the first teacher hired. The school's development in its early years was shaped in part by the course of my relationship with Mark.

Krishnamurti returned to Malibu from India in February 1975, and a few days later he composed a two-page statement intended to define and preserve for the future the fundamental purposes of the school. It would be excellent academically, but it was meant to educate students for the whole of life, not merely to pursue a profession. It was not intended to mold, shape, or condition students to accept traditional norms or to meet preconceived goals or expectations. On the contrary, in a radical break with the past, the school would seek to "uncondition" its students in a process that entailed unconditioning the teacher as well. In this way the student would come upon a way of living that was psychologically free and harmonious, both inwardly and outwardly. Such a result would affect all those with whom the student came into contact, and ultimately it would affect the consciousness of the world.

Krishnamurti may not have fully anticipated whether, or to what extent, the trustees of the KFA would be supportive of this project. They might not have presented him with outright opposition, but such a school could not have formed any part of their initial interest in the roles they had assumed. As the primary officer of the foundation, Erna had acquired her position by virtue of her sense of injustice over Rajagopal's mismanagement of assets intended for Krishnamurti's work. She excelled in guiding and managing the legal battle that ensued. An entirely different set of skills and frame of mind, however, were required in order to assume responsibility for an elementary and secondary school. Erna's contradictory relationship to that function was a critical factor in the school's development and revealed the limits of Krishnamurti's insight into her character.

In June 1975, Indira Gandhi declared a state of emergency in India, during which civil liberties were severely curtailed. Krishnamurti and his associates were uncertain whether he would be safe to give talks there under these circumstances, especially given his frequently expressed views regarding the limitations and dangers of authority. As a result, his annual sojourn in India, scheduled to begin in early fall, was cancelled.

This decision proved to be propitious for the Oak Grove School, as he was in Ojai for most of its first year. The school opened its doors at the east end residence in September 1975. It began with half a dozen students ranging in age from nine to eleven, with two teachers, one for art and one for academic subjects. As the sole academic instructor, I felt keenly the magnitude of my responsibility. My only experience as a teacher had been in a tutorial setting, and I was ill equipped to manage group instruction. The students varied widely in aptitude and temperament, and among them were three who presented behavioral issues. It was not an auspicious way to begin, for a school with so lofty a set of intentions.

I met Krishnamurti for the first time under the broad branches of the pepper tree a month after the school opened its doors. He shook my hand with a gentle grip and asked if we had met previously;

then he escorted me and a few others into the living room of Pine Cottage. His manner was warm and friendly, and he talked about the purposes of the school in a fairly relaxed and casual way. He assured me that we would have many opportunities to discuss all the issues that would arise.

Over the course of the next six months, Krishnamurti conducted fourteen meetings with teachers, staff, parents, trustees, and other friends of the school. These meetings lasted an hour or an hour and a half, and they were attended by forty or fifty people. Krishnamurti entered the room punctually and sat in a simple, straight-backed chair, looking quietly around the room for a long moment before he began to speak. With an attitude of earnest inquiry, he described the need for a school that would serve as a light of intelligence in a dark and destructive world. His extemporaneous opening remarks lasted for ten or fifteen minutes until he arrived at a question or issue for general discussion. What followed was an open-ended conversation in which everyone could participate.

Krishnamurti's educational philosophy was designed to cultivate an atmosphere of freedom where students would excel both academically and in their behavior without the imposition of external restraints or artificial forms of motivation. The traditional strategies employed in schools to elicit good behavior were discarded in favor of genuine relationship and doing the right thing for its own sake. Reward and punishment were considered equally counterproductive in this endeavor. Most forms of competition and the comparison of one child with another were also incompatible with the purposes of the school. The challenge for the teacher was to create an atmosphere of care and a quality of relationship within which the child would not only cooperate but flower to the fullest extent.

In one of the meetings, Krishnamurti described the residential secondary school at Brockwood Park, and he said that it functioned without the exercise of any form of authority. Instead there was extensive discussion with the students in order to elicit their agreement to various practical rules, including adherence to a regular schedule, such as a time for lights out at night. He seemed to suggest that something similar was possible at Oak Grove. However, our students were younger than those at Brockwood, and they presented behavioral challenges that exceeded my ability to handle without recourse to some form of authority.

We kept a dozen chickens in a coop at the east end residence, and one day at the end of the lunch period, one of our students refused to leave the coop and return to the classroom. No amount of dialogue could solve the problem in that moment, and I was torn between dealing with that child and my responsibility to the other students in class. This incident epitomized for me the inadequacy of Krishnamurti's philosophy and precipitated a meeting in which I succeeded in winning from him a concession. He agreed that a principle of "cause and effect" could operate so that a student's behavior might cause him or her to lose certain privileges. This would not be a punitive action because it was not designed to inflict pain or discomfort. It was a relief to discover that some creative adaptation was possible in the application of his principles to the realities of daily life in the school.

The issue of authority was also a source of controversy and confusion in the administration of the school as a whole. During the early years of the school, the teachers sometimes felt that Mark Lee made decisions within their jurisdiction without consulting them; and he in turn was often opposed in unpredictable ways by Erna. There was a general lack of clarity regarding who was responsible for what. I attempted to fill that void by drawing up a kind of constitution for the school, spelling out the distribution of responsibilities for teachers, staff, director, and trustees. The audacity of my proposal earned me the enduring enmity of the Lilliefelts, although Krishnamurti regarded it with benign good humor. He did not support it, however, and he urged me to have more trust in the actions taken by my "elder brothers."

In spite of its difficulties, including a chronic financial deficit, the school grew and prospered, especially after it moved to the Oak Grove property in the heart of the Ojai Valley. Krishnamurti took an active interest in the design of the new school buildings and was closely involved with the architects. He wanted the buildings to blend organically into the land and to have a timeless quality in the simplicity and elegance of their design. Families moved to Ojai from elsewhere in California and beyond specifically to enroll their children in the school, and the resulting potpourri of students, teachers, trustees, and dedicated parents ensured a rich and turbulent blend of energies.

After three years, I felt exhausted emotionally by the demands of the school, especially since I had been identified by the trustees as a potential troublemaker. I was granted a leave of absence with the assurance that my position would be available when I returned to the school after a year or two. As events unfolded, my decision to leave temporarily proved to be advantageous in ways I could not have foreseen.

Another new development in Krishnamurti's work was highly significant and has not yet been fully appreciated. His philosophy is widely assumed to represent a species of religious doctrine or a set of spiritual beliefs, but that assumption overlooks the substance of his message. The fundamental thrust of his teaching addresses the concrete actualities of daily life. His message is factual, secular, and psychological, not abstract, mystical, or metaphysical. To be sure, it contains a religious dimension, but of a kind far removed from churches and priests, heaven and hell, or any form of deity. His constant concern is with issues such as fear, envy, desire, violence, love, and psychological freedom. The new development in his work capitalized on this pervasive feature of his philosophy.

Most of Krishnamurti's teaching was expressed from a public platform or in group dialogues. Less conspicuous but also significant were the countless interviews he conducted with individuals seeking guidance or clarity regarding pressing problems in their lives. The entire three volumes of *Commentaries on Living* consist of actual, recollected dialogues of this kind. In these interviews, Krishnamurti engaged in a kind of therapy, albeit without the accoutrements of fifty-minute sessions or a recognizable technique.

For these reasons, Krishnamurti's work came to the attention of Dr. David Shainberg, a psychiatrist engaged in private practice in the city of New York. Shainberg was invited to a conference of scientists held at Brockwood Park where he met Krishnamurti and developed a relationship that continued for many years. In April 1975, he arranged a two-day conference in New York consisting of Krishnamurti in dialogue with twenty-five psychologists and psychiatrists, representing a variety of therapeutic modalities. These conversations, recorded and transcribed, provide a penetrating study of the manner in which his philosophy may fulfill some of the functions of psychotherapy.

In the first conversation, one of the therapists raised the issue of fear. Few topics are more central to Krishnamurti's philosophy; and fear and its close cousin, anxiety, are near the top of the list of issues that drive people to seek therapy. It represented an excellent point of departure for mutual exploration. Krishnamurti's approach, as he explained many times from the public platform, dispenses at the outset with dealing with any particular form of fear. Whether it is a fear of death, illness, public opinion, or anything else is an entirely secondary matter. To deal with fear at that level, he maintains, is like trimming the branches of a tree—an endless and ultimately futile endeavor. He insists on approaching the subject in terms of its root cause, the source of all fears.

It soon became evident that such an approach was not in the repertoire of the assembled psychotherapists. None of them had even conceived of addressing fear in this manner. The conversation proceeded in various directions, but Krishnamurti persisted in returning to this approach. His intention was concrete and practical in the sense that he aimed to actually eradicate fear—the discussion was not just an intellectual exercise. "Is it possible to be totally free of fear?" he asked. "I say, yes. For me, yes. I'm not conceited, arrogant, stupid. I say it is possible. I know it is."

He brought out the relationship between fear and thought: "The root of fear is the whole movement of thought." Thought is "excellent," he said, when applied to ordinary tasks in the outer world; but when it is employed in an effort to become something better inwardly, it becomes illusory and generates fear. "When I exercise thought as a means of becoming something, then that is the very essence of fear." To suggest that psychological self-improvement is inherently dysfunctional runs counter, of course, to received ideas and conventional wisdom. Nevertheless, this view is central to Krishnamurti's philosophy and is symptomatic of the idiosyncratic quality of his point of view.

The second conversation explored more fully the role of the "me" and its constant concern to improve itself and achieve something more than what it is. The ending of fear is possible, he maintained, only when the illusory nature of the "me" is understood. Psychological nothingness, in this sense, is the condition for complete security and intelligence.

Krishnamurti also raised the question whether action is ever whole, or is the product of conflict or fragmentary motives or desires. He said analysis, the central tool of therapy, is intrinsically fragmentary and therefore self-defeating for purposes of harmonious, holistic action. In so doing, he knew he was intruding upon essential therapeutic terrain: "Therefore we must put away all analysis. To say that in front of you—forgive me." Fortunately, this comment elicited good-natured laughter, and a moment later he again acknowledged the sensitivity of this issue: "And therefore each analysis is incomplete. Am I saying something utterly against all your grain?"

The conversation throughout the two days was lively, freewheeling, and touched upon many topics near to the hearts of psychotherapists, including dreams and the unconscious mind. At one point the dialogue turned somewhat personal, as one of the participants asked Krishnamurti, "Did you ever have a sense of a 'me,' a sense of self, in your own life?" "No, sir, hardly ever," Krishnamurti replied; but this glimpse into his own state of mind was not pursued.

The two dialogues in 1975 were followed by three more in 1976 and an additional three in 1977. By the time of the second dialogue in 1976, Krishnamurti had established a firmer footing with the therapists, and he was no longer quite so deferential. He shifted the framework of the conversation entirely. After some introductory remarks by one of the therapists, Krishnamurti asked, with a touch of biting humor, "Can we leave the patient alone for the time being? or the victim." He wanted to address the larger question of whether radical change could occur in the culture at large so as not to produce so many people in need of therapy.

The therapists laughed at the "victim" remark, but they were not prepared to let go of their role. They said their profession requires them to address the needs of actual individuals who are seeking immediate help:

> Shainberg: He is there, he is talking; this person is sitting there in front of you, in your office…
>
> K: I have met many of them—dozens of them—not only in this country, but in Europe and India—hundreds of them. Are you offering them a palliative?

Krishnamurti wanted to shift the terms of the conversation away from the patient and toward the therapist himself. He did so by asking again whether their approach was fragmented or holistic.

> I come to you as a patient or a victim. I am fragmented; I have problems with my wife and with my society, with a dozen things—fantasies, illusions—and how are you going to deal with me? Holistically or fragmentarily?
>
> And, you know, you cannot cure human ailments partially. You may pacify, give him an antidote, and so on, but you haven't cured him. So how will you deal with that?
>
> Therapist: Well, obviously, I would have to deal with myself first.
>
> K: Why don't we do that? Here we are, sitting together for a couple of hours. Why don't we deal with the question: "I am fragmented. What am I to do with it?" Not the victim, not the patient; leave those poor chaps alone. Here we are.

With this foundation established, Krishnamurti pursued the question of fragmentation in terms of the therapists themselves. Were they actually aware that they are fragmented? How does one come into contact with that fact—not as an idea or a theory, but as an actuality? He offered this answer:

> I know it because there is a contradiction in my life. I say one thing and do another. I have one desire opposed to another desire, one thought opposing another. That is a fact. So I realize there is a contradiction. There is an opposition, conflict. In that state, there is fragmentation.

The conversation was now taking place on more meaningful territory, in Krishnamurti's view, because it was dealing with the actual lives of the people with whom he was discussing. After pursuing it at this level for some time, however, his impatience returned in another form. He evidently felt the focus on fear and fragmentation had gone on too long, and there was much more to address.

> We are discussing superficially now, aren't we? We don't go very deep. Sir, there is the whole problem of death, sorrow—you follow?—if there is God, if there is no god—if there is something in life really holy, sacred. What does it mean to be really religious? You might spit on all that, but it exists; man demands it.
>
> And apparently we don't touch any of that, but say, "Well, I have got some neurotic people—how am I to cure them?" Do we take life as a whole, in which is included fear, love, hate, ambition, money, position, prestige, death—you follow?—if there is eternity, if there is something which is beyond time. Apparently that doesn't interest you. Right, sir?

After this acknowledgement of another dimension of life, the conversation returned to the psychological issues with which the therapists were primarily concerned. The dialogue led inexorably to the relationship between consciousness and time, including Krishnamurti's basic distinction between chronological time and the more subtle and elusive psychological time. After an extended examination of this topic, he assumes for the sake of discussion that his listeners have understood what he has said so far. In the following passage, he adopts the role of the therapist, and he speaks in the first person as if he were one of them:

> I have understood my consciousness, which is the past, and I am free of that past. My mind is not caught in that, and therefore there is no future. No future. You understand, sir? No becoming—not becoming better. There is no future, psychologically. That means time has stopped. [And then the crucial point:] Is that a theory or an actuality?

Of course, chronological time does not stop. Krishnamurti is referring to psychological time: he says there is no future of that kind; it does not exist.

> Can time have a stop? If it stops there is no fear. Now, to find out whether time can stop—time psychologically, not chronologically. It's quarter past twelve chronologically. Psychologically, there is no tomorrow. Actually, there is no tomorrow—except thought says there is tomorrow.
>
> Sir, if you have no tomorrow, what happens, actually? What happens inside you? Tomorrow you are going to have a lovely time—that's dropped. You are going to meet that woman or that man—dropped. You follow, sirs? There is no tomorrow, psychologically. Can you face that? Total emptiness.

The emptiness to which Krishnamurti referred is not something to be avoided or dreaded, as most of us tend to assume; rather it is the source of energy, creativity, and compassion. But that can only occur when the emptiness is an actuality for the individual, an event that is evidently very rare.

Mary Zimbalist lamented that the dialogues with psychotherapists were somewhat scattered and plagued by diversions and irrelevant comments. Nevertheless, taken collectively, the conversations represent a rich and wide-ranging resource for anyone interested in therapy or in Krishnamurti's philosophy or both. Several additional dialogues of this kind were conducted in 1982, 1983, and 1984, and none of this material has been edited and published. No doubt there are many passages in the transcripts that can be reduced or eliminated, but the portions that remain could provide the lineaments of a new form of therapy. In any case, these dialogues represent a wealth of material that so far has remained unexplored even within the communities of people interested in Krishnamurti's philosophy.

Another manifestation of the increased activity that occurred after the lawsuit was the completion of the second of Krishnamurti's three diaries. Unlike *Krishnamurti's Notebook*, this one contained no references to his "process" or to the mysterious energy or entity he had referred to as "the other." It consists of observations about life, relationship, and consciousness, including incidents from his childhood and youth, and recollections of individuals who had come to seek his counsel. It also contains scenes from nature, remarkable in their vivid detail, comparable to the many scenes that appear in *Commentaries on Living*.

The diary consists of forty-five entries, each one about two pages in length. It was started at Brockwood Park in September 1973, but the last eleven entries were composed in Malibu and Ojai in April 1975. Published in 1982 as *Krishnamurti's Journal*, this brief volume forms an accessible introduction to some of the essential elements of his philosophy.

Among the many topics explored in the *Journal* are space, order, and time, joy and pleasure, sleep and dreams, beauty, knowledge, freedom, death, and love. The entries follow a fairly consistent pattern. Each one begins with a long paragraph (as many as twenty sentences) describing an encounter with a tree, river, mountain, or some form of wildlife. There follow two or three paragraphs developing a theme or set of insights regarding some aspect of consciousness and the human condition. The entry typically closes with a very short paragraph that returns to the observation of nature with which it began. The net effect is to enclose the insights into dysfunctional humanity within a broader framework of beauty and order.

Interwoven among the passages are numerous comments regarding the meaning and significance of meditation. At times it seems as though the *Journal* consists largely of the fruit of that state of mind.

Any form of conscious meditation is not the real thing: it can never be. Deliberate attempt to meditate is not meditation. It must happen; it cannot be invited.

The complete elimination of the meditator, the experiencer, the thinker, is the very essence of meditation.

Meditation itself is the movement of peace. It is not an end to be found; it is not put together by thought or word. The action of meditation is intelligence.

Meditation is the emptying of consciousness of its content.

Meditation is the complete transformation of thought and its activities.

Krishnamurti's descriptions of himself include one of his few memories from childhood, standing on the banks of a wide river at the age of fourteen. Also included is a moving scene in which he and his brother visited their orthodox Brahmanical father after not seeing him for fifteen years. In another passage, a visitor asked whether his teachings reflect his own authentic experience. He replied, "It would be utterly vain and stupid if it were merely verbal structures of thought; to talk of such things would be hypocrisy."

Krishnamurti also shared some observations, expressed in the third person, regarding his characteristic states of mind. Among these comments, the following two are perhaps the most revealing.

He only discovered recently that there was not a single thought during these long walks, in the crowded streets or on the solitary paths. Ever since he was a boy it had been like that; no thought entered his mind. He was watching and listening and nothing else. Thought with its associations never arose. There was no image-making. One day he was suddenly aware how extraordinary it was; he attempted often to think but no thought would come. On these walks, with people or without them, any movement of thought was absent.

He always had this strange lack of distance between himself and the trees, rivers and mountains. It wasn't cultivated; you can't cultivate a thing like that. There was never a wall between him and another. What they did to him, what they said to him never seemed to wound him, nor flattery to touch him. Somehow he was altogether untouched. He was not withdrawn, aloof, but like the waters of a river.

No description or summary of the *Journal* can capture the scope, depth, and subtlety of its psychological insights. They explore a wealth of varied issues, but they are unified by interconnected threads pertaining to time, thought, and knowledge, and their limiting effects on the mind. The scenes from nature, with their luminous, diaphanous prose, provide a point of entry into the reflections on consciousness. These passages contain references to forests, mountains, oceans, and rivers, as well as encounters with monkeys, a tiger, a mother bear and her cubs, crows and owls, scolding blue jays, screeching parrots, squirrels, a bobcat, a tarantula, several snakes, and a baby elephant and its mother. The following scene, selected in part for its relative brevity, may serve to suggest the poignant, evocative quality of these descriptions.

There is a single tree in a green field that occupies a whole acre; it is old and highly respected by all the other trees on the hill. In its solitude it dominates the noisy stream, the hills and the cottage across the wooden bridge. You admire it as you pass it by, but on your return you look at it in a more leisurely way. Its trunk is very large, deeply embedded in the earth, solid and indestructible; its branches are long, dark and curving; it has rich shadows. In the evening it is withdrawn into itself, unapproachable; but during the daylight hours it is open and welcoming. It is whole, untouched by an axe or saw. On a sunny day you sat under it; you felt its venerable age; and, because you were alone with it, you were aware of the depth and the beauty of life.

As the middle child among the three diaries, the *Journal* may be somewhat overlooked. If so, that would be regrettable. It has a more consistent structure than either of its siblings and a more coherent point of view. In any case, each of the diaries represents a priceless supplement to the vast record of the public talks.

The first volume of Mary Lutyens's three-part biography of Krishnamurti appeared in 1975 under the title *Years of Awakening*. It recounted the period from his birth until the dissolution of The Order of the Star. It was largely concerned with the theosophical milieu in which he was raised, a context that Lutyens treated sympathetically, perhaps because she herself was raised in that environment. Its primary mission, however, was simply to record the highly unusual sequence of events with fidelity to facts. She was successful in that endeavor, albeit with a certain sacrifice of drama, color, or reasonable inferences from the facts. The narrative is strictly chronological and rather dry in places, but it performed an extremely valuable service in providing the foundation for all subsequent research. Krishnamurti read parts of it and commented favorably on it.

The manuscript of his first diary, recovered in the lawsuit, was published as *Krishnamurti's Notebook* in 1976, the year following the appearance of *Years of Awakening*. After he read a review of the *Notebook* in the *Guardian* newspaper, Krishnamurti decided to compose his own review as if he were a modern scholar. Mary wrote that he was laughing as he did so, but the review is entirely serious. It does not address many of the features of the *Notebook*—the process, the encounters with "the other," the scenes from nature—but instead examines some of the elements of his philosophy, including the limitations of knowledge, the deadening effects of tradition, and the significance of "the observer is the observed."

The review is noteworthy for what it reveals about Krishnamurti's awareness of the relationship between his own work and what others have said. He compares it to the Upanishads, Vedanta, and the findings of modern psychology. He says that Vedanta is close to his work insofar as it advocates freedom from knowledge, but it does not go far enough. His own philosophy, he feels, must at first seem somewhat devastating to anyone who finds security and comfort in knowledge; but another kind of energy, a new dimension of consciousness, is possible with freedom from the known.

The hypothetical reviewer adopts a personal approach and describes his own familiarity with existing literature as well as the impact of the book on him:

> As far as I have come in my studies, I have not found the phrase "the observer is the observed" with its full meaning. Perhaps some ancient thinker may have said it, but one of the most important things that Krishnamurti has found is this great truth which, when it actually takes place, as it has occasionally happened to me personally, literally banishes the movement of time.
>
> Let me add here that I am not a follower nor do I accept Krishnamurti as my guru. To him the idea of becoming a guru is an abomination. With critical examination, I find this book totally absorbing because he annihilates everything thought has put together. It is a shocking thing when one realizes this. It is a real physical shock.

In April 1977, a month before his eighty-second birthday, Krishnamurti was diagnosed with benign prostatic enlargement, a condition very common among men his age. It has the effect of impeding the flow of urine through the urethra. If it were not treated, the condition could worsen unexpectedly and cause a blockage, with potentially dangerous consequences. As a result, he agreed to undergo a procedure the following month to correct the condition. Although the procedure entailed removal of prostate tissue, it did not require a surgical incision, as access to the prostate was through the urethra. Nevertheless, an anesthetic and overnight hospital stay were unavoidable.

Krishnamurti had always felt the line separating his life from death was thin, and he must take precautions not to cross that line carelessly. A general anesthetic, for example, was too great a risk; and even with a spinal anesthetic, he warned Mary that she should keep him engaged in conversation as much as possible. She reserved a room adjoining his in the hospital so that she could be with him at all times, except during the ninety-minute procedure itself. When he emerged from the operating room, it seemed as though all was well, for he was alert, in good spirits, and not in pain. Later that evening, however, events took a different turn. The following morning he dictated to Mary an account of what had occurred.

When the pain arrived and became more severe, Krishnamurti felt his body "almost floating in the air," although he acknowledged that the feeling may have been illusory. A few minutes later he sensed the presence of what he called "the personification of death." At that point, there seemed to occur a dialogue of sorts between his body and death. Death "seemed to be talking to the body" insistently, but his body refused to yield to death's demand. The body was tempted to yield, but it "realized that it was not responsible for itself." It understood that another entity was involved, one that was even stronger than death. In order to protect the body, this other entity intervened, and now the conversation was among the body, "this other," and death. "One felt very strongly and clearly that if the other had not interfered, death would have won."

Krishnamurti did not describe the content of the conversation, but he emphasized that neither the body nor the other entity had any fear of death. The absence of fear was what allowed the conversation to proceed "freely and profoundly.... It was as though the other was acting as an umpire in a dangerous game of which the body was not fully aware." Moreover, "The quality of conversation was urbane." There was no trace of sentimentality or excessive emotion; rather, there was "a great sense of humor" among the three entities. "Fear never entered this conversation, for fear is darkness and death is light."

Three weeks after he dictated his description of this event, Krishnamurti added a few more remarks. "Of course," he began, the three entities were not "three separate activities on their own, but it was a humorous whole moving together without distinction among them." This caveat would seem to contradict some of what he had said previously, but he added that words were not able to describe "this strange movement." It was "a conversation without word, without thought."

In an aside to Mary as he was adding this postscript, Krishnamurti asked her, "You know what I mean by 'the other'?" He answered his own question: "The mind that is inhabited by K."

The dialogue occurred within an ethereal ambience, one which reinforced and refined the dramatic quality of the narrative. Referring to himself in the third person,

> Lying in bed he saw the clouds full of rain, and the window lighted up, the town below stretching for miles. There was spattering of rain on the window pane.... There was thunder

and lightning, and the conversation went on. It was like a whisper in the wind... a song without beginning or an end.

Krishnamurti insisted that the dialogue with death was "not illusory or fanciful." It warrants attention in part for the light it sheds on the essential nature of Krishnamurti as an individual. His body "realized" that it was responsible to something else, another entity that was stronger than death, more dominant; and that entity was none other than "the mind that is inhabited by K."

The suggestion that he "inhabited" a mind that was somehow other than himself shines an oblique light on the mystery of who he was. The essential quality of Krishnamurti was a puzzle that he himself was not able to solve, but information from several sources combines to suggest some possible answers. The clues that emerge from this dialogue will form an important piece of the puzzle when we draw together the available evidence and attempt to discern what it all reveals.

The acceleration of activity in several spheres following the settlement of the lawsuit—the opening and development of the school; the meetings with psychotherapists; the new publications—were all secondary to the public talks, the primary expression of Krishnamurti's teaching. After the recovery of the Oak Grove property, he began giving talks there for the first time since 1966. Beginning in 1975 and every year thereafter, he held between six and ten talks and dialogues in the Oak Grove each year. With the advent of Oak Grove School, he also conducted several meetings each year with teachers, parents, and school staff. These were in addition to special conferences, including a twelve-part series of meetings with a selected group of scientists.

The publication of the first volume of Krishnamurti's biography and of the *Notebook* in consecutive years represented a high-water mark in the trajectory of his career. With these two books, the possibility was erased that Krishnamurti could become a forgotten figure amid the turmoil of the twentieth century. The opening of the school, the conversations with psychotherapists, the completion of the *Journal,* and the numerous talks and dialogues were also highly significant. These events underscore the beneficial effects of the break with Rajagopal; and collectively they constitute a super-nova of psychological insight in the unfolding manifestation of his philosophy.

Chapter Twelve

MEETING THE MAN
FROM SEATTLE

Even at the age of eighty, Krishnamurti's robust physical health and youthful vitality were extraordinary. He had the energy and demeanor of a man in his thirties, according to Mary, and he dominated the room in dialogues with people whose average age was half of his. These are not merely the subjective impressions of people close to him but characteristics conspicuous in the videotapes of his talks and discussions. A lifetime of vigorous daily exercise, healthful vegetarian diet, and abstinence from alcohol, drugs, and even caffeine were no doubt contributing factors in this result. Psychological health and emotional balance were also highly conducive to this outcome.

On the other hand, Krishnamurti's philosophy embraces the inevitability of death without any form of avoidance or fear, and he had to confront the prospect of what would become of his work when he was gone. He addressed these issues with a sustained focus in eleven meetings with representatives of the English, Indian, and American foundations. These meetings, conducted in Ojai in 1977, represented Krishnamurti's comprehensive reflections on the meaning and significance of his teachings. The two conversations with KFA trustees in 1972 revolved around the nature of himself as an individual, but the more extended series in 1977 examined his philosophy and what would become of it after he was no longer present to express it.

The point of departure for the inquiry was what responsibility the trustees would have after Krishnamurti died. What would keep the foundations functioning in harmony and with a coherent, unified sense of purpose? To what extent had the trustees themselves understood or "imbibed" the meaning of his teachings? At the core of these issues was an even more central concern: what was the actual significance and value of Krishnamurti's life's work?

Within the first minute of the first dialogue, Krishnamurti made the blunt assessment that no one had fully understood what he was trying to convey.

> I feel there must be amongst us some who have, if I may use the phrase again, drunk at the fountain, so that they see the truth for themselves and express it in their daily life. I think that is one of the major issues, as far as I am concerned, because for the last fifty-two years, one has talked a great deal about all these things, and I find—I hope you will forgive me for saying this—there is not one person who has seen that thing for himself and goes on with it. Please understand, I am not disappointed that there is no one so far; I am not looking for anybody to carry on, but I think we should consider all this.

This was not the only time he made this observation, and it cannot be dismissed as a casual, offhand, or merely introductory remark. He did not repeat it in these meetings, but it formed the implicit basis for much of what followed.

The first order of business was how to ensure that the schools and foundations would remain united and continue down a common path. Krishnamurti fulfilled that function by means of his annual round of global travels and his relationships with the individuals involved. Who could step into these shoes in his absence? The prospect that any one person could do so was not even entertained: from the outset, the only options considered involved the collective action of some kind of group. A few trustees proposed that each foundation could contribute two members to constitute an "apex" group that would travel each year to visit and consult with all the schools and foundations. This proposal seemed to suggest a hierarchical structure imbued with some kind of authority and was met with pointed opposition. Once the concept of apex was removed, however, it was agreed that two or more members from each foundation would gather together and talk on an annual basis.

Krishnamurti invoked the image of a putative "man from Seattle" to represent an individual who would come to Ojai in the future to find out more about his philosophy. The man from Seattle had explored Zen, the Upanishads, Christianity, and other approaches to life and found them all inadequate or illusory. He had heard about Krishnamurti and read one of his books, and he came to Ojai to meet with people who had known him and studied his teachings in depth. He wanted to find out what it was like to be in Krishnamurti's presence and to discover whether the teachings could really help resolve his issues. He wanted to meet the people who had lived and worked with Krishnamurti and find out whether they had anything meaningful to offer.

Krishnamurti asked pointedly whether any of the fifteen trustees with whom he was discussing would be able to meet the challenge posed by the man from Seattle. This inescapably cast a light upon whether they had sufficient understanding of the teachings to convey them to someone else. It would not be enough to quote him or refer someone to one of his books; nothing would suffice except a living engagement with people who had understood the teachings for themselves.

In one of the early conversations, Krishnamurti seemed to accept that the trustees might have understood the teachings only partially. If so, they could speak to the man from Seattle on that basis. In a later dialogue, however, he reversed himself and rejected the possibility of a partial understanding. He made the case that if one has understood one psychological issue completely, it opens the door to understanding all issues.

> I think if you have understood a part, you have understood the whole. If you have understood, say, for example, the meaning of fear—all its implications, the whole of the structure and nature of fear, which is thought, the ego, all that—if you have understood one thing completely, you have understood the rest. Sorry I am so emphatic.

Ultimately, what seemed to matter most in these dialogues was the personal relationship of each trustee to the teachings: whether they regarded them as essential to their lives, and protecting them as their highest responsibility. If it is "your baby," Krishnamurti said, one would go to any length to care for it. He said that the teachings were sacred because they were an expression of truth; they were like a mine that contained "more and more and more gold" for anyone willing to explore them fully. The question was whether the trustees recognized and embraced the value of the teachings and were consumed with understanding them. If they were, the foundations would form a vessel containing the fire of understanding; and, in that spirit, intelligence would flower.

Krishnamurti repeatedly compared his own departure with the years following the death of the Buddha. If he had lived at that time, he maintained, he would have traveled any distance to meet the people who had known the Buddha and find out what he was like. None of the trustees questioned or challenged this comparison during the meetings or asked what it implied. But someone must have spoken to him about it, because in the seventh conversation he went out of his way to say that he did not mean to suggest that he was the Buddha. "I would never do that. If that is in your mind, please wipe it out." He substituted the metaphor of learning from a great violinist—"let's move in that direction, it is better than the Buddha."

The trustees were unable to meet or challenge Krishnamurti with respect to many of the issues he raised, even though he urged them to do so. "Don't come to me with a little bucket," he admonished.

> I have ten years; for God's sake, use me! You have a deep well, full of water. We have come to a point where K says, "For God's sake, use him, learn, get everything you can out of him. You have a very short time."

And yet none of the trustees was able to be frank and acknowledge their lack of understanding. They responded to many questions, but they remained curiously passive regarding the most essential issue—whether they had undergone the kind of transformation he considered imperative. At the end of eleven meetings, the situation appeared to remain exactly as he had said at the beginning: no one had fully understood what he was trying to convey.

Among the many issues broached during these discussions was one that is relevant not only to the trustees but to any student of Krishnamurti's work. How is one to evaluate or assess whether his teachings reflect a direct engagement with truth, or merely consist of some set of ideas he has borrowed from another source? If he were merely repeating something he had heard, the potential for distortion or self-deception would be substantial. Because so many people profess to have access to insight or wisdom, how is a listener to discern who is authentic and who is not?

One trustee suggested that someone may be persuasive and convincing, but whatever he or she says must be tested for logical coherence and fidelity to facts. If there is something said that is self-contradictory, for example, it cannot be entirely true. Krishnamurti acknowledged that the teachings must be logical, but the most reliable form of discernment, he said, is to perceive directly by listening with a quiet mind. If the spoken word is the expression of a valid perception, it will naturally be logical without effort. Logic alone, by contrast, cannot lead to truth. These distinctions help to distinguish Krishnamurti's work from other forms of inquiry.

⁓

During its first five years of operation, the Oak Grove School underwent a metamorphosis. The enrollment mushroomed from half a dozen to over sixty students, ranging in age from five to fourteen. The teaching staff grew to a dozen, including specialists in art, physical education, French, ceramics, and yoga. The school migrated from the east end residence to the Oak Grove property a few miles away that was to be its permanent home. Three buildings were constructed there: one for administrative functions that included upstairs residential quarters for Mark Lee and his family; a spacious multi-purpose room with massive wooden pillars, French doors, and a charming, undulating roof; and a series of connected classrooms, each with its own deck, extending at length through the oak trees and meadows. Altogether it was a massive transformation from the school's humble beginnings in 1975.

Much of the credit for the school's growth belonged to Mark, whose dedication to Krishnamurti's work was deep and undeniable. He brought to the enterprise a gift for assessing and selecting every nuance and detail of the furnishings, gardens, and landscaping, as well as an overall atmosphere of beauty and care for the environment. He represented the school well in interviews with prospective teachers and parents, and he was adept at interacting with trustees and the many and varied visitors and guests. It was not hard to see why Krishnamurti regarded him with special affection and had cultivated his engagement with the work of the schools for more than a decade.

Over the course of these five years, Krishnamurti conducted

some thirty meetings with teachers, trustees, and members of the staff. The purpose of the meetings was to convey the deep intention of the school, an aim that went well beyond mere academic instruction. The essential idea was to educate students for the whole of life, but that opened up an avenue into all of Krishnamurti's philosophy. Most schools implicitly or deliberately function as agents for conditioning students to the norms and principles of society, including the virtues of tradition, competition, and identification with the nation and its flag. Oak Grove, by contrast, was intended to uncondition the mind of the student and so facilitate the awakening of intelligence.

Krishnamurti drew a sharp contrast between intelligence and the intellect. He associated the intellect with knowledge, logic, and thought. In his view, intelligence is a free and fluid capacity, a form of perception, not bound by accumulated knowledge from the past. Only such a quality of mind was capable of understanding the whole landscape of consciousness. Ultimately the aim of the school was to precipitate a psychological transformation in the teacher as well as the student.

Such far-reaching objectives were not easy to convey to teachers occupied with the daily challenges of classroom management and academic instruction. Yet Krishnamurti did his utmost in meetings that lasted an hour, an hour and a half, or more. These meetings had an unusual quality due to his manner of interaction and demeanor. There were no rules, no set agenda, no parameters for participation, and yet his presence generated an atmosphere of discipline and austerity. In principle, anyone was free to speak at any time, and he encouraged active inquiry, including challenging whatever he had to say. In practice, however, the teachers were unable to interact with him much of the time in any meaningful way. Many issues were explored, some at great length, but the net effect on the teachers was more subliminal than anything they were able to implement in their classrooms.

Several factors contributed to this state of affairs. Among these were Krishnamurti's deeply serious attitude and his aura of exceptional order and clarity. These qualities had the effect of inhibiting anyone who could not meet him on a similar plane. This effect could have been overcome because he also radiated friendliness and good will. The situation was exacerbated, however, by the presence of trustees who tended to sit in the rear of the room and contributed nothing to the dialogue. They were much older than most of the teachers and had a somewhat remote relationship with the school. Under these circumstances, the teachers felt vulnerable and exposed; and their jobs, they felt, were potentially on the line.

Even with all these factors in play, a better result might have been achieved had Mark Lee played a more active role in these discussions. As the director of the school, it was his responsibility to lead the charge, as it were, to contribute whatever he could to the questions and challenges Krishnamurti posed. By his own willingness to expose himself, he could have shown how to interact with Krishnamurti in a meaningful way. In fact, however, he rarely spoke at all, apart from occasionally introducing a question at the outset of a meeting. He left it to the teachers to fend for themselves, almost as if it were not necessary for him to participate, because he had nothing to learn.

Mark's inability to lead the teachers effectively in meetings with Krishnamurti was symptomatic of a more general lack of rapport with the teaching staff. Many of those attracted to the school were imbued with a progressive ethic consonant with the zeitgeist of the 1970s and '80s. Although he was not much older than most of the teachers, Mark was a creature from an earlier era, a provenance which suited him well to interact with the trustees, but out of step with the cultural ethos of the faculty.

The tension generated by this difference might not have been insuperable in itself, but it was compounded by another factor. Mark had a tendency to act in a way that some of the teachers interpreted as disingenuous or manipulative, perhaps because he was blinded at times by vanity or self-interest. An attitude of resentment and mistrust had simmered under the surface of events for years, but it finally boiled over in the fifth year of the school. In the spring of 1980, the teachers requested a series of meetings with Krishnamurti for the purpose of airing their grievances. These meetings were deemed too sensitive to record, and the rebellion marked a turning point in the administration of the school.

The teachers complained rather bitterly about their relationship with Mark, and several threatened to leave the school. The prospect of a mass exodus was alarming and would have damaged the school's reputation. Krishnamurti encouraged the teachers to express themselves, to "lay their cards on the table" without fear of repercussions or consequences. He defended Mark up to a point; he said that even the most able administrator might get tired or distracted at times and make mistakes; and he encouraged everyone to bear in mind the deep intention of the school. He said the intention represented a "common ground," a place where everyone could stand together and cooperate. He asked the teachers to overcome their differences in that spirit.

I had taken a sabbatical from the school after three years, in part because I shared some of the misgivings that came to the surface two years later. My efforts to correct the situation had proven counterproductive and left me identified by the trustees as a possible troublemaker. My time away from the school not only insulated me from criticism when trouble emerged, but somehow even enhanced my status in the eyes of the trustees. During my absence, I continued to attend the meetings that Krishnamurti conducted with the teachers, including those in the spring of 1980. Because the meetings had not been recorded, he wanted someone to make a written record of what had been concluded. To my surprise, he turned to me at the end of the last meeting and asked me to write a statement summarizing what had occurred.

I composed a document titled "Responsibility and the Common Ground" that expressed these results in simple declarative sentences. In addition, I went somewhat beyond my mandate and included a delineation of the respective responsibilities of teachers, director, and trustees. The document I composed somehow met with the approval of Krishnamurti and the trustees and was accepted.

No document or agreement could have succeeded by itself, however, in quelling the spirit of rebellion that had consumed the teaching staff. Implicit in the teachers' complaints was the hope or expectation that Mark would be replaced as director of the school. This was a remedy that went far beyond what the trustees were prepared to consider. They had their own reservations about Mark, but no one on the horizon was remotely capable, in their view, of replacing him.

Nevertheless, the trustees accepted the need for some kind of structural change to alleviate the tensions that had arisen. With no advance notice of the agenda, I was invited to attend a meeting with the trustees and Mark where Krishnamurti asked me to consider becoming co-director of the school. I would be responsible for educational matters while Mark would look after administrative affairs. We would be "like two horses yoked," he said, an image he reinforced with his hands, palms together, as in the gesture of namaste.

I regarded this proposal with an acute sense of ambivalence. I respected Mark and admired him in many ways, but I shared some of the teachers' misgivings, and I was not sure we were compatible to the extent that would be required. On the other hand, I was not prepared to say no to Krishnamurti. I trusted his judgment more than my own; so I swallowed my uncertainties and accepted his offer. I sensed that my decision was momentous and the road ahead would be rocky; but the dimensions of the challenge I had agreed to face exceeded the scope of my imagination. The problems in the administration of the school had only begun to emerge; and they would require, and continue to receive, Krishnamurti's close attention in the years ahead.

The resolution of the lawsuit provided access to a cornucopia of assets in the form of land, securities, cash, and documents. Nevertheless, Rajagopal had not battled for six years for nothing, and the legal success was not achieved without a cost. He fought to retain control over every item in the empire he had amassed. Among these was the right to maintain possession of a trove of archival material of somewhat unknown dimensions. It included, at a minimum, the original handwritten manuscripts of Krishnamurti's books, as well as invaluable correspondence from the early days with Annie Besant, Leadbeater, Nitya, and others prominent in the TS. Rajagopal succeeded in preventing an inventory of the archives, and the terms of the settlement stipulated only that it would revert to the KFA upon his death. In the meantime, the KFA trustees would have the opportunity to inspect this material after the lawsuit was settled.

This resolution entailed a certain degree of trust that Rajagopal would behave with a modicum of good will after the long legal battle and permit access to the archives without further delay. This assumption was put to the test four months after the lawsuit had been brought to a close. Krishnamurti, Mary, Erna, and Theo made an appointment in April 1975 and went to the offices of the K&R foundation, where they were met personally by Rajagopal. Mary wrote that he had an angry look, "the glare of the disturbed." His presence was not necessary for the purpose at hand, but he took the opportunity to embark upon a diatribe. Why did they want to inspect his archives? Could he inspect the archives of the KFA? Why had he been "vilified" by the KFA? And so it went, for forty minutes.

No one argued with him or replied until he challenged Krishnamurti directly. Rajagopal said they had once been on friendly terms, but now he would not speak. With that Krishnamurti stood up and declared that if Rajagopal wanted a resumption of their friendship, he should resign from his position and "do penance." Until then, he said, he would have nothing further to say; and he left the room. This declaration propelled Rajagopal into a show of cooperation. He opened a few drawers containing files of transcripts of discussions, and he brought out some of the old letters, as well as photographs of the two brothers from their childhood.

Additional meetings followed that month with similar results. Erna requested to see the archives without Rajagopal present, and he refused. He said Krishnamurti had broken the settlement agreement by telling him he should resign. Most disturbingly, he said he no longer had manuscript copies of the *Commentaries on Living*—"I think they were destroyed." He said he alone would decide what material did or did not constitute archival materials; and, when asked what that meant, he refused to answer any further questions. Mary wrote, "We left in a blast of anger and semi-hysteria."

Other obstacles unrelated to the archives arose in the efforts to implement the terms of the settlement. Rajagopal had failed to disclose the existence of easements that affected KFA's access to some of the property that had been recovered. He also sent members of his foundation to a hearing of the local planning commission to protest holding Krishnamurti's talks in the Oak Grove. (Permission was not denied.) Most significantly, the settlement allowed Rajagopal to republish some material, provided it had been written after 1926 and without alterations from the original version. Purely by chance, the KFA discovered that he was negotiating with Harper & Row to bring out a volume of Krishnamurti's early poems, including one written before 1926, and with hundreds of changes to the original texts. Hurried negotiations with the publisher and the threat of legal action were required to prevent these departures from the terms of the settlement.

In spite of the voluminous evidence of Rajagopal's corrupt behavior, he still had something in reserve that shocked and astonished the KFA trustees. Donald Ingram-Smith, an Australian newsman and old friend of Krishnamurti, was invited by Rajagopal to pay him a visit. During the course of their meeting, early in 1980, Rajagopal dropped into the conversation news of a donation he was about to make to the Huntington Library in Pasadena, a repository of historical documents of all varieties. The donation would consist of Krishnamurti archival material that Rajagopal had collected over the years. He claimed all this material now as his personal property and designated it as the Rajagopal Historical Collection.

Rajagopal must have known that Ingram-Smith would convey this information to the KFA, where it would land like a bombshell. Now all his obfuscation regarding the content and whereabouts of archival documents came into focus. It was hard to know which was greater, his audacity or his mendacity. Apart from the perverse pleasure he took in frustrating the purposes of the KFA, Rajagopal's motivations for this maneuver were evidently mercenary, since the donation no doubt yielded a substantial charitable deduction on his tax returns. The claim that this material represented his personal property not only ran profoundly against the trust that had been invested in him; it also illuminated the devious contours of his consciousness: all these documents that he had accumulated for decades, he maintained, belonged to him!

The scope and volume of the material that Rajagopal claimed as his personal property almost defies description. It took years just to develop a complete inventory. His meticulous attention to detail was on full display in the orderly and exhaustive quantity of material he had accumulated. Letters, photograph albums, interviews, articles, transcripts, handwritten manuscripts, books, pamphlets, business records, and every other form of memorabilia was included. The correspondence files alone filled thirty-six boxes. Each box contained dozens of files, and each file contained as many as fifty letters. When the inventory was finally completed years later, the

Rajagopal Historical Collection required 158 pages to describe all the items it contained.

The KFA had escaped the necessity for a resumption of legal action in connection with the republication of Krishnamurti's early poems. This new challenge to the plain terms of the settlement was of another order of magnitude. Appeals to the Huntington Library were to no avail. It had been negotiating with Rajagopal for over a year for access to the documents and saw no legal basis not to accept them. The only apparent recourse was to go to court again.

Krishnamurti, Mary, and Theo were in India in December 1980 when the letter arrived from Erna informing them of the resumption of legal action. Theo's normal demeanor was reserved and dignified, but when he learned that his wife was engaged in another lawsuit, he broke down in tears. Krishnamurti devoutly wished for nothing more than to be released from any further interaction with Rajagopal, but his hopes would not be realized for the foreseeable future. He told Mary he felt stronger now than he had ten years earlier, and he was ready for whatever the battle might bring. Even so, he could not know how severely his resolve would be tested in the years ahead.

The succession of violations of the settlement agreement elicited numerous comments by Krishnamurti regarding the character of Rajagopal and Rosalind. Some of his remarks were short and to the point: "Those monsters" or "That crook!" He declared that his only regret in life was his association with them. He even entertained the idea that he should encourage the Rajagopals to "repent." They had been exposed to the teachings but had "spat upon them," and so they were vulnerable to some inchoate kind of damnation. Upon reflection, he concluded that any effort to encourage them to repent would be futile.

Krishnamurti recalled a persistent pattern of verbal and physical abuse beginning as far back as 1935. He reported two instances when Rosalind shoved him down the four steps of the patio at Arya

Vihara. On one of these occasions, he was caught by a friend; on the other, he was knocked unconscious. He said she walked out of the room when he spoke to the teachers at Happy Valley School. A friend of Erna's offered the opinion that the Rajagopals' objective had been to destroy Krishnamurti personally as well as the teachings. When Erna reported this to him, he thought it over for a day and then said, "I think that is so."

Of course the question arose repeatedly why he had tolerated so much abuse. Krishnamurti himself was baffled by it. The only explanation he could offer was that he had accepted it as a given, as the irrevocable state of affairs. Beyond that, he said he simply did not care at the time. He attributed his passivity in part to a lack of maturity; he did not mature fully, he maintained, until the age of sixty-five. Now, he told Mary, he would not have tolerated for one minute what he had endured for so many years.

Krishnamurti said that all during the war, while living at the east end residence with the Rajagopals, he had been unable to meditate. Pupul Jayakar asked if he had changed in any meaningful way, and he said very little until after he separated from them. Significant inward developments only began to occur at that time.

∽

Another consequence of the lawsuit settlement was the opportunity to remodel and enlarge Pine Cottage. For this purpose, Mary hired the distinguished architect Charles Moore. She had decided to sell her house in Malibu and use the proceeds to transform the cottage into a residence that she and Krishnamurti could live in for the rest of their lives. After they were gone, ownership of the property would revert to the KFA.

The remodel supplemented Krishnamurti's original rooms with an adjoining bedroom and bath for Mary. An entirely new wing of the cottage was also constructed, featuring a capacious, high-ceil-inged living room, suitable for large meetings, with tall windows, a skylight, and massive hearth and fireplace. The extension also included an ample dining room, well-appointed kitchen, and an office room for Mary. The square footage of the new rooms dwarfed the original Pine Cottage and transformed the modest dwelling into a beautiful (but not opulent) home.

Krishnamurti and Mary moved into the house in March 1978. He was enchanted with the final result. He commented repeatedly on the exceptional quality of the atmosphere it generated. In his last diary, he described his impressions of driving into the Ojai Valley and entering his home. From his description it is apparent that, for him, the valley and his residence were not entirely separate entities. The atmosphere of the house was redolent of the valley and repre-sented a distillation of the valley's essence:

> You enter into this valley, which is almost like a vast cup, a nest. Then you leave the little village and climb to about 1400 feet, passing rows and rows of orange orchards and groves. The air is perfumed with orange blossom. The whole valley is filled with that scent. And the smell of it is in your mind, in your heart, in your whole body.... Each time you come to this quiet, peaceful valley there is a feeling of strange aloofness, of deep silence and the vast spreading of slow time.
>
> The mountains that morning were extraordinarily beautiful. The majesty, the vast sense of permanency is there in them. And you enter into the house where you have lived for over sixty years and the atmosphere, the air, is, if one can use that word, holy; you can feel it. You can almost touch it.
>
> As it has rained considerably, for it is the rainy season, all the hills and the little folds of the mountain are green, flourishing, full—the earth is smiling with such delight, with some deep quiet understanding of its own existence.

Chapter Thirteen

DAVID BOHM

Krishnamurti never suffered from any shortage of people eager to engage with him in dialogue. Among these were many prominent intellectuals who were attracted to his philosophy in spite of his insistence on the limitations of the intellect. Aldous Huxley and Pupul Jayakar were among the individuals of this kind; but even with the participation of people of this caliber, he sometimes expressed dissatisfaction with the level of their understanding. Of all those with whom he discussed, however, there was one who was able to meet him consistently on his own level. Theoretical physicist David Bohm stands preeminent in the quantity and quality of conversations he conducted with Krishnamurti and in the fruitful results they achieved.

Bohm made important contributions at an early age to the foundations of quantum mechanics, but his insights were so revolutionary that decades elapsed before they were fully appreciated. His interests encompassed not only theoretical physics but philosophy of science, cosmology, and the study of consciousness. He was drawn to Krishnamurti's work in part due to similarities with the implications of quantum theory, including the inextricable connection between the apparatus used to observe and the phenomena under observation. He initiated a meeting in 1961, and the two men found they had an immediate rapport.

Bohm was an expatriate American, driven out of the United

States by the House Committee on UnAmerican Activities. He had a highly promising career as a professor at Princeton before he was forced to leave the country in order to find employment. He had settled into a chair in theoretical physics at the University of London when he met Krishnamurti and began attending the annual talks at Saanen. His understanding of Krishnamurti's work was profound and his skill in dialogue unequalled.

Among the most successful series of s Krishnamurti conducted was one with Bohm and David Shainberg, the psychiatrist who arranged the meetings with therapists in New York. Conducted in May 1976, these conversations were the first of his dialogues to be videotaped in color. The three men assume distinctive personas, with Shainberg in the role of the common man; he is receptive but somewhat skeptical, and given to the kind of question that might occur to someone unfamiliar with this work. He is short and slouching, with prominent sideburns and scruffy hair, and a cheerful, inquisitive demeanor that lifts the dialogue into another key. Bohm and Krishnamurti act as his mentors, alternately clarifying and challenging him and one another. The videotapes are available under the title *The Transformation of Man*, while the transcripts of the dialogues were published as *The Wholeness of Life*.

Over the course of their quarter-century collaboration, Bohm and Krishnamurti engaged together and with others in well over one hundred recorded dialogues. Bohm was a fixture on weekends at the school at Brockwood Park, and he consulted regularly with the trustees in England regarding administrative issues. He was almost equally involved with the American foundation and the Oak Grove School. He was in many respects a known quantity, and it was generally understood that he enjoyed a sterling reputation within his primary world of science. Even so, very few of those associated with Krishnamurti appreciated the magnitude of Bohm's contribution to the foundations of theoretical physics.

Bohm attended graduate school at the University of California at Berkeley under the wing of J. Robert Oppenheimer, then the leading light of the American physics community. Even before he finished his PhD, he made enduring contributions in several fields. Among other discoveries, he found an important characteristic of plasma now known as Bohm diffusion. He accepted a position as assistant professor at Princeton, where he explored physics and the philosophy of science with Einstein at the Institute for Advanced Studies. His main focus of research was quantum mechanics, which deals with the behavior of electrons and other subatomic particles. The textbook he wrote, *Quantum Theory*, surpassed all others in its lucid account of the strange behavior of matter at that level.

Although it forms a central pillar of the discipline of physics, quantum mechanics is notorious for the confusing, inexplicable phenomena at the subatomic level. Among the bizarre and paradoxical features of the quantum world is that electrons behave differently when they are observed than they do when they are not under observation. Much of the quantum world, moreover, is held to be irrevocably unknowable, beyond the reach not only of our existing instruments, but beyond any possible observations or measurements. This essential barrier to knowledge was underwritten by the equations of John von Neumann, a mathematician whose work was regarded as impregnable.

In 1951, Bohm published a pair of papers that knocked the support out from under this hallowed principle. He detected a flaw in the reasoning of von Neumann, an assumption that was not necessarily valid. He opened up that aperture in the armor of quantum theory and drove a truckload of unsuspected possibilities through it. The paterfamilias of the physics community promptly went into a state of denial. The elder statesman, Oppenheimer himself, said shamelessly, "If we cannot disprove Bohm, we must agree to ignore him." On the other hand, a few recognized the significance of what

Bohm had accomplished. The young prodigy John Bell said of Bohm's work, "In 1951, I saw the impossible done."

It has taken decades for Bohm's contribution to receive the respect it deserves, and today it stands near the center of a roiling mass of still unresolved issues. If the physics community itself was unable fully to appreciate Bohm, it is not surprising that those near Krishnamurti regarded him as simply another brilliant scientist. His manner was so modest and unassuming that it was easy to over-look the actuality that Bohm was a bona fide genius, a man whose intellectual powers far surpassed the merely talented and gifted. His contributions to theoretical physics, philosophy of science, and cosmology were comprehensive, highly original, and profound.

When Krishnamurti left Ojai in May 1975, he returned to Brockwood Park, where he stayed for several weeks until the Saanen gathering in July. During that period, he conducted a series of twelve recorded dialogues with Bohm. The two men had engaged in many conversations previously, individually and with others, but this was the first extended series with only the two participating. It was a unique and important opportunity.

By a stroke of serendipity, these conversations occurred very shortly after the release of the first volume of Mary Lutyens's biography of Krishnamurti. Bohm had read an early copy of the manuscript, and he used the opportunity of these dialogues to question him about it. He asked whether Krishnamurti's fundamental insights had first occurred in association with some particular moment, event, or experience. Krishnamurti said no; his point of view had always been fundamentally the same. There was, however, a long, gradual process of clarifying what his teaching was and how to express it. Rather remarkably, Bohm did not mention in this context the three-day episode culminating under the pepper tree, although that event was treated at length by Lutyens and presented as if it were a major turn-ing point. Nor did Krishnamurti refer to that experience in his reply.

Bohm also asked about the nature and significance of Krishnamurti's "process." Would others have to endure something similar in order to realize his insights or state of mind? Krishnamurti was unhelpful when it came to elucidating the meaning of the process; but he offered the observation that to face suffering without any form of escape generates an intensity of energy. Evidently, he felt the process served that function. He also speculated that perhaps the process might bear some relationship to kundalini, although he made a point of not endorsing the idea. He was clear and emphatic, however, that it was not a prerequisite for anyone else to undergo something similar in order to share his insights into consciousness.

Another feature of these dialogues consisted of some refinements Bohm introduced into the vocabulary Krishnamurti employed. He was fascinated with the root meanings of words, and he examined the etymology of *reality*, *actuality*, and *truth* in an effort to bring these terms into alignment with Krishnamurti's philosophy. The result was a significant shift in the way Krishnamurti used these terms, not only during these conversations, but subsequently for several years.

The twelve dialogues were transcribed, edited, and prepared for publication when they came to the attention of Mary Lutyens. As a key member of the publications committee, she objected strongly to the dialogues appearing in print. She felt the new vocabulary was unfamiliar and overly intellectual; and she rebelled against the implication that Bohm might seem to be the dominant partner, as if he were teaching Krishnamurti. She went so far as to count the number of lines that each man spoke, and she chafed at the fact that Bohm had more. She felt that it conveyed a wrong impression of the actual relationship between the two men and might be misunderstood by the reading public.

Lutyens was alone in her objections, but she threatened to resign from her role as a trustee of the English foundation if the publication went forward as planned. As Krishnamurti's biographer

and his close and lifelong friend, her role was somewhat indispensable, and she succeeded in bringing the book to a halt. As a kind
of compromise, selected excerpts from a few of the dialogues were
published with other material in *Truth and Actuality*; but most of the
dialogues remained unpublished for many years.

The task of communicating to Bohm what had occurred fell to
Krishnamurti. He evidently broached the matter in a fairly casual
manner, with little appreciation for how it would be received. As a
form of compensation, he promised Bohm that they would conduct
another series of dialogues that would in fact be published in full.
The failure to publish the existing dialogues as planned, however,
represented a serious disappointment to Bohm and precipitated a
conflict in their relationship.

Had Bohm been seen for what he was, the difficulties he
encountered with publication of these dialogues might never have
arisen. The publication was cancelled solely due to Lutyens, who
succeeded by some inexplicable combination of argument and
influence in persuading Krishnamurti to drown this incomparable
litter of offspring. Had she understood that Bohm was a towering
figure in his own right, and not just another of Krishnamurti's part-
ners in dialogue, she might have hesitated to act with such arrogant
certitude.

There was one individual, however, who appreciated Bohm's
work as a scientist, and with whom he could share the disillusionment that followed the decision not to publish. Fritz Wilhelm was
a professor of physics from Germany who had been introduced
to Krishnamurti in Saanen. He was tall, young, bearded, and glib,
fluent in English and self-possessed. He was sufficiently interested in
Krishnamurti's work to give up his professorship in favor of a plum
assignment in Ojai. Although he was new to Krishnamurti and his
circle, Wilhelm was plucked out of obscurity and offered an important role with little advance vetting of his qualifications.

One of Krishnamurti's pet projects, often discussed but seldom realized, was to create places where serious people could immerse themselves in the teachings for two or three weeks at a time. Such a setting would need to have a pristine, meditative atmosphere, natural beauty in abundance, and one or more individuals with whom a visitor could discuss and inquire into the meaning of his work. Wilhelm was selected to fill that role in what was called an Adult Center soon to be established in Ojai.

Wilhelm had been working in that capacity for a year in 1977 when Krishnamurti conducted the series of meetings with the international trustees to discuss their responsibilities after he was gone. His involvement is mentioned several times in the meetings and not always in a way that reflected appreciation for the work he was doing. A meme emerged to the effect that he was engaging with visitors in a form of group therapy, as if he were moderating another of the self-help groups that were sprouting like mushrooms in the cultural landscape of that era. Krishnamurti's intention for the Adult Center was that guests should explore issues germane to the human condition, rather than their personal attachments, addictions, or other idiosyncratic forms of dysfunction. The general, not the particular, was the avenue into the teachings, and the view emerged that Wilhelm was not attentive to that distinction.

Wilhelm had his own grounds for disappointment with the role to which he was appointed. He had envisioned long walks and hours of personal engagement with Krishnamurti. When little of that materialized, he developed a degree of alienation toward the enterprise as a whole. He was closely associated with the teachers' revolt against Mark Lee, but his sense of discontent was larger and more amorphous. Krishnamurti gave him increasing attention, in the form of numerous meetings, with the aim of remedying whatever ailed him. These efforts were not successful, and Wilhelm left the Adult Center and Ojai in 1980.

Well before Wilhelm's departure, he had formed a close bond with Bohm. The two men shared a common interest in physics, the philosophy of science, and the work of Krishnamurti. Bohm and his wife spent six weeks each year in Ojai, staying in an upstairs apartment over the KFA offices that came to be known as the Bohm flat. While in Ojai, he was accessible for the kind of endless conversation that Wilhelm craved with someone of that caliber. The two men bonded not only over their shared interests, but also over a measure of discontent regarding Krishnamurti himself.

Bohm's displeasure found expression in four letters he wrote to Wilhelm in 1979 and early 1980. In these letters, he developed a comprehensive indictment of Krishnamurti's personality and point of view. At the core of his critique was the acute conflict he felt regarding the dialogues that had been pulled at the last minute from the path of publication. Mary Lutyens's stated apprehension was that the dialogues falsely conveyed the impression that Bohm was leading or teaching Krishnamurti. Since Krishnamurti had capitulated to Lutyens's reservations, was he trying to protect the image he projected to the world? Krishnamurti, according to Bohm, seemed to have a distorted sense of himself, conditioned by Theosophy, in which he had some form of infallibility or exclusive access to truth. Bohm felt literally "crushed," he said, with physical pain in his chest, by the contradictions he perceived in Krishnamurti's personality.

In point of fact, the pain in Bohm's chest was probably due more to the condition of his arteries than to any currents of emotion. A year later he was diagnosed with arterial sclerosis, which required multiple bypass surgery. Moreover, a month after he had written the last of these letters, Bohm wrote again to Wilhelm and partially repudiated his previous remarks. He said they failed to reflect his positive regard for Krishnamurti, and he pointedly downplayed the significance of what he had said. Such comments were subject to misinterpretation, he now said, and he even asked Wilhelm to destroy the letters containing disparaging remarks.

The new series of dialogues that Krishnamurti had promised Bohm were initiated in Ojai, shortly after these letters were written, in April 1980. One of the distinctive features of these dialogues consisted of something Krishnamurti described, an event that had occurred a few months earlier. His treatment of the topic of meditation, and his own experience of it, were highly unusual in many respects. Among the remarkable features of his meditation was that it often occurred when he was asleep. The meditation persisted after he woke up, and so confirmed the nature of what had been taking place.

One night in Rishi Valley, late in 1979, Krishnamurti's meditation deepened in a manner that he considered extraordinary. Three months later, in Ojai, he composed a description of what had occurred. His meditation, he maintained, had reached "the source of all energy," the absolute beginning and end of all that is. He acknowledged that people might think he had imagined it or wonder how he could know such a thing; but he declared "with all humility" that it was so.

Two months after he had composed this account, Krishnamurti and Bohm commenced the series of fifteen dialogues that collectively represent their most important work together. Half an hour into the first conversation, Krishnamurti described what he had experienced in Rishi Valley, and the meaning of that event is woven through the series. Bohm provided the appropriate terminology to discuss what had occurred: he suggested that Krishnamurti had reached "the ground" of the universe, the source of all that is.

The primary theme of these dialogues was introduced early on. Krishnamurti raised the question whether humanity has taken a "wrong turn" in its evolutionary development. He and Bohm agreed that must have been the case by virtue of the conflict, confusion, and disharmony endemic in the human condition. Their dialogue ranged over a wide array of topics, but the source and nature of the wrong turn occupied center stage much of the time. Krishnamurti located the essential error in the ubiquitous desire to improve oneself psychologically, to become something more or better—more virtuous, wise, wealthy, famous, or successful in any arena. This incessant drive he calls the process of "becoming," and he maintains that it arises through the illusion of psychological time.

Here it is crucial to emphasize (as noted previously) that Krishnamurti distinguishes psychological time from the ordinary chronological time that we measure by the calendar or the clock. He acknowledges that chronological time is an obvious and inescapable fact; but psychological time represents the arena within which the ego or self seeks to improve or become something that it is not. Psychological time, he maintains, is illusory; it does not exist; it is an artifact created by thought. To see the false nature of psychological time represents a deep insight that eliminates the source of fruitless conflict.

These dialogues were published in full, as Krishnamurti had promised, in a book called *The Ending of Time*. (The title is misleading since it must appear to anyone not familiar with Krishnamurti's vocabulary to refer to ending chronological time.) With this publication, the breach of trust Bohm had endured was partially repaired. Krishnamurti's own capacity for insight represented a recurrent theme of the dialogues. The conversations therefore provided an opportunity for Bohm to explore his misgivings about Krishnamurti himself, if he had so desired. Nowhere, however, is there any hint of the reservations he had expressed to Wilhelm. *The Ending of Time* formed the pinnacle of the quarter-century collaboration between the two men.

Additional portions of the 1975 dialogues were published many years later as *The Limits of Thought*. To this day, however, approximately half of the series remains unpublished. To continue even now to withhold publication of the entire series in a single volume represents an enduring mystery and an incomprehensible decision on the part of those responsible for Krishnamurti's work.

⁓

Krishnamurti's debt to Erna Lilliefelt was immeasurable, and his trust and confidence in her were correspondingly great. While Mary rescued him personally from the Rajagopals, Erna rescued him legally, and in the process she recovered the intellectual, monetary, and real property that were the tangible fruit of his life's work. She was a formidable adversary for Rajagopal, a woman with the rare combination of perseverance, acumen, and integrity to see the need to do battle with him and to win. She devoted year after year of painstaking labor to the long struggle, with little reward other than the certainty of the merits of her case. Krishnamurti had good grounds for his reliance upon her.

The very qualities that made Erna a worthy warrior in the legal arena were supremely unsuited for someone invested with responsibility for a school. Up against Rajagopal, she could be hardnosed and uncompromising, driven and meticulous, consumed with the bottom line, and function day to day with little affection or joy in her heart. The great irony of Krishnamurti's deep commitment to the Oak Grove School was that Erna, by virtue of her pivotal role in the KFA, was ipso facto responsible as well for the school; and almost everything she did in that arena systematically undermined what Krishnamurti was trying to achieve. His blindness to this reality was almost on a par with his acquiescence to the crimes perpetrated by Rajagopal.

During my years as a teacher at the school, I was largely insulated from the effects of Erna's interactions with the school.

As co-director, however, I found her impact was immediate and profound. A very small harbinger of what was to come occurred shortly after my appointment, on the last day before Krishnamurti and Mary departed Ojai. Erna decreed that my wife and I would not be permitted to bring our two cats to live with us in the upstairs apartment at Arya Vihara—notwithstanding that several other cats were in residence on the property. Only the last minute intervention of Krishnamurti himself succeeded in reversing this edict.

A far more serious decree was imposed by Erna two months later, and this time no one was available to whom to appeal her execrable judgment. Prior to my appointment to the role of co-direc-tor, it had been understood that I would return as one of the primary homeroom teachers, a full-time job in itself. But after my appoint-ment, Erna determined that budgetary considerations dictated that I would have to perform the two jobs of homeroom teacher and co-director simultaneously. Mark Lee offered no objection to this decision, and I had no allies with sufficient influence to stand up to Erna. I rather meekly acquiesced, with little or no resistance. I must have felt cowed and powerless to avert an open invitation to confusion or paralysis or worse.

A twist of the knife occurred a few weeks into the school year. One morning Mark announced to me cheerfully that Krishnamurti had asked him to drop everything and go immediately to India for an indefinite period of time. No reason for this sudden expedition was given. I would be left behind to fill the role of both directors and homeroom teacher all at the same time until further notice. Before I had a chance to fully absorb the implications of this plan, Mark had packed up and left town.

I learned many years later, from the memoirs of Mary Zimbalist, what had precipitated this exercise in absurdity. Evidently one of the trustees, a close friend of Mark's, was traveling with Krishnamurti in India and suggested out of the blue how great it would be for

Mark to join them there. Perhaps they felt that he had been through a rough time the previous spring and needed this trip to boost his morale. There was certainly no objective requirement for his presence. According to Mary's memoir, Krishnamurti endorsed this idea, provided that Erna sign on and approve it. This she did without hesitation and without consulting me. Indeed, no one consulted me about it, in spite of the fact that the entire burden of the arrangement fell upon my shoulders. But only Erna knew I was already working two jobs. Only she had the knowledge and the authority to put a stop to this moronic idea, and she offered no objection at all.

Mark was gone for six weeks. After a month, with no communication from him and no clue when he would return, I mentioned to Erna that I was considering sending him a telegram, asking when we could expect him to come back. Erna felt the cost of such a telegram, some fifteen dollars, was an unnecessary expense, and she counseled me against sending it. I sent it anyway and thereby incurred her unending wrath. Two years later, she cited this incident, with bitter hostility, as dispositive evidence why she was unable to work with me in a cooperative manner.

Krishnamurti often wondered why Oak Grove exhibited signs of dysfunction. He devoted long hours in meetings with teachers, trying to convey his educational philosophy, in part as a remedy for the school's problems. Erna and the other trustees reinforced his apprehensions and clucked together nervously, uncertain what could be done. The possibility that Erna herself was the source of many of the school's problems evidently never crossed his mind. It would require years of further turmoil before the simple truth of the matter finally became manifest to him.

Krishnamurti's educational philosophy was dedicated to psychological freedom, unconditioning, and the cultivation of intelligence, but Erna brought the mentality of a bookkeeper to the enterprise. She saw everything through the prism of financial profit and loss, and in that calculus the parents were prized as a source of income, and the teachers were lamentably the school's greatest expense. Krishnamurti's schools in India and at Brockwood Park were boarding schools, unlike Oak Grove, where students went home to their families at three o'clock each day. Krishnamurti and those near him had never had to deal with the close proximity of parents, and they were completely unequipped to anticipate what that would entail. With her accountant's cap firmly in place, Erna was driven to elevate parents to a position of power in the administration of the school. This was precisely the wrong approach, another reflection of her poor judgment in all things related to education.

In my second year as co-director, the burden of performing two jobs was eliminated from my portfolio, and the potentiality of the dual directorship was beginning to show some promise. It was a little too late, however, for the first year had begun on such a wrong foot, and a ripple effect of negative consequences was already underway. Two of the parents had been vocal and aggressive in criticizing our biology teacher, whose selection of a textbook did not meet with their approval. I was slow and too distracted to intervene in time, and, while I temporized, these parents brought their concerns directly to Erna. They leveraged their complaint into a wholesale indictment of the administration of the school, and they found in Erna a receptive audience. She in turn conveyed her concerns to Krishnamurti as soon as he arrived in Ojai in February 1982.

The parents in question were a psychologist and a psychiatrist. They were in business together in a therapeutic setting, and Erna was in thrall to their professional credentials. The dominant figure of the two was Tom Krause, who was tall, bearded, slow talking, and intense. His diminutive sidekick was John Hidley, whose manner was more subtle and refined. Krause had two children enrolled in the school and Hidley had four, so their personal investment in it was substantial, and their clout with Erna was magnified accordingly.

Within a few weeks of Krishnamurti's arrival in Ojai, Erna invited Krause to lunch for the purpose of meeting him. Krishnamurti, according to Mary, said that Krause seemed "serious"; and, on the strength of that and Erna's recommendation, he was suddenly elected to the board of trustees of the KFA. His unofficial job description entailed the exercise of special responsibility for the school.

As if this were not enough, Krishnamurti began to suggest a new concept for the school administration. At Brockwood, he had been exploring the possibility of a committee rather than a single individual at the helm, and he seemed eager to transplant this idea to Oak Grove. With Erna's support, the committee concept took shape rather quickly, and its members were selected before the idea itself had been fully examined and absorbed. Mark and I were members ex officio, and we were to be joined by Krause, one other parent, and one teacher. The teacher would be left to Mark and me to designate, but the trustees would choose the second parent. In practice, that meant Erna would make the selection, and she delegated that responsibility to Krause. He chose Leslie Hidley, the wife of his business partner, John.

Putting the clients of a business in the role of managing the managers is a recipe for disaster in any ordinary enterprise. It would not work in a bank or an auto shop or a law firm. In the context of the Oak Grove School, the prospects for success were even worse. It was comparable to putting the patients in charge of an asylum. But in the spring of 1982, the potential downside of this arrangement was not yet apparent. Krishnamurti charged the committee with the mission of "driving" the school, as he put it, focusing its energies on the essential psychological work at the core of its intention. In principle this might not have been a bad idea. In practice it led to a wicked maelstrom of conflicting personalities and energies.

Krause had little serious interest in Krishnamurti's work—he later converted to Catholicism—notwithstanding that his children were enrolled in the school. He had even less administrative expertise. Krishnamurti had yielded to Erna's judgment in elevating him to a position of dominance in the school, and the consequences nearly capsized the school before it had fully matured. It would take two years, however, for the fruit of the poisoned tree to ripen and for Krishnamurti to take corrective action. Even then he continued to rely without question on Erna's judgment. What it would take to open his eyes fully was the issue on which the future of the school depended.

In the summer of 1981, Bohm underwent triple bypass surgery to correct the heart condition that had been plaguing him intermittently for years. Krishnamurti visited him the day before the operation and placed his hands on him to transmit a healing energy. According to Mary's memoirs, Bohm was very fearful of the impending surgery. After the procedure, his blood pressure dropped precipitously, and his life seemed to hang in the balance. Krishnamurti and Mary held him strongly in their consciousness and strove to provide some form of spiritual support through the moment of crisis.

Krishnamurti asked Mary if Bohm was dependent upon him. Mary said that he was very invested in the relationship and had suffered in recent years due to an apparent reduction in the frequency of their conversations. With the benefit of hindsight, this explanation makes little sense. The most important and sustained conversations between the two men had occurred only the year before, and the issue that had troubled Bohm was not the lack of meetings but the failure to publish the 1975 dialogues. Mary's lack of insight into his state of mind serves as a reminder that her memoirs, so good in many respects, were partial and incomplete in others.

Krishnamurti told Mary that Bohm might be suffering from an inner conflict, due to a contradiction between his commitment to psychological inquiry and the demands of his day job in theoretical physics. He said that after Bohm had recovered, he would urge him to forget about quantum mechanics and cosmology and give himself fully to his work with Krishnamurti. Such a conversation evidently did occur two or three years later, but with consequences far removed from those intended.

⚬

In 1982, the year following his surgery, Bohm brought to Ojai a celebrated but controversial figure, someone newly prominent on the horizons of scientific discourse. Rupert Sheldrake was the author of *A New Science of Life*, a book that offered a radical new theory to account for the origin of species. Like Bohm himself, Sheldrake was a maverick, a daring provocateur. Their differences, however, were as important as their similarities. Bohm's revolutionary contributions to theoretical physics were generally discounted when first published, but have subsequently gained increasing respect. Sheldrake's ideas, by contrast, received widespread attention from the outset, but have shown little promise as the years have gone by. Nevertheless, he had an impeccable academic pedigree from Cambridge and Harvard, and he was a darling of progressive intellectual circles in England. He found a sympathetic reception in Bohm, whose tolerance for intellectual unconventionality resided deep in his DNA. It was a match made in purgatory.

Sheldrake's commitment to science was leavened with a religious streak. He had a fondness for churches, ashrams, and other centers of worship, coupled with an acerbic skepticism regarding certain gurus and priests. He brought to the lunch table at Arya Vihara a gift for entertaining anecdotes that revealed the hypocrisy of some of the religious leaders he had encountered. He was sufficiently astute to recognize that Krishnamurti was cut from another cloth entirely. At the same time, he was not intimidated by Krishnamurti's reputation, and he was able to hold his own in dialogue or any other forum that required him to think fast on his feet.

For these reasons, Sheldrake was a good candidate for conversations with Krishnamurti. He had the right combination of receptivity, verbal skill, and independence of mind, and Bohm was on hand to serve as a facilitator if the dialogue took an untoward turn. A series of meetings was arranged with Bohm, Sheldrake, Krishnamurti, and John Hidley, the psychiatrist and business partner of Tom Krause.

It was a dialogue in four parts, spread out over three days. Hidley took the lead and initiated an inquiry into the sources of psychological disorder. The clinical setting of the office of a psychotherapist represented the hypothetical point of departure. Krishnamurti quizzed Hidley regarding the treatment of a patient suffering from depression. He wasted no time in bringing the central issue into focus. Is not the self—the "me," the ego—the origin of most if not all psychological disorder? Is it not an inherently isolating factor in consciousness, an ineluctable engine of division and disharmony?

Hidley pointed out that the standard approach of most therapy is to accept the self as a given and work toward repairing or improving the sense of identity. The possibility of eliminating the self altogether is never seriously considered. Bohm, Hidley, and Sheldrake testified to the powerful inward feeling of the reality of an enduring self, a psychological entity at the center of consciousness. The illusory nature of that sense of reality represented a crucial feature of Krishnamurti's philosophy.

Sheldrake served the useful function of challenging some of Krishnamurti's familiar assertions. The tendency of the individual to identify with some larger group—the family, a particular religion, a nation-state—is intended to generate security but in fact, according to him, leads to division and insecurity. Sheldrake succeeded in moving him to concede that in certain limited circumstances, identification with a group does indeed produce safety and security for the individual. Exchanges of this kind helped refine and elucidate the meaning of his statements.

In the third of the four dialogues, the inquiry arrived at the core of Krishnamurti's understanding of consciousness. The conversation penetrated to the relationship between the observer and the observed, including his insight that the observer "is" the observed. He devoted a great deal of attention in his public talks to the effort to illuminate the meaning of this statement, but a shroud of confusion surrounded it nevertheless. Sheldrake, Hidley, and Bohm succeeded in drawing out his perspective on this issue with unusual clarity.

In the final dialogue, Krishnamurti posed a series of questions about religion and what is sacred. He began by asking whether anything produced by thought can ever be considered sacred. Too quickly, the other participants agreed that it cannot. No one argued, for example, that thought can embody exquisite forms of beauty and order, as in a poem, dance, or symphony. What he had in mind were the symbols and images normally associated with religion, including holy books, rituals, and supernatural events enshrined in myth. By excluding all of this from anything sacred, organized religion fails a crucial test.

At this point Sheldrake introduced an astute objection. Although religious ideas and imagery are expressed in thought, he suggested they are intended to point to something beyond themselves, something numinous and ineffable. Krishnamurti acknowledged that may be the intention, but he insisted that such an intention can never be realized. No one can discover or come upon whatever lies beyond thought, he said, unless and until the existing disorder in consciousness is resolved. The effort to go beyond is doomed, he maintained, if it proceeds from a state of mind already in confusion and conflict.

This point of view distinguishes Krishnamurti as a religious philosopher. He acknowledges the existence of something sacred, but he offers no description of it or pathway to it. On the contrary, he insists that the only thing one can do is to give attention to one's existing state of mind. His philosophy, accordingly, consists of the straightforward exploration of the actual daily life of the ordinary individual. The substance of his teaching is secular and psychological, and even his idea of true religion is oriented in a similar direction. Religion, he maintains, consists of "the accumulation of energy to find out whether it is possible to be free." Such an intention or action would normally be regarded as secular if it were not characterized otherwise.

There can be no doubt that Krishnamurti's teaching contains a deep religious dimension. The nature of what he regards as religious, however, has nothing to do with faith, or the hereafter, or some supernatural figure guiding events on Earth. It has everything to do with a state of mind that is orderly and whole, a mind that is healthy and sane. That is why his philosophy is almost exclusively psychological. Only a mind that is sane, he would say, can discover that which is immeasurable.

Chapter Fourteen

LOS ALAMOS

The commencement of the committee structure inaugurated a dark period in the early history of the Oak Grove School. Erna Lilliefelt's negative attitude was not buffered by the committee but amplified through Tom Krause and Leslie Hidley. They were on a mission of sorts to rein in what they viewed as the unruly and irreverent teaching staff. In fact, the teachers were normally quiescent, dedicated to their classrooms, and passive with respect to the administration. But they were imbued with a progressive, anti-authoritarian ethos that set them apart from the conservative mentality of the trustees. Krause and Hidley represented the business end of a cattle prod designed to keep the faculty in line.

Mark Lee aligned himself with the Krause-Hidley faction, and, in so doing, magnified the implicit division between the two directors. He was sufficiently circumspect to make his position ambiguous until I initiated a frank conversation with him late one afternoon. I told him I felt the committee was dysfunctional and had cast a "shadow" over the school. As co-directors, it was our responsibility to do something about it. Without consulting me or even warning me, he conveyed my apprehensions straight to Krause and the trustees. They reacted to my incipient resistance to their authority with alarm, and I had to backtrack to keep the peace. In this manner, Mark made the direction of his loyalties very clear.

After that episode, my frame of mind deteriorated. The weekly meetings of the committee were long, unpleasant, and unproductive, and they had the enervating effect of suffocating in its cradle every creative impulse or idea. I was dedicated to the work of the school, but this was not that work, and I could see no way out. The collective weight of Erna, Tom Krause, and Mark Lee was more than I could overturn or tolerate.

I met with Krishnamurti to submit my resignation. I lacked the courage or clarity, however, to tell him what the actual issues were. I said I was not well suited to my job, which required me to meet with too many people and fragmented and dissipated my energies. He surprised me by saying he was counting on me to look after the school far into the future, after he was gone. That was not a reply I could easily discount.

I thought it over for a week and met with him a second time. I said I still wanted to resign. He looked at me rather quizzically and asked what I would do instead. He even floated the idea that I could travel with him. By some alchemy, he gradually made me realize that my heart was still engaged in the school; and, in some intuitive way, I felt he would be there to support me. I agreed to try to stay on for a while longer.

In the fall of 1983, yet another layer of oversight was added to the already unwieldy administrative structure of the school. At the suggestion of Krause, the trustees agreed to create a school board after the fashion of other private schools. At Oak Grove such a board was superfluous because the KFA already had responsibility for the school. The fledgling school was saddled with two directors, the existing five-member committee, as well as the trustees, so the addition of a school board represented an administrative tumor growing out of control.

Krause appointed himself chairman of the board, and he added John Hidley, his business partner, as one of its seven members. Now Krause was a member of the KFA, and of the school committee, and the school board, while his partner Hidley was on the board, and Hidley's wife served on the committee. The net effect was surreal in its disproportionate delegation of responsibility to a tiny segment of the school community. Yet Mark and the trustees behaved as though the whole arrangement made perfect sense; and Krishnamurti was in India, far removed from the madness. Resistance, under these circumstances, was beyond my capabilities.

Two months after it had been formed, the school board took a decision to intervene in a sensitive matter that was symptomatic of the culture of the school. It was our custom for students to address teachers by their first names. This had been the case from the earliest days of the school, and it was a uniform practice from the youngest to the oldest grades. No one at the school, parents or teachers, considered the practice problematical, and it was understood to reflect the kind of close relationship that the school was aiming to cultivate. It was, in any case, an embedded habit.

The board was unanimous in its decision to overturn the custom of using first names. Mark Lee fell in line and actively supported the change in policy. I abstained from voting on grounds that the board had no business intervening in a matter of this kind. I said the decision intruded on the province of the teachers and that negative consequences were likely to ensue. My objections were summarily dismissed; no one had the courtesy even to pretend to consider what I had said. The board had the bit between its teeth and was determined to plunge ahead.

Word of the board's decision filtered through the school community with an incendiary mixture of outrage and astonishment. Few people had even heard of the school board, and the influence of the Krause-Hidley faction had so far remained subterranean. Now a spotlight illuminated the whole ungainly administrative structure, and teachers and parents alike were alarmed and furious. The only question was how they would register their objections.

This was the state of affairs when Krishnamurti arrived in Ojai in February 1984. A document was delivered to him the first day he sat down at the lunch table at Arya Vihara. It had been signed by about half of the parents of children in the school, some three dozen signatures. The document consisted of several pages presenting a comprehensive indictment of the top-heavy structure of the school administration. The attitudes and behavior of the school board were targets of special attention, while the teachers were described as dedicated and responsible. It was a call to action, but of what form was left unspecified.

The language of the document was framed in generalities, and Krishnamurti had trouble understanding what it was all about. He turned to me, sitting next to him, and asked me to explain what the problem was. I felt caught in the crosshairs, as the table was attended largely by trustees. All I could say was that there was a problem of communication in the school. He received this vague and insipid response with undisguised incredulity: "*Communication?*" he said. "If I had an issue with Mrs. Zimbalist, and I told her it was a problem of 'communication,' she would throw a brick at me!" His scathing response did nothing to alleviate my discomfort, and I retreated into silence.

A meeting was held at the school to which all the parents and teachers were invited. Krishnamurti sat alone on the low stage of the assembly room and looked out calmly over the sea of simmering discontent. He invited anyone who wished to speak to say whatever was on their mind. The comments of the first few parents were desultory and unfocused, and Krishnamurti began to show signs of impatience. Then a man stood up and spoke in a language that resonated with him. "There is fear in the school," the man said. He described the somewhat amorphous conflict in psychological terms that intersected with Krishnamurti's intention for the school.

With that, the tide began to turn. The trustees might have been hoping that the parents would raise their voices, behave badly, and discredit themselves, but nothing of that kind occurred; and now Krishnamurti was engaged on the parents' behalf. If there was fear in the school, he vowed, he would seek out its source and eradicate it. "I will go after it like a terrier," he pledged.

Over the course of the next few weeks, he conducted numerous meetings with individuals and groups from every corner of the school community. The trustees enjoyed an initial advantage by virtue of their access to him and the trust he invested in Erna. He also met twice with the teachers, however, with no one else present. He was predisposed to honor and appreciate the role of the teacher, and, with the benefit of hindsight, those meetings may have proven pivotal.

After about a month, Krishnamurti called me into Pine Cottage one afternoon with a friendly and cheerful demeanor. He had reached a tentative conclusion, he said, and he wanted to know how I felt about it before taking any action. He had determined that the primary source of the conflict roiling the school community was the participation of Krause and the Hidleys. He was proposing to dissolve the school committee and remove the Krause-Hidley faction from any further involvement in the school and the foundation. I greeted these words with unalloyed wonder and joy.

A week or two later, Krishnamurti and the trustees met with Krause and Hidley to secure their resignations. The following day, he described the meeting to me in detail. It was long and arduous. Krause did not want to relinquish his position, and he countered every argument with arguments of his own. He employed a gesture to predict what would happen to the school without his involvement: he held his hand out flat, palm facing the floor, and made a short, sharp downward motion. He finally agreed to resign provided that Erna would state forthrightly that she personally requested it. When she assured him that was the case, the meeting came to a close.

Krishnamurti had made good to a remarkable degree on his

promise to root out the source of fear in the school. But he was not yet finished. A few days later, I walked into Mark's office and found him sitting at his desk with tears in his eyes. He had just learned that the trustees had decided to relieve him of his position too. It was a stunning turn of events. The axe had fallen on almost every tree in the administrative forest of the school.

Although I was spared, I was not untainted in the eyes of the trustees. They felt there was blame enough to implicate everyone, and they were not prepared to leave me in charge of the school. Some other remedy, another candidate to step into the role of director, had to be found. As luck would have it, such an individual appeared on the school's doorstep at that very time.

Terry Doyle was a bear of a man, six feet two inches and robust, a former Marine with tattoos on his arms. He owned and operated a training center for martial arts in Northern California, but his interest in education had deep roots. He had founded a private secondary school with a progressive program, and he was well versed in Krishnamurti's educational philosophy. He came to Ojai for several days to visit the school and find out if there was a place for him.

The trustees greeted Terry warmly. Theo Lilliefelt advocated strongly on his behalf; he had discovered letters Terry wrote to Krishnamurti years earlier, describing his efforts to adapt the teachings to classroom practices. He was invited to lunch at Arya Vihara, where he displayed a warm and relaxed demeanor and a serious approach to educational issues.

I talked with Terry several times without realizing what the trustees had in mind. I considered him a plausible candidate for some role at the school—perhaps a houseparent for our handful of boarding students. But Krishnamurti surprised me one day at lunch by asking whether I could foresee a position for Terry; it was rare for him to weigh in on hiring decisions. At the end of the meal, I followed him out the back patio and asked what he envisioned for Terry to do.

He gestured expansively with a wave of his arm and answered with a single word: "Everything." With that, he disappeared into the orange groves on his way back to his cottage.

And so it came to pass that Terry was appointed director of the school. He was to have responsibility for the secondary section, while I would remain in charge of the elementary school. He moved into his new role with confidence and aplomb. In a meeting with the trustees, he said he would like to nail Krishnamurti's statement of intent to the front door of the school. Yet he also had the audacity to propose a change in the document's wording, which was not only accepted but precipitated a wholesale revision of the statement. It was a very auspicious beginning.

Krishnamurti had met the crisis in the school with an admirable ability to respond to difficult circumstances. One might question the wisdom of his decisions, but he was not unable to take action when it was called for. Most striking was that he overturned everything Erna had put into place, although he continued to invest complete trust in her. His action served as a somewhat humiliating rebuke of her judgment, but she bore it with apparent good grace and tolerated the inexorable shift in the wind. The trustees took pity on Mark and carved out a new position for him: director of development, responsible for fundraising and recruitment of students, but with no lines of authority to the school.

The question remained whether the new administration would prove to be durable and effective. The committee structure and the Krause-Hidley faction were imposed on the school in a somewhat peremptory manner, with insufficient foresight and very negative consequences. A great deal of confidence was now being invested in Terry Doyle with a similar absence of the kind of careful, sustained assessment that his role would seem to require. Whether the judgment of the trustees would prove to be more reliable this time was the issue that remained to be determined.

The explosion of Krishnamurti's activity in America following the separation from Rajagopal continued during the years that Oak Grove was enduring growing pains. Among his many other engagements, he traveled to New York for public talks and conferences in 1982, 1983, and 1984. Carnegie Hall was the venue for his talks in 1982, a forum that Mary found particularly suitable, as she sensed that the walls retained memories of the music of her favorite composers. The hall was sold out for each of the talks, and she wrote that his presence, alone on the stage, filled the auditorium.

Krishnamurti spoke to some two hundred delegates of the United Nations in 1984. He had been invited by the *Pacem in Terris* committee of the UN to speak in the Dag Hammarskjöld Auditorium. He pointed out the inevitability of war when individuals are divided by sectarian conditioning along religious, ethnic, and national lines. He challenged the audience to consider whether any organization could bring about peace, or whether conflict begins within the individual and can only be solved at that level. These remarks might have been somewhat controversial in that setting, but his talk was warmly applauded and well received.

Krishnamurti spoke twice each year in 1983 and 1984 in the Masonic Hall in San Francisco. He was greeted there by various people he happened to encounter in stores and restaurants. These trips were also the occasion for lunch with Alain Naudé, who made his home there. Krishnamurti felt Naudé should have initiated a meeting, but Mary called him instead. The visits were friendly, but Krishnamurti later confided that he felt Naudé had inwardly drifted away.

In March 1984, Krishnamurti spoke at the National Laboratory Research Center at Los Alamos, New Mexico, where the atomic bomb was created during World War II. J. Robert Oppenheimer, the scientist in charge of The Manhattan Project, selected this site for its natural beauty and its remote location, in order to ensure the extreme secrecy of the project. Today Los Alamos is a city of some twenty thousand, and the research center located there continues to produce some of the nation's most highly sophisticated weapons of war. The potential for irony in extending an invitation to Krishnamurti to speak there was not lost on him or his audience.

The topic for the symposium was Creativity in Science. No doubt those who suggested this theme envisioned an element of creativity in scientific investigation itself. Perhaps they were wondering how to cultivate or maximize that element. But Krishnamurti began by associating science with the accumulation of knowledge; indeed, science was the quintessence of knowledge, "gathering more, and more, and more." But knowledge is always limited, "whether now or in the future," because it is based on experience and consists fundamentally of thought. The question then became, what place has thought as knowledge in creativity?

In the equations of Krishnamurti, anything limited must lead to conflict, and "conflict can never, under any circumstances, bring about creativity." Therefore knowledge cannot be the ground on which creativity can occur or flourish. He recognized that this point of view might be controversial, especially in a setting like Los Alamos. "You may totally disagree with this. I am sure you do, because, to most of us, thought is extraordinarily important—which means the intellect, which is only part of the human being."

Krishnamurti acknowledged the contribution of knowledge in creating civilization, but he questioned whether human beings are actually civilized. "What are we, after forty-five thousand years as *Homo sapiens*? What have we become? Most human beings are terribly confused, uncertain, though they may not admit it—not only seeking physical security, but also inward, psychological security." True creativity, he maintained, requires freedom, and "psychologically, inwardly, we have no freedom."

Creativity can only occur when the activity of thought has subsided. "It is only when the brain is absolutely silent, not inquiring, not searching, but quiet, still, that there can be creativity." He conceded at the end of the talk that knowledge can produce a limited form of creativity, but not a "holistic perception" in which the individual personality does not enter. "Then only is there this thing called creativity."

⌇⌇

The second lawsuit brought by the KFA against Rajagopal, filed in the Superior Court of California, derived from a select subset of the issues that were contested in the first lawsuit. The tangible elements of real estate and financial assets had been recovered and ownership transferred to the KFA. What remained at issue were the more ephemeral items consisting of documentary evidence of Krishnamurti's life and career: letters and photographs; original manuscripts of poems, articles, books, and essays; notes of meetings and discussions; and film and audio recordings. In view of the notoriety of his early life and the length of his career, the quantity of archival material of this kind was immense and its value beyond measure. The revelation that Rajagopal had donated most of this material to the Huntington Library was as inexplicable as it was outrageous. He had designated it as the Rajagopal Historical Collection and now claimed that it fell entirely outside the parameters of the settlement.

The initiation of the second suit required Rajagopal to disclose the contents of the archives and submit to a deposition to explain his rationale for calling any of it his own. However, he exhibited a protean gift for inventing impediments and grounds for postponement. The lawsuit was filed in December 1980, and the production of documents and his deposition were scheduled for January 1981. What followed instead was a blizzard of motions and memoranda, court dates scheduled and delayed, proposals for settlement offered and withdrawn, changing of attorneys, and continuous excuses of ill health. The net effect was to push any meaningful action well into 1982.

Annie Vigeveno, one of the K&R trustees, proposed that Krishnamurti and Rajagopal meet face to face in her home in an effort to solve all the issues under dispute. Krishnamurti was willing to meet with him provided that members of the KFA were present, and the meeting was scheduled for March 21, 1982. He had undergone surgery to correct a hernia three weeks earlier, and his activities were still limited as a result. Nevertheless, he made the effort to travel across town and confront Rajagopal one more time. He arrived at the home of Vigeveno with the Lilliefelts and Mary Zimbalist.

When they arrived, Vigeveno was present along with one other K&R trustee, but Rajagopal was nowhere to be seen. The K&R trustees gave no reason for his absence, and they offered no apologies. They had not called in advance, they said, because they only learned at the last minute that he would not be present; but Krishnamurti noticed that the circle of chairs did not include one for Rajagopal. In any case, he and the KFA trustees left the Vigeveno residence without further delay. Krishnamurti told Mary he would never agree to meet with Rajagopal again.

A few weeks later, Rajagopal made one gesture of conciliation, perhaps to compensate for his recalcitrant behavior. He delivered to Pine Cottage five boxes of valuable archive material. These boxes contained documents that were not collected originally by him but had been forwarded from India. The KFA considered the recovery of this material an important development.

No further production of documents occurred until July 1982. At that time, Rajagopal sent to the KFA attorney a random and disorganized collection of papers, none of which had any historical value or significance. After eighteen months, no inventory of the archives had occurred, and the lawsuit began to seem like an exercise in futility. The case could not proceed to trial on the basis of material that the KFA had not seen and could not prove existed. The trustees were forced to entertain the possibility of settlement on a more limited basis. Perhaps it would be sufficient to concede the existence of the Rajagopal Historical Collection, provided he would agree to relinquish the material to the KFA upon his death.

Terms of settlement along these lines, however, were vitiated by another provision that Rajagopal insisted upon. He refused to accept any settlement unless the KFA agreed never under any circumstances to file another lawsuit against him. Such a provision was almost impossible to accept. It would have allowed him to ignore and violate everything he had already agreed to.

At the end of two years, Rajagopal had danced and dodged around every date set for the production of documents and had not yet submitted to his deposition. Even while he eluded every effort to pin him down, his attorneys were demanding the opportunity to question Krishnamurti. To do so was extraneous to the issues under dispute, but it fell within Rajagopal's rights, and it was suitable for purposes of harassment and delay.

In March 1983, Krishnamurti submitted to questioning for several hours over the course of two days. Toward the end of the second day, the interrogation took an ugly turn. In a maneuver that was tantamount to blackmail, the attorneys posed a series of questions regarding Krishnamurti's past relationship with Rosalind. On the advice of counsel that the questions were irrelevant to the issues at hand, Krishnamurti refused to answer. Rajagopal's attorneys then declared they intended to go to court to insist that he answer the questions.

According to Mary, Krishnamurti was prepared to follow through and appear in court for this purpose. The KFA trustees, however, felt the matter had gone far enough. At least the lawsuit had led to the recovery of the five boxes of important material from India. Otherwise, Rajagopal had succeeded in exhausting their patience, and their obligation to protect Krishnamurti personally exceeded the necessity to continue to pursue a fruitless course of action. In order to spare him the stress and publicity that would have attended a hearing in court, they decided to withdraw the lawsuit two years and five months after it had been filed.

But Rajagopal was not content to let the matter rest at that. Six weeks after the lawsuit was dropped, Krishnamurti was in the midst of delivering his annual series of talks in Ojai. Immediately following one of the talks, as he was leaving the Oak Grove, one of Rajagopal's trustees handed him a thick envelope. It contained notice of a new lawsuit, filed in Superior Court that morning, brought by the K&R Foundation against the KFA.

The primary complaint in the new suit was for breach of contract. Because the KFA had withdrawn the second lawsuit before going to trial, Rajagopal charged that it was a malicious prosecution, intentionally designed to inflict emotional distress. Another ground for action consisted of something Krishnamurti had said in a phone call to Radha. In the course of discussing with her the legal proceedings, he had said he was afraid that Rajagopal might be suffering from some kind of mental defect. On this basis, Rajagopal brought charges of slander.

It had been fifteen years since Krishnamurti formally disassociated from KWInc, and eleven years since the first lawsuit was filed. Litigation had been ongoing for five and a half of those years, and this new action represented the third lawsuit in the sequence. The damages Rajagopal claimed totaled nine million dollars; and the suit held each of the trustees of the KFA personally liable for the full amount.

The legal drama might have distracted Krishnamurti from his mission, but evidently it did not. Even as those events were unfolding, in the spring of 1983, he composed the third and last in his series of diaries. *Krishnamurti to Himself* was distinctive in several respects. It was dictated into a recorder rather than written out by hand, and the entries were longer than in the previous journals. The topics addressed do not include anything personal, such as his process or encounters with "the other." It is limited to descriptions of nature and psychological reflections, although here the two categories are interwoven and flow into one another. The diary consists of only twenty-seven entries, but it is rich in imagery, dense in meaning, and poignant in its observations of the plight of man on earth.

One of the passages describes a spring morning in Ojai.

> It was really a most extraordinarily beautiful morning. The high mountain was there, impenetrable, and the hills below were green and lovely. And as you walked along quietly, without much thought, you saw a dead leaf, yellow and bright red, a leaf from the autumn. How beautiful that leaf was, so simple in its death, so lively, full of the beauty and vitality of the whole tree and the summer. Strange that it had not withered. Looking at it more closely, one saw all the veins and the stem and the shape of that leaf. That leaf was all the tree.

To observe so closely is to initiate a relationship with nature, and without a connection of that kind, he said, it is impossible to have right relationship with human beings. If we had a deep feeling for nature, he maintained, we would never kill animals to satisfy our appetite or vivisect for purposes of research. We would find other ways and means, but human beings evidently love to kill.

In several entries, Krishnamurti described the special quality of the atmosphere of the Ojai Valley. He recalls climbing the trail far above the valley and looking down from a great height. There one has left behind everything, and one feels as if a guest on the earth, with no sense of separation. Why has mankind broken up the world politically, ethnically, religiously? How long will it take to learn to live without conflict and violence?

In the sixth entry, dated March 15, Krishnamurti receives a visitor who has come to inquire with him. During the course of this and the next two passages, we learn that the man lives alone in a house by the sea. He was raised in a comfortable home and entered into his father's business, where he rose to the top position and prospered. He married and had two daughters, but his life was shattered when his wife and children were killed in a car accident. He has come to inquire into the meaning of death—what is its significance, and why we are afraid of death. He has engaged in conversations of this kind with priests and gurus but has not found clarity or a sense of deep understanding.

According to Krishnamurti, living and dying go together; one cannot be understood without the other. The death of the physical organism is fairly simple, part of nature; but what does it mean to die psychologically? What is it that dies? Is it not the self, the sense of individual identity? That entity is put together by thought, and thinking is shared by all human beings. The individual, therefore, is not separate from mankind.

Is it possible to face death completely—to live with it, psychologically? To do so is to end all attachment on a daily basis, without any motive. Such a state of mind is the entryway to another dimension of consciousness. "The roots of heaven" are in the process of living and dying as a single movement.

Many of the entries address an array of topics with a common set of underlying themes. What is the future of humanity? What are the actual causes of war? Is it possible to cultivate a quiet, serious mind? Can the quality of order we observe in nature become part of our own daily life? These questions are explored in terms of time, thought, and knowledge, each of which is limited and therefore the source of fragmentation and conflict.

Krishnamurti receives several other visitors during the course of this journal. One is an eighteen-year-old boy, a student who is good at sports, capable in his studies, but somewhat apprehensive about the future. What is he being educated for, he asks, and what does life hold in store for him? Krishnamurti orients the conversation around mediocrity—not in one's career or profession, but in one's inner life. Mediocrity in that sense means a life of problem after problem, conflict and contradiction, and little sensitivity to beauty or access to intelligence. Life is demanding and cruel; it is vast and complex; it extends "from horizon to horizon." The antidote to mediocrity is inward observation—to be a light to oneself.

One of the entries, dated April 23, retells the parable with which Krishnamurti announced the dissolution of the Order of the Star. In the original story, a man was walking with the devil when they observed someone ahead of them pick up a piece of the truth. The man says to the devil, "That is a bad business for you." The devil is nonchalant. "Oh, not at all," he says. "I am going to let him organize it."

In the new version, there is no devil, but two friends are walking together on a path in the hills. One of them happens to pick up "something ravishingly beautiful, sparkling, a jewel of extraordinary antiquity." He has discovered a piece of the truth; and, while the details differ in this rendition, the outcome is the same: truth can never be captured by any organization, and the effort to do so is inimical to freedom.

One of the entries recommends that a secondary school should teach both science and religion. Science is the objective cultivation of knowledge, without regard for personal opinion or received authority. Religion, in Krishnamurti's view, is psychological freedom, a state of mind that is open to the unlimited. Religion in this sense is a form of science, he says, in that it is factual and free; but it goes beyond knowledge to embrace truth, a dimension timeless and eternal.

Krishnamurti is known for his teachings as expressed from a public platform and not as a writer of scenes from nature. But his nature writing warrants greater attention: his descriptions are precise, full of vitality, and imbued with an intuitive sense of kinship and sympathy. He perceives a tree or a mountain as full of dignity; the morning awakens with a sense of "adoration" for the beauty of the dawn. "Killing a deer is like killing your neighbor." This diary is populated with squirrels, blue jays, quail, a bobcat and a tiger, and a mocking bird doing somersaults in the air. The pellucid portrayal of sunlit clouds, mountain streams, the night sky, and many other natural scenes is on a par with the work of John Muir, Loren Eisley, and Annie Dillard.

The diary as a whole is rather like what the man discovered who picked up a piece of truth: an extraordinary jewel. It represents a distillation of the essence of the teachings—grounded in freedom, one with nature, and steeped in compassion and intelligence.

Chapter Fifteen

WASHINGTON, D.C.

Mark Lee's tenure as director of Oak Grove School lasted nine years and concluded in June 1984. The circumstances that led to the loss of his position must have been difficult for him to understand and absorb. On the other hand, he had reason to reflect with pride on what he had accomplished. The school had grown from half a dozen students to over one hundred, ranging in age from five to fifteen. He played a central role in the design of several school buildings, each an inspired work of architecture; they were fashioned for individual purposes, but united by the common themes of natural materials, sensitivity to the land, and a spirit of warmth and good taste. He served as a steady, stabilizing force that enabled teachers and families to uproot their lives and move to Ojai in order to participate in the school. He helped create and cultivate a central feature of a Krishnamurti school: an atmosphere of care and consideration for others, a welcoming place where students would feel safe and protected. His contribution represented a significant and enduring element in the overall edifice of Krishnamurti's work.

Terry Doyle moved into his role as Mark Lee's successor with a degree of confidence bordering on bravado. He interacted easily with all the major constituencies—students and teachers, parents and trustees—but he may have underestimated the nature and magnitude of the challenge that he faced. Oak Grove was a beautiful campus with well-behaved students, but the crosscurrents and undertow within the community were fierce and formidable. The proximate cause of Mark Lee's dismissal was that he cast his lot with Krause and Hidley, a narrow faction with disproportionate power and an agenda at odds with the intent of the school. But these circumstances were merely symptomatic of deeper divisions, and the challenge for any administrator to avoid offending one group or another was deceptively difficult. Time would tell whether Terry was equal to the challenge.

The first sign of trouble occurred halfway through the summer. Several weeks before the opening of the new school year, Erna called a meeting with Terry, Mark, and me to discuss the prospective budget for the year ahead. I had a bad feeling about this event. Any meeting with Erna was likely to be unpleasant, and discussions about the budget—the issue that most inflamed her gut apprehensions about the school—even more so. So I took the unprecedented step of deciding not to show up. (Let Mark and Terry handle it, I thought—I needed a break.)

My telephone rang several times, unanswered, during the course of this meeting. It was Terry calling, desperate for my presence and participation. He told me later what had transpired. The largest item in the school's annual budget consisted of salaries for teachers—notwithstanding that, by any reasonable standard, they were poorly paid. Erna seized upon this item in the budget to unleash a torrent of invective and condemnation of the faculty. Perhaps she was still smarting from the role the teachers had played in displacing Krause and Hidley, her hand-picked agents to monitor and manage the school. But Terry was shocked by the degree of disrespect she expressed; and, in the weeks that followed, he repeatedly cited this experience as an epiphany in his understanding of the culture of the school.

I was grateful to have Terry play a leading role. Mark Lee and I had arrived at a stalemate of energies, and Terry, with his beard and imposing physical presence, brought an entirely new spirit to the enterprise: optimistic, free-wheeling, unguarded. But he was also somewhat impulsive, and he made two personnel moves early on that had very unfortunate and far-reaching consequences. As a result, I was watching him somewhat warily, wondering if he really had the chops to manage the highly charged, unwieldy enterprise of the school. It was a test not only of his skill, but also of the trustees' judgment in investing so much confidence in him, based upon a minimum of exposure and observation.

Three weeks into the new school year, an episode occurred that represented for Terry a moment tantamount to the fate of the Titanic. He had endorsed the idea of a committee structure (without parents) to administer some of the routine, practical aspects of the school. At first it seemed the new committee would consist of a few teachers and the bookkeeper, along with Terry and me. But late one afternoon, he informed me of his intention to appoint two of our most difficult students, both tenth-grade boys, as members of the committee. He saw this as a solution to the behavior problems the boys presented, as well as an expression of his egalitarian, inclusive attitude toward the school as a whole.

I considered this idea quixotic at best and probably a recipe for chaos. I told Terry we would have to present his proposal to the teaching staff for their consideration; and fortunately a meeting of teachers was scheduled for the following afternoon. When he proposed his idea in that forum, it was met with muted but chilly disapproval. Terry quickly caught the drift of the prevailing sentiment. He did something then that no one anticipated: in an apparent fit of pique, he got up and walked out of the meeting.

But it was more than a fit of pique: Terry suddenly decided that he had had enough. He told me first thing the next morning that he had made up his mind to resign his position. He mentioned again the meeting with Erna during the summer and said he had realized he was not suited for his role. I tried to talk him out of it, but he was unyielding.

Krishnamurti, Mary, and the Lilliefelts were in Brockwood Park at that time, attending an international meeting of the three foundations. Terry had to call Erna and tell her what he had decided, and she and Theo had to leave precipitously and hurry home. Under the circumstances, the options available to the trustees were very limited, and they turned to the only reasonable solution open to them. Erna met with me the morning after she arrived and asked me to assume the role of sole director of the school.

I regarded these events with little joy in my heart. It was not a script I would have written for myself. I lacked the social skills that Mark and Terry had in abundance, and I doubted that Erna would support me for long. I wanted to create a school that was wholly original, whereas she, in my judgment, wanted a school that was entirely conventional. We had clashed repeatedly in the past, and nothing in the new arrangement seemed to portend that was likely to change.

But just as the trustees had little choice in offering me the position, I had little choice but to accept. My commitment to the school was adamantine, and I could not fail to answer the call when the enterprise was in jeopardy. I accepted without provision or qualification, but not without a heavy dose of apprehension. I marveled at the turn of events that had led Erna to make this offer to me. I knew she was only acting on Krishnamurti's behalf. Nevertheless, I could only wonder at the depth of ambivalence that had brought her to this result.

The lawsuit filed by Rajagopal, claiming damages of nine million dollars, appears with the benefit of hindsight to have been brought primarily for purposes of harassment. No real effort was ever made to bring the case to trial or actually collect any money. Instead, a long series of legal actions took place preliminary to trial, which kept alive the threatening cloud and consumed endless quantities of time and attorney fees. Foremost among the efforts to inflict discomfort or distress was to require Krishnamurti to continue the deposition that had precipitated the withdrawal of the second lawsuit.

Rajagopal's suit was filed in May 1983, a few days before Krishnamurti's departure from the United States. Negotiations to fix a date for his deposition began during the summer. The KFA pleaded to the court to allow him to defer his appearance until the following February, the time of his next scheduled visit to the United States; but the judge refused. As a result, after the talks in Saanen that summer, Krishnamurti postponed his annual trip to India and returned to the United States.

His deposition took place over a period of three days in September. One might assume that an interrogation of that length would have covered a wide range of topics, but that was not the case. The inquiry revolved around a narrow set of events and legal issues. Many of the questions tested his memory of fine points and minor details of meetings and events that had occurred ten, twenty or more years in the past. Other questions were intended to fix the boundaries of the archival materials that Rajagopal could claim as his own. For example, would the KFA claim ownership of a book that Rajagopal had purchased for himself? Obviously not, but an exhausting number of questions of that variety were posed.

The harassment reached its pinnacle toward the end of the third day. At that time, the questioning suddenly turned to Krishnamurti's past relationship with Rosalind. Had it ever been sexual in nature? He admitted without hesitation that it had, and he said it had come about at Rosalind's request. Her conjugal relationship with Rajagopal had ceased, and Krishnamurti went to bed with her because "she wanted it." She was "the aggressor," he said; and, as a result, he engaged in sexual activity for the first time in his life at the age of thirty-eight. Shortly thereafter, he informed Rajagopal by letter of what had occurred. There was no doubt that he knew about it, in part because the nature of the relationship was apparent to others. Moreover, he had told people about it. Krishnamurti identified by name two people Rajagopal had told, and he indicated there were others as well.

The attorney asked whether Rosalind had ever become pregnant, and Krishnamurti acknowledged she had at one time. He said Rosalind told him she "wanted it out," and he had said that such a decision was hers to make. Asked whether he had supported her to obtain an abortion, he replied simply that he had no money. The attorney also asked whether she had ever become pregnant again, and he said not to his knowledge. The sexual relationship ended, he said, around 1950.

The most crucial point was that Rajagopal had known about the relationship from its inception and never expressed any objection until many years later. Krishnamurti also brought out that Rajagopal had frequently threatened to expose what had occurred and attempted to use that threat as an explicit form of blackmail. Faced with this threat, Krishnamurti had told Rajagopal, "Go ahead." It is worth noting that Krishnamurti's version of events was testimony given under oath.

The deposition of Rajagopal was delayed repeatedly, in part because he prevailed upon the court to impose strict restrictions regarding the scope of the examination. Somehow he succeeded in limiting the period about which he could be questioned to events that occurred after June 1977. This limitation precluded any inquiry into his conduct for his entire tenure, more than forty years, working on behalf of Krishnamurti. Had Krishnamurti secured a similar

restriction for his own deposition, the vast majority of questions put
to him would not have been permitted.

By March 1984, the depositions had been taken, and the case
could have proceeded to trial. Evidently that was not a result that
Rajagopal actually wished to achieve. The case went into abeyance
for close to a year, and the KFA began preparing to move to have the
charges dismissed. At that point, Rajagopal and his attorneys began
to negotiate terms for settlement, none of which contemplated any
actual payment of monetary damages. All he really wanted were
assurances that he would not be sued again, as well as some face-sav-
ing statement to the effect that he had "done nothing wrong." In
exchange for this, he was prepared to settle his claims and dismantle
the K&R foundation and turn its remaining assets over to the KFA.

Negotiations of this kind continued throughout 1985. Each time
the terms of settlement were agreed upon, Rajagopal introduced
some new caveat or addendum that sustained and prolonged the
process. At one point, Erna flew to England to obtain Krishnamurti's
signature on final documents before he departed for India, only to
have Rajagopal change his mind yet again. By the end of the year, the
case still remained unresolved.

The endless nature of the negotiations suggested that their only
purpose was to sustain a program of harassment. This led Krishnamurti to express on several occasions his private assessment of
Rajagopal. He told Mary he regarded him as "dirty," "unholy," and
even "evil." He deeply wished to have nothing more to do with him,
and he lamented that the lawsuits sustained a connection that he
wanted completely terminated.

Rajagopal occasionally offered expressions of good will, which
fed the illusion that he might change course and become cooperative.
After one of the public talks, he met Krishnamurti outside the Oak
Grove and shook his hand. In the car driving back to Pine Cottage,
Krishnamurti felt sickened by this physical contact. "What has

happened to my hand? It is not my hand," he declared, and he held it out the window in an effort to rid it of some pollution. When he got home he washed his hand at length until he felt it was his own again.

Part of what disturbed Krishnamurti consisted of telepathic communications. At times he felt that "those two" were directing hostile thoughts toward him across the Ojai valley. If he were far away, in Saanen or Brockwood Park, he felt he was beyond the range of what could reach him. But within the valley, he had to take measures to protect himself. He could put up a mental barrier, he said, which consisted of a state of inward emptiness; then the negative energy would be re-directed to its source. Krishnamurti in turn employed telepathic or paranormal communications of his own. He attempted to project some kind of positive, beneficent energy toward Rajagopal—"angels," he called them, though he added they were nothing like the sentimental images we associate with that term. He did so in an effort to induce Rajagopal to recover a sense of decency, but he doubted that his efforts had much effect.

In April and May 1985, Krishnamurti dictated two letters, addressed to Rajagopal, intended to describe the whole course and quality of their relationship. He said the bullying behavior had commenced shortly after the death of Nitya. It was a continuous pattern from the beginning, but it increased in intensity after World War II. Krishnamurti used to keep a diary recording many of the incidents, such as an occasion when Rajagopal made a "frightful scene" over some talcum powder that he had spilled in the bathroom. Rajagopal alternated between "subservient and sycophantic" behavior and aggressive bullying to obtain his objectives.

The letters included several references to heavy drinking, evidence that suggested Rajagopal may have been alcoholic. He was depressed in the morning and his workday did not start until two in the afternoon. He was observed weaving drunkenly late at night on many occasions. A mutual friend reported that Rajagopal would consume half a bottle of Johnnie Walker whiskey during the course of a single conversation.

Krishnamurti described a dossier compiled by Erna, consisting of some two hundred pages, recording a litany of instances of Rajagopal's mismanagement of assets. He gave one example: Rajagopal had used KWInc funds to construct an apartment over the office building at the east end residence, and then transferred ownership of it into his own name. He then sold the apartment to the K&R Foundation, and used the proceeds to purchase for himself a house owned by the daughter of one of his trustees. He kept two sets of books, one secret and one for public review, in order to conceal numerous transactions of this kind.

In the end, Rajagopal had made himself into a wealthy man "by some extraordinary, cunning means." He was motivated in part by jealousy. He had said that he had the brains while Krishnamurti had the looks, and that the Theosophical Society should have chosen him for the role of World Teacher. What he had done was "incredible, ugly, monstrous." Nothing that he owned belonged to him—not the land, not the house, not the papers. "What a petty, mean, dishonorable, blackmailing man you have become."

The two letters were never sent because the trustees felt that they would not facilitate resolution of the lawsuit. But one day a future historian may compose a complete accounting of Rajagopal's behavior, and these letters will provide some guidance for that purpose. Also central to such research will be the dossier Erna compiled. Much remains to be unearthed before the entire dimensions of Rajagopal's immoral and criminal behavior are fully exposed.

Milton Friedman (not to be confused with the economist of the same name) was a speechwriter in the Ford and Reagan administrations until he resigned in protest over deleterious environmental policies he was expected to defend. He was invited to meet Krishnamurti in 1984 by Patricia Hunt-Perry, a professor of philosophy at Rutgers University. Friedman made a favorable impression on Krishnamurti and suggested he consider speaking in Washington, D.C. The proposal met with approval, and plans were set in motion for the talks to occur the following year.

Krishnamurti spoke for a second year at *Pacem in Terris* of the United Nations before he and Mary traveled to Washington in April 1985. They were met by Friedman and Hunt-Perry and spent a week there visiting the countryside as well as selected buildings and monuments. Krishnamurti was deeply moved by the Lincoln Memorial and noted similarities with the structure of the Parthenon. The majesty of the memorial and what it represented made him feel, he told Mary, as if he "could have cried."

A reporter for the *Washington Post* visited with Krishnamurti and interviewed him at length. His article of over a thousand words appeared on the front page of the *Post*. What he wrote was reasonably accurate, although Mary and Krishnamurti cringed when the reporter described her as his "disciple." The reporter referred to him as "the great Indian teacher and philosopher," but was careful to add, "Understand, he is not a guru. He can't bear gurus…. He uses no incense, no sitars, no drama." The article included excerpts from the public talks as well some paragraphs about David Bohm and his involvement in Krishnamurti's work.

The talks were held in the concert hall of the Kennedy Center and were scheduled on consecutive days. The auditorium was full for each talk. Krishnamurti had no difficulty speaking for six or eight days in a series of public talks, but now, in his first and last opportunity to address the nation's capital, he had to convey the primary themes of his philosophy in just two talks.

As was his custom, he began by negating any implicit or

conventional expectations for what he intended to do. His talk was not a lecture; it was not meant to convey any body of knowledge or set of information. Nor was he engaged in any form of entertainment or effort to please his audience. Rather, he and they were taking part in a mutual exploration, a journey together, a form of inquiry into daily life. The intention was to investigate in a manner that was objective, dispassionate, impersonal—to see facts as they are, without bias, speculation, or any kind of ideology. He and they were "going to talk together about the whole of our existence, from the moment we are born until we die."

During several thousand years of human history, mankind has engaged in constant warfare and demonstrated little capacity to find another way of life. "So we are going to observe together this extraordinary phenomenon: how man, after these thousands of years, still remains a barbarian—cruel, vulgar, full of anxiety and hatred." What is the origin of conflict, and is it possible to learn to live without it? In this context, Krishnamurti introduced one of his most fundamental insights. "Where there is division, there must be conflict. That is a law." Indeed, we may call this Krishnamurti's Law. It is unique to his philosophy and the only statement he made of its kind—categorical, repeated, and designated as a law.

One of the central factors that serves to bring about division, he said, is organized religion. Krishnamurti categorized the major religions according to their respective ideas about God. Buddhism is unique in that it posits no god; Hinduism, by contrast, has some three hundred thousand. "That's rather fun, you can choose whichever god you like." Christianity and Islam are each based upon a book and each has only one god. Religion based upon a book produces people who are "bigoted, narrow, intolerant"; and every religion divides one group of people against everyone else.

One of the themes of the first talk consisted of the source of fear and whether it is possible to live without it entirely. "If you have no fear psychologically, then there is tremendous relief, a great sense of freedom." Insofar as fear is psychological rather than biological, its source lies in thought and time. He asks the audience whether they have ever given attention to the nature and significance of the process of thinking. "What is thought? Probably very few people have asked this question. The speaker has been asking this question for sixty years." This inquiry opens the door to the crucial insight that the thinker is not separate from his thoughts—"the thinker is the thought."

The second talk resumed with an effort to understand "the whole structure of our psychological being, our whole existence." To undertake such an inquiry requires self-examination, and the instrument for that purpose is the process of relationship. In "the mirror of relationship," one may observe one's own anger, jealousy, and possessiveness. The typical relationship between two individuals involves the construction of an image, a picture or concept of who the other person is, based upon their past behavior. Because it comes from the past, such an image serves as a filter through which we observe the person in the present. In this manner, the past colors and distorts the immediate perception of the person.

Relationship is also limited by the pursuit of pleasure. The memory of a delightful moment leads us to seek to repeat or perpetuate that moment, and so engenders pleasure, "the other side of the coin of fear." Pleasure and fear go hand in hand because each one represents a projection, mediated by thought, of some future experience. But love is not pleasure; it is not thought; it "cannot be invited or cultivated." Love arises spontaneously through the negation of what it is not.

Krishnamurti concluded the second talk by asking, "Is there something that is sacred, eternal, that is beyond all the reaches of thought?" A religious mind, he maintained, is one that is capable of inquiring deeply, and for that "there must be total freedom." This led to the question of what is meditation. He paused to castigate every form of system for meditation: "the Zen method, the Buddhist meditation, the Hindu meditation, and the latest gurus with their meditation. They are always bearded, full of money…."

Real meditation "has nothing whatever to do with method, system, practices; therefore it can never be mechanical. It can never be conscious meditation." Actual meditation is a state of mind that is entirely attentive: "attention now to everything, every word, every gesture, every thought: to pay complete attention, not partial." Such a mind is not cluttered with theories, problems, conflict, and knowledge. In that state of mind there is space, the emptiness of space, and within such emptiness there lies tremendous energy.

> So when there is that space and emptiness and therefore immense energy—energy is passion, love, compassion, and intelligence—then there is that truth which is most holy, most sacred…. And it has no path to it except through one's own understanding of oneself. Then there is that which is eternal.

When Krishnamurti returned to Ojai after the Washington talks, he was nearing his ninetieth year. Among his characteristics were his youthful vitality, exceptional physical fitness, and mental acuity. But after the Washington talks, I observed on two or three occasions that he was holding his hand against the side of his stomach. Something about this gesture was subtly disturbing. It seemed to suggest that he might not be invincible, and thoughts of his mortality began to assume a more concrete character in my mind.

At that time, I had been serving as director of the school for most of the academic year. My brief tenure so far was marked by an absence of the kind of disturbance that had characterized my predecessors. Neither the teachers nor the parents were visibly upset about anything. On the other hand, I had found it necessary to reverse two of Terry Doyle's most egregious personnel decisions, and both actions ran afoul of the sentiments of certain trustees. I had had to fire a man who was living openly with two women, a man whom Theo Lilliefelt—conservative in all his tastes and attitudes—had taken an unaccountable liking to. Another dismissal earned the ire of a trustee who was one of Erna's personal favorites. For these and other reasons, I knew I was on thin ice.

The prospect that Krishnamurti's time on Earth might be nearing an end precipitated an action that I had long considered but never had the courage to undertake. I was convinced that his attitude toward Erna was based on a partial and selective set of observations and evidence. There was a side to her personality that I doubted he had ever witnessed. In his presence, her whole demeanor brightened and assumed an aspect of congeniality and good cheer. This was entirely unlike the face that she presented to the world in his absence: dour, all business, and merciless to anyone who got in her way.

The difficulty that Erna posed was nothing remotely like what Rajagopal had done. She was a woman of genuine rectitude who never would have mismanaged a penny of foundation funds. On the other hand, her motivations were narrow, as far as I could discern. Her interest in the teachings seemed very limited and secondary to her primary concerns: securing the financial condition and the public image of the foundation. Moreover, she had nursed a long-standing attitude of disapproval of me, possibly based upon some obscure threat she felt I posed to her authority. If it were not for Krishnamurti's support, I knew I had no more chance of remaining in my position than the proverbial snowball in hell.

I finally resolved to speak up and express my concerns. Krishnamurti's departure from Ojai for another nine months was only two weeks away, and this might be my last opportunity. I met with him in his cottage and conveyed my apprehensions in brief but forthright terms.

Krishnamurti listened patiently and responded without resistance or any defensive reaction. He replied by recounting the history of Erna's involvement in undoing the malfeasance of Rajagopal. He emphasized the weeks she had spent before the KFA was formed, burrowing into the bowels of the county bureaucracy, unearthing real estate transactions dating back thirty years. I couldn't argue with any of that. I was reduced to warning that my tenure as director would be very short if she could act with impunity and do as she pleased. With that he sat up a little straighter and spoke in a more formal way. He said he understood that I was speaking in my official capacity and telling him that "Mrs. Lilliefelt" was not supporting me in my role. I knew that he meant he would take it up with her unless I objected. With a sense that this was not going to end well, I agreed.

Three days later, I was called in to meet with Krishnamurti and Erna in the spacious living room in the new wing of Pine Cottage. He repeated what he had undoubtedly already conveyed to her—that I felt she was not supportive of me—and asked for her response. She categorically denied it. She acknowledged no trace whatsoever of animosity or ill will or any feeling of negative judgment or disapproval. Her only concern was for the welfare of the school, she said, and she would do everything in her power to help me make it a success.

I found the whole encounter intimidating. I was not able to challenge or contradict her to any degree. Krishnamurti re-stated what he understood her to be saying, and he added, "Mr. Moody is rather inarticulate, for some reason." The conversation turned in another direction, and nothing was resolved.

I felt at the time that I had discharged my responsibility. I did what I could to bring the issue to Krishnamurti's attention. He had his own extensive experience of Erna, and nothing I could say was likely to overcome the weight of his impressions. Nor did I know what the future would hold. Perhaps we could revisit the issue when he returned to Ojai the following year.

When he departed a few days later for distant shores, I hoped for the best, but I had the gnawing feeling that I should have done something more, perhaps much more. The circumstances posed what seemed like an impenetrable quandary.

Krishnamurti speaking in the Oak Grove

Krishnamurti and Mary Zimbalist

Krishnamurti and Pupul Jayakar

Krishnamurti and David Bohm circa 1978

Erna Lilliefelt

Theo Lilliefelt

Mark Lee with Oak Grove students in 1975

The multi-purpose Pavilion at Oak Grove School

Living room extension of Pine Cottage

The pepper tree circa 1980

Scott Forbes (seated)

Erna Lilliefelt with Krishnamurti circa 1978

Krishnamurti at lunch with Pupul Jayakar and David Moody. Seated next to Krishnamurti is Friedrich Grohe. Partially visible next to Grohe is Vivienne Moody. At the far end of the table on the left is Michael Krohnen.

Chapter Sixteen

SCOTT FORBES

Among the members of the audience in Saanen in 1972 was a newcomer, a twenty-four-year-old American, then residing in Paris. Scott Forbes was a dealer in antique furniture, with offices in Geneva; he had traveled widely and was fluent in French. He also had a well-developed interest in psychological issues. He had studied Freud while still in his teens and was living in Paris in part to explore the work of a French mystic. On the strength of a recommendation from a friend, Scott had hitchhiked from Paris to Saanen in order to hear Krishnamurti speak.

Two years after his first exposure to Krishnamurti, Scott gave up his business buying and selling antique furniture and went to work as the maintenance man for Brockwood Park. In another school, the role of maintenance man might be considered secondary or of inferior significance, but in the egalitarian setting of Brockwood, he was on an equal footing with all the teachers and staff. In a compound as old and complex as Brockwood, his role called for an unusual set of talents, including not only mechanical aptitude and familiarity with tools, but also versatility and creative problem-solving skills. Scott brought all this and more to the job, as he was energetic, dedicated, and a quick learner.

At that time, only a handful of films and video recordings had been made of Krishnamurti's talks and dialogues. Scott saw the need for a vastly increased commitment to recording Krishnamurti on video, and he devoted increasing amounts of time to this project. He excelled in mastering the fine points of technological innovations, and, within a few years, recording Krishnamurti's talks and some of his dialogues on video became standard procedure. This development might have been inevitable at some point, but Scott deserves credit for implementing it at an early and accelerated pace.

His hands-on engagement with the recordings brought Scott into personal contact with Krishnamurti right before and after each public talk in Brockwood and in Saanen for several years. Most of the teachers encountered Krishnamurti mainly in the context of staff meetings for the purpose of exploring the teachings, where the possibility of demonstrating mastery of the business at hand was minimal. Scott found another avenue for cultivating a relationship with Krishnamurti, one that enabled him to be seen in an arena where he excelled; and eventually this relationship blossomed to an extent almost without parallel.

By the early 1980s, Scott had become part of Krishnamurti's most intimate circle of associates. He often joined Krishnamurti and Mary for dinner in their private quarters at Brockwood and stayed after dinner to watch TV with them. He began to accompany Krishnamurti in his morning exercises, and even to massage his feet when they were swollen at the end of the day. He was consulted on matters large and small and in many respects was treated by Krishnamurti and Mary as if he were their son.

Krishnamurti left Ojai on May 24, 1985, and traveled with Mary to Brockwood Park, where the administration of the school was in a state of turmoil. Partly for that reason, Scott began to spend even more time with him, tending to daily affairs and consulting about the ongoing issues in Brockwood as well as in Ojai and India. He kept notes of these interactions and of the conversations they had and brought this material together in a book published in 2018. His observations supplement Mary's and represent a cornucopia of new information and insight into Krishnamurti's behavior, thoughts, concerns, and states of mind.

Dorothy Simmons was a tall, large-boned Englishwoman with a strong personality. She had served as Brockwood's director from its inception in 1969 until she suffered a heart attack in 1983. At that time, a committee of four teachers and staff was formed to administer the school in her absence; and, after she had recovered, the committee continued to function to some extent. As a result, a chronic tension developed between Dorothy and the committee, as she did not wish to relinquish her authority. The effects of this tension infected the students and staff and were very disturbing to Krishnamurti. When he returned to Brockwood in May 1985, resolving this issue was his highest priority.

Krishnamurti's response to the problems at Brockwood threw an oblique light on what had transpired at Oak Grove School the previous year. He began by meeting with members of the Brockwood committee on almost a daily basis, without Dorothy or the other teachers even being aware of it. He cultivated this group and added a few more people to it over a period of weeks. He brought them into a cohesive force with a sense of mutual trust and a common purpose. When he felt they were ready, he asked them to select a new director of the school. He had prepared the soil in such a way that Scott was their all-but-inevitable choice. Scott's book makes it clear that this was the result that Krishnamurti had intended from the outset.

The contrast with what had occurred at Oak Grove was stark. The appointment of Terry Doyle had occurred with no consultation with the staff whatsoever. On the contrary, Krishnamurti's time and attention had been with the trustees, testing and questioning whether they approved of the appointment. At Brockwood Park, the trustees were not even informed of the decision to appoint Scott director until a week after the decision had been made.

Somewhat similarly, Krishnamurti lavished an abundance of

attention on Scott in an effort to train and groom him for his role. None of that occurred with Terry Doyle or with me when I replaced Terry. Krishnamurti complained repeatedly about the Ojai school and foundation, according to Scott, but evidently without reflecting on the enormous disparity in the time and manner of his interactions with the people involved. No doubt he invested his energies according to some inner calculus, the merits of which are difficult to assess.

Mary recalled Krishnamurti's talks in Washington, D.C. as the "last blaze" of his normal energy and strength. By the time of his talks in Ojai a few weeks later, he was beginning to complain of nausea and stomachaches. These symptoms gradually became more pronounced over the course of the summer and were accompanied by a suite of additional manifestations of some unidentified illness.

Scott observed that Krishnamurti's regular afternoon walks were conducted with diminishing enthusiasm, and that he navigated minor obstacles with less than his normal nimbleness. He required more time to rest during the day, and his appetite for food, never large, decreased further. His sleeping patterns were disturbed to the point that he began to take a quarter tablet of Halcion, a mild sedative, each night. Similarly, he began to drink a cup of mild tea before his afternoon walks, with beneficial effects. Chalet Tannegg was no longer available for rent in Saanen, and Krishnamurti's new room there was dark and devoid of any view. This would have bothered him at any time, but now it was a source of significant disturbance.

When the public talks began at Saanen, Krishnamurti's reserve of vitality was so low that those around him began to debate how long he could continue at that venue. Not until the fourth talk, according to Mary, did he exhibit his characteristic depth of energy and perception. Before the series had concluded, a decision was taken that held ominous implications for the future: 1985 would be the last time he would speak in Saanen. He had been coming there for twenty-five years, and the announcement that this year would be the last was met with a solemn sense of impending loss.

Another symptom of Krishnamurti's illness was behavioral and psychological. He began to express a degree of irritability and a critical attitude that was new and uncharacteristic. Mary was the object of much of his annoyed attention. He corrected the way she walked and how she performed her morning exercises. He found fault with her tendency not to complete one task before taking up another, and he noticed and commented when he felt she was not attentive to her gestures and even her facial expressions. He asked her to drive more slowly and to adjust the position of her thumbs on the steering wheel.

Mary accepted all of this with grace and good humor, but it came to the point where she told him that his attitude had become more critical, with "a roughness that is unlike you." He took her observation to heart and responded in a forthcoming manner, without defensiveness. He reflected on what she had said for some time and then told her she was right. "It is my fault and it must stop. We've been together a long time, and I love you deeply. The body has become hypersensitive. Most of the time I want to go away, and I mustn't do that. I am going to deal with this. It is unforgiveable."

The critical attitude Krishnamurti brought to bear on Mary was representative of a broader and deeper assessment of his schools and foundations. He was particularly disturbed by Pupul Jayakar and the relationship of the Indian foundation to the other two. The right to edit and publish talks and dialogues had been a source of contention for several years. The English foundation had primary responsibility for copyright and publications, and the Indian foundation chafed at having to submit to editorial decisions taken in England.

In the summer of 1985, the matter was brought to a head when Pupul issued an ultimatum. Either England must share the copyright with India, she said, or else the Indian foundation would go its own way and publish one book every three years on its own. Krishnamurti was shocked to be challenged in this manner, and he regarded it as symptomatic of a deeper sense of division among the foundations. Such a situation was anathema to his work and something he intended to address in India later in the year.

His attitude toward the American foundation was negative for different reasons. His greatest concern was that he felt insufficiently engaged during the three months he spent in Ojai each year. He had exhausted the ability of the teachers to interact with him in a meaningful way, and the trustees had not arranged new places for him to speak or interesting people with whom to hold dialogues. Mary conveyed this concern to Erna, who responded defensively in a letter, recounting all that the KFA had accomplished over the years. Krishnamurti hastened to reassure her and to affirm his appreciation for all that she had done.

Nevertheless, Krishnamurti was troubled with who could carry on his work in America after he was gone. He told Mary that she was the only one in Ojai whom he trusted completely; and, as a result, she would have to assume greater responsibility there. Evidently no one else had his complete confidence—not Erna or Theo, nor Mark Lee, and not me.

To entrust Mary with that degree of responsibility was rather ironic in view of her poor understanding of events at the school and the foundation. In sharp contrast to her detailed appreciation of circumstances at Brockwood, she was curiously removed from the currents of people and events in Ojai. When she reviewed entries in her diary regarding Terry Doyle, years later, she could not even remember who he was. The manner in which she recorded events at the time often reflected a distorted view or virtual blindness to the most salient facts. The pattern of relative neglect of the Ojai school by Krishnamurti and Mary may have been a byproduct of the attention consumed by the lawsuits and their corresponding confidence in Erna. In any case, relying upon Mary under these circumstances was symptomatic of the difficulty in finding people truly dedicated to understanding the teachings and living in their light.

⁓

Krishnamurti's illness occurred in association with premonitions of his death. These seemed to consist not of a vision or presentiment of the future but rather of some private knowledge to which he had access. He raised the issue on multiple occasions with Mary, but his predictions of the timing of his death were highly inaccurate. He had a valid inner sense of his impending end, but his ability to gauge when it would occur was seriously flawed.

On the day he left Ojai for Brockwood Park in May 1985, Krishnamurti told Mary he could not predict the timing of his death, but he had the feeling he would live another ten years. Ten weeks later, he revised this estimate to "probably" another five to ten years. He made this statement even after his illness had become sufficiently severe to cause the cancellation of future talks in Saanen.

One morning shortly after Krishnamurti and Mary returned to Brockwood from Saanen, the symptoms of his illness became more acute. His breakfast of buckwheat triggered several episodes of vomiting, accompanied by weakness so pronounced he had difficulty standing up and stepping out of the bathtub. "Death is always so close," he told Mary.

Later that day, in the context of discussing his travel plans, he said, rather remarkably, "My life has been planned. It will tell me when to die, say it is over. That will settle my life." He cautioned that when he stopped giving talks, his life would be finished. Even then, however, he repeated his estimate that he might have ten years left to live. He did not explain who or what had planned his life or why he believed that to be the case, and Mary did not ask.

Two weeks later, he reiterated his feeling that "it's all been carefully planned." On this occasion he acknowledged his uncertainty regarding the timing of his death—"It may be tomorrow, it may be in ten years"—but he expressed no uncertainty regarding his "strange feeling" that his life had been "completely planned."

In spite of his advancing illness, Krishnamurti was still capable of conducting his regular activities and the affairs of daily life. In September, he and Mary traveled by train eighty miles to London, and she wrote in her diary, "It was a warm, soft late summer morning. He looked not over forty, standing in immense elegance at the Petersfield station: young, attractive, with a dignity that is both aloof and intensely unassuming."

In that setting, he recounted to Mary a conversation in which Scott had asked if he knew how long he would live. He had told Scott that he did know, but he would not tell him. With Mary, he expressed less certainty: "I think I know. I have intimations." But it would not be right to tell anyone, he said; and, in any case, "It won't be for quite a while."

Later that month, Mary questioned him again. On this occasion, he said he knew "more or less" when he would die, but that it would not be sudden or right away. He then offered a glimpse into the background from which his intimations evidently had their source:

It is all decided by someone else. I can't talk about it. I'm not allowed to. Do you understand? It is much more serious.

There are things you don't know, enormous, and I can't tell you. It is very hard to find a brain like this, and it must keep on as long as the body can—until something says, "Enough."

These remarks open a window into issues deeper than whether Krishnamurti was able to anticipate the timing of his death. They belong in a larger category of observations that shed light on his essential character. These issues are the subject of a subsequent chapter.

Krishnamurti left Brockwood Park for India on October 24, four months to the day after he had left Ojai. In spite of his illness, he and Mary had decided that she would not accompany him on this trip. On the morning of his departure, she asked him directly whether she would ever see him again. "Yes, I'll be back," he replied.

When Krishnamurti left Brockwood in October 1985, he had less than four months left to live. Eleven weeks of that time were spent in India, distributed among Rajghat, his school in the north; Rishi Valley, his school in the south; and Madras, where the headquarters of the Krishnamurti Foundation India (KFI) were located.

Krishnamurti founded several schools in India, but those at Rajghat and Rishi Valley were the oldest and the largest. The Rajghat educational center was located in Benares (also known as Varanasi), adjacent to the Ganges River. It was established in 1934 and consisted of some two hundred acres, with facilities for three hundred residential students as well as a women's college, an agricultural school, and a free hospital for the neighboring villages.

Krishnamurti stayed at Rajghat throughout the month of November. He held a series of meetings with Buddhist scholars and gave three public talks in Benares. His main order of business, however, was to install a new director of the school. The man he selected was Padmanabhan Krishna, a highly regarded professor of physics at the University of Benares. Dr. Krishna was in his late forties and had studied Krishnamurti's work since his teenage years. The appointment was made in part on the basis of an intuitive recognition of Krishna's orderly and insightful mind. The two men had a strong mutual sense of trust, and subsequent events demonstrated that this was one of Krishnamurti's most outstanding and successful appointments in any of his schools.

Before Krishnamurti had left Ojai in the spring, he and the trustees of the three foundations agreed to schedule an educational conference, with representatives from all the schools, to be held in Rishi Valley in December. My wife, Vivienne, and I left Ojai in late November and spent a week at Brockwood Park before continuing on to India. Vivienne had by that time become an important part of the work of the KFA. She had formed a close bond with Mary, who appointed her to create and manage a library of Krishnamurti books, audio, and video tapes, located in Arya Vihara, open to the public three days a week. She performed her function with warmth, grace, and skill and was widely appreciated by visitors as well as trustees.

We arrived at Rishi Valley in late morning on a day that Krishnamurti was conducting a meeting with teachers, and we were ushered into the back of the room. He was sitting cross-legged on the floor, as were most of the teachers, and leaning back against a wall. He did not seem to me to be sitting with his normal energy and upright posture. I had not seen him for six months, and my immediate impression was that something was seriously wrong.

He invited us to join him for breakfast the next morning. He was propped up in bed when we arrived, leaning against some pillows, and he gestured for us to sit with him on the bed. After a few preliminaries, he began to speak more seriously. "I may be going," he announced; and, as if to underscore his meaning, he pointed to his folded clothes, visible on open shelves, and invited us to take whatever we liked. He proceeded to tell us about the changes he had made at Rajghat, as well as some difficult issues he would have to address in a few weeks with the KFI. It was unmistakably the story of a man putting all the pieces of his life in order.

Krishnamurti's personal physician was Dr. Parchure, a lively and dedicated man who now attended to his physical condition on a daily basis. I sought him out as soon as breakfast was over and asked a series of questions about the medical state of affairs. He told me that Krishnamurti was becoming increasingly weak and might not continue to be able to walk in the foreseeable future. He was running an erratic fever, his appetite was poor, and he was losing weight. But the doctor was unable to diagnose the source of these symptoms.

I found the whole set of circumstances confounding and inexplicable. It seemed inconceivable that every effort was not being made to determine a diagnosis as soon as possible. In my judgment, Krishnamurti should have canceled all his scheduled talks and returned to the United States for immediate medical attention. I went to see him shortly after speaking with Dr. Parchure and attempted to convey this point of view. His attitude struck me as somewhat fatalistic. He brushed aside my concerns and said he would have further tests done in a few weeks in Madras.

I persisted and discussed how he could return to the United States as soon as possible. His normal itinerary took him back to Brockwood Park from India, and his existing airline ticket followed that route. I managed to persuade him to fly instead from India straight to California via Singapore as soon as he had concluded his business in Madras. To my surprise, he not only agreed but also gave me his plane ticket and passport and asked me to go ahead and make those arrangements for him.

Scott Forbes arrived in Rishi Valley a few days later and immediately got wind of what was afoot. He came to my room and told me to turn over the ticket and passport to him. I did so and he implemented the plan I had initiated. I was somewhat relieved to have him take care of it, as he was far more familiar with the intricacies of travel to and from India.

The compound at Rishi Valley was similar to Rajghat in its

physical dimensions, enrollment, and complexity. It was a virtual village in its own right, with residential quarters for hundreds of students and staff, huge vegetable gardens, its own sources of energy production, and almost every ingredient for a self-sustaining community. Afternoon walks with Krishnamurti were a daily ritual, with a dozen people or more spread out behind him like the tail of a comet. He seemed to feel completely in his element there.

The educational conference was intended to facilitate a sense of unity among the schools. Meeting together was supposed to enable the several schools to share their varied approaches to their common purpose. But none of the schools' representatives could articulate their approach with force and clarity, and the net effect was to illuminate differences more than to cultivate a common ground.

One of the differences revolved around whether to invite Krishnamurti to participate. Radhika Herzberger, the primary organizer of the event, was Pupul's daughter, and she carried herself with authority. She had concluded that Krishnamurti was too ill to be involved and should conserve all his energy for other purposes. I felt he would want to participate and should at least be invited to join us. I went to see him in his room right before the first meeting and again before the last meeting and urged him to be present. He was happy to do so, and in both cases he made an important contribution. The last meeting turned out to be his final dialogue with teachers—the last of many hundreds—and is included in *The Future is Now*.

Vasanta Vihar is a six-acre compound located in Madras, north of the Adyar River. It is just a few miles away from the Theosophical Society headquarters on the south side of the river, where Krishnamurti had been brought into the fold in 1909. The Star Publishing Trust, under Rajagopal's direction, had purchased Vasanta Vihar in 1933 to serve as the headquarters for Krishnamurti's talks and publications in India. Rajagopal refused to relinquish control over the property when Krishnamurti separated from him, and it had been the subject of a lawsuit in its own right. As a result of the legal proceedings, brought by KFI, it was restored to Krishnamurti's control in 1976 and had served since then as residential and office facilities for the work of the foundation.

Krishnamurti left Rishi Valley on December 22 and traveled by car for five hours to Madras and his room at Vasanta Vihar. In charge of the facility were a married couple, Pama and Sunanda Patwardhan. Sunanda held a doctorate degree in sociology, and she and her husband had been students of Krishnamurti's work for many years.

His dissatisfaction with the administration of his work in Ojai and England paled in comparison with his sense of disturbance over the state of affairs in India. At the core of his concern was the conviction that no one had fully absorbed the meaning of his teachings or taken them seriously. Mary recorded two instances in the preceding months when he lamented, "No one has changed." What exactly he meant by that or how it could be detected were somewhat open questions, but his teaching called for a transformation in the nature and structure of consciousness, and he seemed to be certain that change of that magnitude had not occurred in anyone.

Krishnamurti's disturbance with the Indian foundation, however, went well beyond this core concern, which applied equally to all. As the dominant personality in the KFI, Pupul was responsible for the sense of division among the foundations, he felt, due to her refusal to accept that the publication rights were vested in England. In addition, he had developed a dissatisfaction with the administration of his work by the Patwardhans. He felt they were misusing Vasanta Vihar as little more than their personal residence, rather than cultivating an atmosphere in which the teachings could take root and flower.

Krishnamurti was highly sensitive to subtle feelings and impressions generated by a room, a building, or a piece of land. He often referred to the atmosphere of a place as a quality that reflected the care and sensitivity of the people who lived or had lived there. The land and buildings dedicated to his work should reflect an atmosphere, he felt, uncorrupted by petty emotional disturbances or conflict; it should convey something special, pure, and even sacred. He was particularly disturbed by the atmosphere he perceived at Vasanta Vihar in December 1985. He sensed a place that was indolent, ordinary, and devoid of the psychological soil conducive to the development of insight and compassion.

Krishnamurti remained in Madras for three weeks. His primary purpose in going there was to deliver a series of public talks, but after they were concluded, he held meetings with the trustees of the KFI on four consecutive days. During these meetings, he secured the resignation of the Patwardhans from the management of Vasanta Vihar. This must have been painful and difficult for all concerned, in view of the number of years they had known him and worked on his behalf.

But even this action was not sufficient to alleviate Krishnamurti's sense of dissatisfaction. He actually declared his intention to resign from the foundation and remove his name from it and all of his schools in India. The threat of this action underscored the depth of his disturbance and implicitly acknowledged that he would not be available to correct the situation in the future. Ultimately, his threat to resign was not realized, but it must have been a shock to the trustees and a difficult message to absorb.

The KFA paid for Vivienne and me to go to India so that I could attend the conference in Rishi Valley, but we were invited to extend our trip to include the Madras events as well. Our room at Vasanta Vihar was in the building adjacent to Krishnamurti's, and the proximity afforded me the opportunity to meet with him privately. His room was located at the top of an outdoor stairway and consisted only of space for a bed, a sitting area with a mat on the floor, two small tables, and a couple of straight-backed chairs. Nevertheless, it had an open and spacious feeling, uncluttered, with an abundance of natural light.

According to Scott, Krishnamurti's time in Madras was occupied with an endless flow of visitors and his chronic sense of dissatisfaction with the place and the people there. My observations and experience of him were entirely different. On the half dozen occasions that I dropped by to see him, he was always available, and our time was never interrupted. His demeanor and disposition were sunny and relaxed.

These meetings were the closest I ever came to interacting with Krishnamurti as if we were simply friends, rather than as his student or the director of his school. We sat together on the mat on his floor and conversed fairly freely, in an open and somewhat personal manner. He said that he was glad to see that I had dropped my habit. I had no idea what he was referring to and looked at him quizzically. He said that while in India I had dropped my habit of not talking. I did not know that I had such a habit, but on reflection it was clear to me what he meant. Without even being aware of it, in India I felt free of the overbearing, judgmental attitude of the KFA trustees and therefore more relaxed and able to speak my mind.

On another occasion he asked me in a somewhat guarded way what was my assessment of Terry Doyle. He pointed to an envelope on his table that contained a letter Terry had recently written to him. He would not tell me what it said, but later I learned the contents of the letter. After being away from Oak Grove for more than a year, Terry had concluded that the administrative difficulties at the school had their source in Erna. Although he was no longer associated with the school, he felt an obligation to convey his considered assessment of the situation.

One day our conversation turned to the persistent puzzle of why no one had undergone the kind of transformation that his teaching pointed toward. He shared with me an ancient Indian aphorism: Under the banyan tree, nothing grows. The banyan is a species of fig, an enormous tree with thick foliage and long extensions that enable it to cover large amounts of territory. So little sunlight reaches the ground that hardly any vegetation grows under the tree. Where there is a man whose influence is similarly broad, the opportunity for others to flower in his proximity is correspondingly diminished.

In spite of his illness, Krishnamurti's daily walks continued without interruption. In Madras, he walked along a promenade that extended for miles adjacent to the very beach in Adyar where he had been discovered so many years before. It was a stirring, memorable sight to witness him striding there in his Indian clothes, with the wind whipping his hair behind his head, and the big waves crashing on one side of the promenade while the sun was setting on the other. How poignant it was to think of him at the same time as a fourteen-year-old boy, playing in the sand with his younger brother, three-quarters of a century before.

One morning I came into Krishnamurti's room and noticed at once a bruise high on his forehead, a discoloration the size of a thumbprint. He said he had gotten out of bed during the night, lost his balance, and fallen against the wall. It was yet another reminder of the weakness and frailty that were gradually overcoming his vitality. I urged him again to cancel his talks and return at once to the United States, but he would not hear of it. Too many people had come to Madras to hear him speak, and his first talk was scheduled for that evening. He lived in order to speak; it was his highest priority, and nothing must interfere with it.

Krishnamurti had been scheduled to have six public meetings in Madras—four talks and two question-and-answer sessions—but these were reduced to three talks as a result of his illness. The meetings were held in the early evening in the large open courtyard of Vasanta Vihar. There was sufficient space for two thousand people, but the audience was tightly packed together, and the crowd overflowed out the front gate and into the street.

The premise of the first talk consisted of the inseparability of the individual from society and mankind. What action is meaningful and responsible in the face of that fact? This question led to the relationship of action to time. Is all action based on the past and the future? Or is there a form of action that is independent of time? "Go into it, this is a tremendously important question." Krishnamurti emphasized that he was not there to provide information or "help." The point of the talk was to engage in a process of mutual deliberation, of thinking together. "And if you don't want to think, get up and go home—much better."

As that comment suggests, Krishnamurti's general feeling of irritability found expression in this talk in his attitude toward the audience. His observations were punctuated by remarks critical of his listeners, including a few comments that bordered on the truculent: "Where were you all educated?" And even, at one point, "You are a rummy crowd."

The end of the talk shifted gears and addressed the nature and meaning of love—not personal or romantic love, but something of another dimension. In the second talk he continued this theme but took it in a new direction. What is the source of all energy, he asked—the original, "primordial" source? "Don't say 'God'," he cautioned. "I don't accept God; the speaker has no god."

By asking for the original source of energy, he was inquiring into something that is not held or confined within any limitations. The field of knowledge, he maintained, is inherently limited, as is thought, which is based upon knowledge. "And from this limitation we try to find the source of energy—you understand?—we try to find the origin, the beginning of creation." To pursue this question requires a state of mind that is free, without fear or any form of attachment. Such a mind itself is without limitation and therefore able to inquire more deeply.

What does it mean to live without attachment? This question led directly into an exploration of death. "Why are we all so frightened of death? What is dying?"

> It must be an extraordinary thing to die. Everything is taken away from you: your attachments, your money, your wife, your children, your country, your gurus, your gods. You may wish to take them into the other world but you can't.
>
> So death says, "Be totally detached." That's what happens when death comes: you have no person to lean on. Nothing. You can believe that you will be reincarnated. That's a very comfortable idea, but it's not a fact.

He rephrases the question in terms of a state of mind that is living and dying simultaneously, every day. "Death cuts you off with a very, very, very sharp razor from your attachments, from your gods, from your superstitions, from your desire for comfort—next life and so on." To enter into such a state of mind while living "means to be totally free. You don't see the beauty of it, the greatness of it, the extraordinary strength of it—while living to be dying." Such a state of mind can only be realized, he says, through experimentation, by trying it out—"not for just a day; every day."

> Death says, "Be free, nonattached, you can carry nothing with you." And love says, love says—there is no word for it. Love can exist only when there is freedom—not from your

wife, from a new girl, or a new husband—but the feeling, the enormous strength, the vitality, the energy of complete freedom.

By a conservative estimate, Krishnamurti delivered at least two thousand public talks subsequent to the dissolution of the Order of the Star. When he seated himself cross-legged on the low platform in Madras on January 4, 1986, it would be for the last time. He was surely aware of that reality.

His talk resumed on the theme of creation, but with a slightly different orientation. What is the origin of life? he now asked.

> What is the origin of all this—the marvelous earth, the lovely evening and the early morning sun, the rivers, the valleys, the mountains, and the glory of the land which is being despoiled? If you begin to question, doubt, as one should, all gods, all gurus—I don't belong to that tribe—if you begin to question all that man has put together through a long evolution down the corridors of history, you find this question asked: What is the beginning? What is the origin?

The discussion on this evening explored several byways before returning to the main theme. Why have human beings always worshipped something more than this world? With what energy have men created religions, churches, temples? "Was it fear? Was it seeking a reward from heaven?" He also examined the significance of the computer and what it holds in store for human consciousness. When the computer begins to work in concert with genetic engineering, as it will inevitably, what will become of the human being? "Your brains are going to be altered. Your way of behavior is going to be changed."

The inquiry then turned to the nature of meditation. Conventional kinds of meditation revolve around forms of concentration, such as maintaining an awareness of an image or a sound or the flow of one's breath in and out. But concentration is always divisive; the mind wanders off and has to be brought back by effort, by an act of will. "The speaker says that that is not meditation at all. That's merely a process of achievement. That's like a clerk becoming a manager."

Is there a meditation in which there is no effort, no will, no concentration? Krishnamurti maintains that there is, but it is "something that has to be absolutely silent."

> So, in meditation which is absolutely no effort, no achievement, no thinking, the brain is quiet—not made quiet by will, by intention, by conclusion, and all that nonsense; it is quiet. And, being quiet, it has infinite space.

These observations prepared the audience for his final remarks regarding his point of departure, the origin of life, the beginning of creation. "No description can ever describe the origin. The origin is nameless; the origin is absolutely quiet; it's not whirring about, making noise."

> Creation is something that is most holy; it's the most sacred thing in life; and if you have made a mess of your life, change it. Change it today, not tomorrow. If you are uncertain, find out why and be certain. If your thinking is not straight, think straight, logically. Unless all that is prepared, all that is settled, you can't enter into this world, into the world of creation.

His final two words were uttered under his breath, scarcely more than a whisper; but they were an unmistakable acknowledgment that this was the last public talk: "It ends."

⌒

Krishnamurti had been scheduled to leave India on January 17, but when he arrived in Madras, he told Scott to change the date to January

12. Two weeks later, he moved the departure date forward again to January 10. He expressed repeatedly his urgent desire to return to Ojai. This was not only a matter of wanting to be with Mary; she could just as easily have traveled to India. It was clearly an expression of where he wanted to die—not India, not Brockwood Park, but in his true home, Pine Cottage, in Ojai. The statement of his preference was limpid and emphatic. It represented a deep conviction of the right way to arrive at the end of his life.

Chapter Seventeen

THAT SUPREME INTELLIGENCE

The flight from Madras to Los Angeles, via Singapore and Tokyo, was long and arduous. Krishnamurti traveled with Scott Forbes, Dr. Parchure, and Adelle Chabelski, a friend from Ojai who had been with us in Rishi Valley and Madras. Although he flew in the first class section, Krishnamurti could not rest comfortably or stay warm, even under several layers of blankets. They arrived in Los Angeles on the morning of January 11 and were met by Mary and Mark. On the drive back to Ojai, Krishnamurti told Mary that he had returned in order to be with her and under her care in Pine Cottage. "I came back to see you and to die. If I die, it's alright. If I live, it's alright. But one must not invite death, and I don't. I came back to be taken care of by you." He did not know when the end would come, he said; but in fact, at that time, he had five weeks left to live.

Krishnamurti's physician in Ojai was Dr. Gary Deutsch, a young general practitioner affiliated with the hospital in Santa Paula, half an hour away by car. The first appointment with Dr. Deutsch occurred on January 13. Tests revealed an extremely high level of blood sugar as well as anemia, and the doctor suggested that Krishnamurti's fever might be the result of an inflammation of the prostate. He recommended that a sonogram be taken of his liver, pancreas, and gall bladder.

The sonogram was conducted at the hospital in Ojai one week later. It revealed the presence of a mass on the liver, a growth or tumor that may or may not have been malignant. Dr. Deutsch said that the growth should be examined with a CAT scan, which was scheduled for January 27.

On January 21, Krishnamurti took a short walk, accompanied by Scott, around the east end residence. It was a distance of about a quarter of a mile, with a slight incline at one point, after which he had to stop and rest. It had been his custom for decades to walk vigorously almost every day; but this short walk was to be his last.

Early the next morning, Krishnamurti experienced acute stomach pains with increasing severity. He was admitted to intensive care at the hospital in Santa Paula, where it was determined that he had a blockage of the bowel. A tube was inserted through his nose into his stomach to drain the accumulation of fluid, which relieved the pain. The reason for the blockage was not determined, but it dissipated after a few days and the nasal tube was removed. In the meantime, an intravenous drip was inserted in his hand to keep him nourished and hydrated. He also received a transfusion of a pint of blood.

The CAT scan on the 27th confirmed the presence of a growth of three inches on the liver as well as calcification of a portion of the pancreas. An attempted biopsy on the 28th to assess whether the growth was malignant was aborted before the needle reached the tumor because it was too painful. The next day, a highly sensitive blood test revealed definitive biochemical markers of a primary malignancy of the pancreas and a secondary cancer of the liver. This was the final piece of information needed to determine the diagnosis.

Krishnamurti was released from the hospital on January 30. The intravenous drip had been moved from a vein in his hand to a larger one under the collarbone, and it continued in place after he returned to Pine Cottage.

Krishnamurti's illness was sufficiently advanced in the summer of 1985 to announce in Saanen that no further talks would be scheduled there in subsequent years. When he returned to Brockwood in the fall, he took great care to ensure the stability of the administration of the school, including the transition from the leadership of Dorothy Simmons to that of Scott Forbes. The process of putting in place a firm foundation for the future continued at Rajghat, where Professor Krishna became the new director of the educational center, and in Madras, where he completed a wholesale revision of the KFI.

It was consistent with this trend of events to undertake a similar effort to stabilize the administrative structure in Ojai. I had foreseen the need for a remedy of this kind the previous May when I spoke to Krishnamurti and conveyed my apprehensions regarding Erna and her assessment of my role. At that time, she refused to acknowledge any degree of doubt or reservation about me, and the matter was left unresolved. Subsequent events made clear, however, what I suspected at the time: that her stated show of support was merely a tactic in a program of duplicity and deception.

Her tactic became manifest the following September when events in the lawsuit required her to travel to Brockwood to secure Krishnamurti's signature on documents before he departed for India. While in Brockwood she leveled a broad indictment of my performance as director, the tenor of which was that I had failed to seize the reins of leadership and take charge of the school. The remedy she proposed was for Scott Forbes to come to Ojai for a period of several months in order to immerse himself in the culture of the school and make a prescription to cure whatever ailed it. Her indictment was completely at odds with what she had told Krishnamurti, in my presence, the previous May. She never conveyed any of her concerns or apprehensions to me, and she never informed me, either beforehand or afterwards, about this proposal to Scott.

When Krishnamurti returned to Ojai in January 1986, he was too ill to take whatever steps were necessary to resolve the contradictions in the administration of the school. Instead he appointed Scott to investigate the matter and make recommendations. "All through Krishnaji's first ten days in Ojai," according to Scott, "he pressed me to talk with people from the Oak Grove School and try to understand the situation there."

At the end of these ten days, before Krishnamurti was hospitalized, Scott conveyed the results of his investigation in a meeting with Erna, Theo, Mary, and Krishnamurti. The conclusion of his inquiry was unequivocal: the difficulty in the administration of the school had its source in the behavior and attitudes of Erna. The school community was unanimous in its assessment that her assertion of dominance was obvious and undermined the authority of the director. The complaint she had lodged in September, that I had failed to take charge of the school, was the result of her own actions and interference.

Scott wrote that it was difficult to say all this forthrightly in front of Erna and Theo, but he felt it was necessary to do so, rather than simply convey his findings to Krishnamurti. The difficulty was compounded by the fact that Mary was "fiercely loyal" to Erna, as a result of all she had done to combat Rajagopal. In spite of the difficulty, no one at the meeting was able to contest anything Scott had said, and Krishnamurti stated that he agreed with his assessment. Scott wrote that he felt he had done "a very good piece of work for the KFA," but he did not expect any thanks for his efforts, and did not receive any.

While all this was occurring, I was completely unaware of what was taking place. Vivienne and I had returned from Madras before our intended departure date because both of us had become ill. When we arrived in Ojai, she recovered rather quickly, but I was bedridden for two weeks with high fever and a body rash whose source could not be diagnosed. By the time I recovered, Krishnamurti had been hospitalized. When he returned to Pine Cottage, another ten days had elapsed, his diagnosis had been confirmed, and the momentum of events had assumed another course and character altogether.

When the outcome of his illness was no longer in any doubt, Krishnamurti called for certain members of the English and Indian foundations to come to Ojai. Although he remained confined to his bed in Pine Cottage, he met with several trustees on February 3, four days after he had been released from the hospital. The purpose of the meeting was to bring a sense of finality to the disagreements regarding publications that had plagued the foundations for years. The primary source of contention was Pupul Jayakar's insistent claim that the Indian foundation had the right to select, edit, and publish talks and dialogues that had occurred in India. In the meeting on February 3, Krishnamurti emphatically rejected that claim. He delegated to the English foundation the exclusive authority to edit and publish his work. The meeting was recorded to guarantee its authenticity.

Two days later, he called a second meeting of trustees along with a few additional people, including me. This meeting had two purposes. The first was to insist upon the clarity of his mind, in spite of his illness and medications. Why he would make a point of emphasizing this fact was not clear, but it seemed that he did not want anyone to call into question later the authority of what he had said about publications in the previous meeting. He took the extraordinary step of instructing Scott, who was holding the recording device, to swear that the recording would be preserved intact and never destroyed or altered. Moreover, when Scott's reply was not sufficiently emphatic, Krishnamurti made him repeat, "I swear" that the recordings would be preserved.

The second purpose of the meeting was to ask those assembled who did not live in Ojai to please go home. There was nothing further to be accomplished, and their continued presence represented a kind of pressure that he found disturbing. His request for people to leave was expressed with great courtesy, but it left no room for doubt about his meaning.

The meeting lasted no more than fifteen or twenty minutes, but it was painful to listen to and to witness. Krishnamurti was sitting up in his bed, and his frailty was plain to see. His voice was pitched at a higher register than normal, and it broke repeatedly in a kind of muffled sob. He apologized and said he did not want to cry, but "the body" rebelled at remaining confined for the indefinite future.

By the time I recovered from my illness, Krishnamurti had been in the hospital for a week, and his diagnosis was all but confirmed. Scott and Mary had been spending most of their time at the hospital, taking turns sitting next to his bed throughout the night. They were both consumed with the new understanding of his illness and the exigencies that followed, including the necessity of being present with him as much as possible. Scott's effort to remedy the state of affairs at the school must have receded from his awareness and become a matter very peripheral to his primary concerns. In any case, he communicated to me what had transpired in only the briefest and most cursory terms. I had no idea that he had been at the school for ten days and spoken to many people, and he said nothing about the meeting where he had confronted Erna in the presence of Krishnamurti and Mary. All I knew was that he had visited the school and made some recommendations.

After Krishnamurti returned from the hospital, I saw him for short periods of time on half a dozen occasions. As my home was at Arya Vihara, I was able to sense the rhythm of activities at Pine Cottage, and I crept into the house and into his room without causing any disturbance several times. Each time I found him lying on his back in his bed, and he could hear or sense when I entered the room. He always offered some quiet word of welcome or asked me to take a seat in a chair by his bed.

On the first of these occasions, without any preliminaries, he went directly to the matter at hand. He told me that from now on I was to be "in complete charge" of the school. He was too weak, however, to explain what that meant or how it had come about. He mentioned nothing about Scott's investigations at the school or the meeting Scott had conducted with Erna in his presence. The end result was simply presented to me as a fait accompli, devoid of any context or sequence of events. As a result, I found it bewildering.

Krishnamurti added, however, that it was important for me to speak with Erna in order to finalize and confirm the new state of affairs. Perhaps he assumed that she would explain all that had transpired and the basis for the new arrangement. In any case, his direction to speak with her was clear, in spite of his weakened condition.

At that time, my tenure as director had lasted a year and a half, and I had made it a point throughout that period to walk with Erna early in the morning two or three times a month. Although she was seventy-five years old, she had a regular habit of setting out from her home at six-thirty each morning and walking a predictable route for an hour or so. I made the effort to join her occasionally in an ongoing attempt to establish some degree of rapport or common basis for relationship. My presence brought little joy to either of us. Conversation was intermittent and revolved around superficial events associated with the school and the people connected to it.

When Krishnamurti told me I needed to speak with Erna about being "in complete charge" of the school, I joined her on her walk the next morning. I waited for half an hour while we walked to see if she would raise the matter, but she was even more remote than usual and said nothing about it. Finally I broached the issue as delicately as possible and asked if I had understood Krishnamurti correctly. She confirmed it tersely, with an attitude as cold as the north wind. She volunteered nothing about the sequence of events that had brought about this result, and her manner made it clear that any further questions would be unwelcome. Her brow was furrowed, her mouth was set, and she kept her gaze fixed on the road in front of her feet.

On my next visit to Krishnamurti's bedside, he asked me immediately whether I had spoken with Erna. He was lying motionless in bed, barely opening his eyes, and his voice was as soft as the sound of a sigh. Nevertheless, his meaning was clear, and I assured him that I had. He absorbed this news with a momentary sense of relief, but he added a new task for me to complete. He wanted to know if I had made an announcement to the school community, informing everyone of the new state of affairs. Such a course of action struck me as strange and unnecessary, and I said that I had not done that. He urged me to do so. He felt it was imperative, and I assured him that I would do as he had asked.

Krishnamurti's health was so precarious at this point, his weakness and frailty so conspicuous, that I found it impossible to challenge him or ask him to summon the energy to explain more fully what was going on. As a result, when he asked me later if I had made the announcement he requested, I said yes when in fact I had not. Nothing fundamental seemed to me to have actually changed, except that Erna had been maneuvered into agreeing to something that held little or no reality for her or for me. I don't think he believed me when I said I had done what he asked; but he let the matter rest, and so did I.

I had several other brief conversations with Krishnamurti during his final days that held more significance for me. I asked why his teaching had not been fully understood, and he said that no one had listened to or absorbed it in its entirety. Given the sense of protection he felt, as well as the fact that his work was not finished, was his illness the result of some kind of "mistake"? He said no, "the body" was bound to malfunction sooner or later. I asked if he were still learning, and he said yes—"that is the problem," because it kept him awake at night.

In my last meeting with him, a day and a half before he died, I held his hand and said I would always remember everything he had told me. He was too weak to reply; but he squeezed my hand with a sudden strength that said more than words could ever have conveyed.

⸺

In Krishnamurti's philosophy, death is not something to be feared or avoided, but rather explored and understood, and even, in a psychological sense, embraced as part of daily life. The question therefore arises whether or how he actualized or enacted that point of view as he approached the end of his life. What he said and did at that time may also shed light on other questions regarding his states of mind and his essential quality or character.

As soon as he arrived in California from Madras, on the drive from the airport to Ojai, Krishnamurti cautioned Mary that she must not leave him alone, even for a few minutes, for the next two or three days. Otherwise, he said, he "might slip away." He repeated this request, to Mary as well as to Scott, several times over the course of the following weeks. In this case, as in so many others, they both refrained from inquiring exactly why he was concerned or what would happen if he were left alone. The spirit of the request, however, appeared to be impersonal. He was concerned for the welfare of "the body," as he put it, as if he felt vulnerable and unable entirely to fend for himself. Among other things, he had work left to do, and if he were to "slip away" unexpectedly or prematurely, important business would be left undone.

Another theme interwoven throughout this period revolved around whether "the other" would remain with him during his illness. Krishnamurti's operating assumption seemed to be that the other would not continue to visit a body that was seriously ill or diseased. The diagnosis of cancer was unexpected to him for this reason. Because the other was still with him from time to time, he had felt sure his body must be fundamentally healthy, notwithstanding the accumulating evidence to the contrary. His conviction about this was not so strong that he doubted the diagnosis; but he was surprised at the result. On occasions when the pain became very acute, the other would leave temporarily, he said. The biopsy in particular had this effect; but when morphine alleviated the pain, the other returned. Indeed, after he had recovered from the effects of the biopsy, the other "took charge" for two consecutive nights—whatever that may mean.

In the meeting with trustees on February 3, Krishnamurti said that Dr. Deutsch had told him the tumor was growing rapidly. He was going to inquire of the doctor whether the tubes could be disconnected or other measures taken to hasten the end. But after talking it over with Mary, Scott, and Dr. Parchure, he decided not to consider such an alternative. The course of action they chose was to let death come in a natural way, in its own time.

I also raised this question in one of my last visits with him. If he felt ready to go, and if he were suffering, would it not be possible to increase the dosage of morphine to a significant or decisive extent? He said no, because that would "look like suicide" and not be the right way for him to depart.

Several times during the last week of his life, Scott and the nurse on duty carried Krishnamurti into the large living room in Pine

Cottage and placed him where he could watch the fire in the massive fireplace. In the evenings, he watched Clint Eastwood movies with Scott or had Mary read to him from a novel by Paul Theroux. His nighttime meditations continued right to the end.

Early in the morning on February 16, the pain in his abdomen became acute and could not be alleviated by injections of morphine. Dr. Deutsch could not be reached for several hours to authorize an increase in dosage. In mid-afternoon the efforts to contact him were finally successful, and at that time the morphine began to be given by means of the intravenous drip rather than by injection. This method succeeded in alleviating the pain, and by evening he was lucid and at peace.

A few days previously, Krishnamurti had told Mary that he loved her, and that "K" loved her, and that she was the closest human contact he had. He asked her to assure him that she would stay with him until the very end. On the evening of the 16th, as he was given medication to sleep, he told her good night over and over again. Then he closed his eyes and drifted off. She and Scott stayed with him on either side of the bed throughout the evening hours, watching the rise and fall of his breath, as it gradually slowed more and more. By his final hour, he was breathing only three times a minute.

At eleven-forty p.m., Scott had the sudden, definitive sense that Krishnamurti was no longer present, although outwardly nothing had changed. The pulse continued slowly and the body continued to breathe, but Scott felt certain that Krishnamurti was gone. Thirty minutes later, shortly after midnight on the 17th, the pulse stopped; and, as Mary Lutyens wrote, the spark had entered the flame.

One of the central tenets of Krishnamurti's philosophy was to deny every form of authority in the psychological field. "Be a light to yourself" was among his most familiar refrains, and its corollary was not to accept the authority of any priest, guru, politician, or psychologist for the purpose of self-understanding. As a result, it was crucially important for his audience not to project such authority onto Krishnamurti himself. For this reason, he rarely spoke about himself, and then only in generalities or in a manner designed to deflect attention.

It seems that Krishnamurti lived in some respects behind a veil designed to shield from others a full awareness of who or what he was. The primary purpose of this veil may have been to minimize the possibility that people would treat him as an authority, in spite of all his admonitions otherwise. Moreover, it might have enabled his inner life to unfold more naturally than it would have if those around him were fully aware of what transpired within him.

In his final days in Ojai, however, Krishnamurti lifted up a corner of the veil for the world to have a better sense of what his life had been like for him. He did so on February 7, two days after his last meeting with trustees, and ten days before he died. This anomalous event occurred in response to a question that had been put to him in writing by Mary Cadogan, the secretary of the foundation in England. What would happen, she asked, to his "focus of energy and understanding" after he died? His answer was the last recorded statement of his life.

In his reply, Krishnamurti emphasized that no one, including those close to him, could possibly understand what his life had been like. For seventy years, he maintained, his body had been "used" by an "immense energy, immense intelligence." It required a very special body, one that had been carefully protected and prepared, for such energy and intelligence to pass through it. The world would not see such a body again for hundreds of years. And after he was gone, that intelligence would go with him.

As these comments were his last recorded statement, they

warrant special attention. They seem to represent a gift, a last gift to humanity, a departing pirouette on the stage of consciousness. They were a revelation, a challenge, and an invitation. The comments were his epitaph, the final message to the s of the World Teacher.

I was telling them this morning:

For seventy years, that immense energy, immense intelligence, has been using this body. I don't think people realize what tremendous energy and intelligence went through this body. It was like a twelve-cylinder engine. And it went on for seventy years. It was a pretty long time. And now the body can't stand any more.

Nobody can understand. Unless the body has been prepared—very carefully protected and so on—nobody can understand what went through this body. Don't anybody pretend.

I repeat this: nobody amongst us or the public knows what went on. I know they don't.

And now, after seventy years, it has come to an end. Not that intelligence and energy—it's somewhat here every day, especially at night. And after seventy years, the body can't stand any more. (The Indians have a lot of damned superstitions about this—that you will, and the body goes—and all that kind of nonsense.)

You won't find another body like this, or that supreme intelligence operating in a body, for many hundred years. You won't see it again. When he goes, it goes. There is no consciousness left behind of that consciousness, that state.

They'll all pretend, or try to imagine, that they can get into touch with that. Perhaps they will, somewhat, if they live the teachings. But nobody has done it—nobody.

And so, that's that.

Chapter Eighteen

THE TEACHINGS IN PERSPECTIVE

Three decades and more have elapsed since the death of Krishnamurti, and the time has come to consider what impact or effect his philosophy has had on society and mankind. If his work had been taken seriously, it would have arrived like an asteroid, with an explosive force and shock waves that reverberated around the globe. Yet only a slender minority of people have recognized the significance of his message, and fewer still have fully absorbed its meaning. What accounts for the discrepancy between the intrinsic value of the teachings and the manner in which they have been received by the world?

Several factors contribute to this unfortunate state of affairs. One is the sheer magnitude of his philosophy—the scope, depth, and all-encompassing embrace of what he had to say. The whole of life fell within his orbit; and ours is an age of specialization, with little or no appreciation for a holistic point of view. We have no experience or familiarity with a window as wide as the sky.

Another factor revolves around the ratio of costs to rewards in the investment of time spent studying the teachings. Krishnamurti emphasized that any form of motive actively interferes with the choiceless awareness that he advocates. Not only is there no immediate payoff in studying his work, but if one approaches it with an expected reward, he warns, one is already on the wrong track. This is not a philosophy that promises that you will get rich quick, or win friends and influence people, or secure a comfortable home in the hereafter. It doesn't lend itself to acquisition, entertainment, or achievement.

There is a third factor of equal or greater significance. By virtue of his name and the country of his origin, Krishnamurti's work falls all too easily into a preconceived category of gurus and other individuals dispensing spiritual guidance or mystical platitudes. These images form a barrier that blocks attention to the actual content and substance of his message. The images are not inevitable, however, and, with some concerted effort, they may be overcome.

In order to correct the misconceptions regarding the content and meaning of Krishnamurti's philosophy, certain intellectual skills may be brought into play: his work may be summarized, analyzed, and compared with the work of others. In any other field, to engage in such activities would be standard procedure and unremarkable. Students of the teachings, however, may hesitate or object to approaching Krishnamurti's work in that manner. He insists that a merely intellectual understanding of his philosophy has little value. Only actual insight—seeing for oneself in a direct, nonverbal manner—can precipitate meaningful, enduring change.

Krishnamurti's reservations regarding the limitations of the intellect, however, were not intended to serve as a wholesale proscription against examining his work in that manner. The intellect may be limited, but he never meant to suggest that it is useless. The point is to see where it is helpful or necessary, and where it has no place.

A related issue may also serve to discourage comparative analysis of Krishnamurti's work. He strongly objected to any form of what he called "interpretation" of the teachings, especially after he was gone. He abhorred the possibility that individuals would claim to have an exclusive or authoritative understanding of his work and present themselves as intermediaries or representatives on his behalf.

However, as noted in a previous chapter, he distinguished between interpretation and simple discussion of the meaning of his work. Objective inquiry intended to explore and elucidate what he said is necessary and appropriate unless and until someone assumes the mantle of authority. To distinguish between interpretation and inquiry of this kind is an art that requires attention and adjustment to circumstances. In any case, the discussion that follows is offered in the spirit of exploration; it is intended to encourage and facilitate further inquiry, and not to suggest that it is the last word.

We begin our analysis with a few of the quintessential statements most characteristic of the teachings.

1. Be a light to yourself.

Meaningful change can only occur on the basis of self-understanding, seeing what is for oneself. There is no authority in the psychological field.

2. You are the world.

The differences that divide people—race, religion, nationality, ideology—are superficial. What everyone has in common are the deeper realities of suffering, loneliness, fear, conflict, and a mind that is dominated by thought. Everyone is fundamentally alike in this respect.

3. Where there is division, there must be conflict.

Krishnamurti calls this statement a "law" because it is categorical and universal, like gravity or the speed of light. Krishnamurti's Law is meant to apply in the psychological field, within the individual and between individuals, where division consists of a false, illusory sense of separation.

4. The observer is the observed.

The psychological entity at the center of consciousness considers itself to be an observer separate from the emotion or state of mind that it observes. In fact, the observed and the observer are one.

5. Time is the enemy of man.

Psychological time is the field in which the individual strives to become something, to improve, to be more or better than what he or she is. But psychological time is an illusion; it does not exist; and the process of "becoming" is futile.

These pillars in the edifice of Krishnamurti's philosophy represent some of the most characteristic features of his work. Each statement clearly falls within the broad parameters of the field of psychology. They are meant to be taken as verifiable facts, not speculations about spiritual states of mind. Moreover, each statement contradicts one of the guiding assumptions of most people. Based upon this sample of the teachings, it seems fair to conclude what Krishnamurti has stated: that he is proposing a transformation in the structure and operation of ordinary consciousness.

Here lies an additional clue regarding the relative lack of appreciation of his work. Krishnmurti has intruded upon the province of a well-developed discipline of knowledge and inquiry. Professionals in the established field of psychology have little incentive to consider the contribution of someone with no credentials, no recognizable methodology, and no empirical findings. If such an individual were merely suggesting a modification within the existing framework, he might warrant some attention; but here is someone who is proposing a wholesale psychological revolution. The sheer audacity of it might well provoke resistance, annoyance, or neglect.

Nevertheless, Krishnamurti's work contains an elaborate and detailed set of principles that support and reinforce his call for a change in consciousness. The scope, variety, and coherence of these principles are not immediately apparent because they are embedded in talks that function on multiple levels. His talks are holistic; they range over a territory encompassing the whole of life. To extract and distill the psychological principles at the core of his work is to engage in a process of analysis that is entirely unlike his own approach.

But if we set aside our reservations and continue to examine his work analytically, several findings emerge. He devotes a great deal of attention to issues familiar in the clinical setting of psychotherapy: anger and aggression; fear and anxiety; desire and jealousy; self-image, identity, and feelings of inferiority; and conflict in personal relationships. The prevalence of issues of this kind throughout the teachings confirms the impression that the primary focus of his work falls within the four corners of the field of psychology.

Another finding that emerges if we take the liberty to examine his work analytically revolves around his treatment of various functions of the mind. Krishnamurti sharply distinguishes between two kinds or families of functions in a way that is unique to his philosophy. One prominent example of the two families consists of his assertion of a fundamental difference between the intellect and intelligence. This distinction is not one that we normally observe or recognize, but it is basic to Krishnamurti's work.

He associates the intellect with the family of functions that includes thought, knowledge, memory, comparison, measurement, and analysis. Intelligence, by contrast, belongs to an entirely different category that includes perception, observation, awareness, attention, and insight. The difference between these two families is one that he brings to bear upon almost every problem or issue that he addresses. To understand his philosophy, it is crucial to examine the basis for this distinction and how it operates in his treatment of particular forms of psychological disorder.

At the core of Krishnamurti's philosophy lies a comprehensive set of insights into the nature and operation of thought. He regards thought as the dominant force in consciousness and daily life, and he maintains that the failure to understand its nature and how it functions is the primary source of illusion and conflict. The two families of mental functioning differ according to whether or not they partake of or employ the operations of thought.

According to Krishnamurti, thought is "the response of memory"; it is the repository of the past; it represents the field of knowledge. We consider that field to be vast, and we are always adding more and more to it; but knowledge, and therefore thought, are always limited in scope. Moreover, thought is inherently fragmentary. It consists of words, concepts, and images, and these each represent something static and defined, a fragment isolated from the context from which it came.

These observations acquire weight and significance in the examination of familiar problems of daily life. Conflict and discord between husband and wife can be traced in part to the manner in which thought as memory actively interferes in relationship. Each partner has formed over time an image of the other, based on an accumulation of incidents from the past. Those images are not merely passive, innocuous memories that one can pick up or put aside like a photo album. Instead they are embedded in the present perception of the other person, so that he or she is seen as if through a filter. That filter serves as a barrier that prevents complete awareness of the person in the immediate present. Conflict and discord inevitably follow.

Thought interferes in relationship because of the manner in which it intrudes upon or participates in perception. The image of the other person is projected seamlessly, effortlessly into our present awareness of him or her. It acts in such a way that we don't distinguish between the image and the present actuality. We feel the image *is* the actual person just as much as whatever he or she is saying or doing now.

In short, we fail to distinguish between thought and perception not merely in an abstract, academic sense, but from moment to moment in our daily lives. A somewhat similar dynamic operates inwardly as well, as the individual attempts to cope with anger, jealousy, grief, and other forms of disturbance.

Above all, the mistaken application of thought distorts our sense of self, the psychological entity that stands at the center of consciousness. We attribute to that entity the ability to think, observe, judge, choose, and analyze, whereas in fact the self is merely an image, an illusory construct derived from the past. To penetrate and dissolve this illusion entails seeing for oneself Krishnamurti's cardinal insight that the observer is the observed. In so doing, the very structure of consciousness undergoes a transformation.

Most of these points and principles are familiar to students of Krishnamurti's work. However, in his teachings, they are scattered throughout the talks and embedded in a larger context. They are drawn together here in order to show that a coherent scaffolding exists, underlying the teachings, that may not be immediately apparent. This scaffolding or skeletal structure represents a consistent, logical, coherent point of view that forms the basis for a new approach to the field of psychology.

Krishnamurti's observations about the nature of thought form a remarkably comprehensive set of insights. The list below consists of statements he has made at one time or another. In his work, each point is explored independently from the others to account for some particular issue or problem under consideration. Here these statements are brought together without reference to any context, in order to show how comprehensive his treatment of this topic is.

1. Thought is the response of memory.
2. Thought is mechanical.
3. Thought is fragmentary.
4. Thought is limited.
5. Thought is a material process.
6. Thought is knowledge.

7. Thought is the past.
8. Thought is time and time is thought.
9. The word (thought) is not the thing.
10. Thought is movement.
11. Thought is division.
12. The thinker is the thought.

What has been provided here is merely a sketch of what could be a far more complete exposition of Krishnamurti's point of view. Several important topics have been left untouched in this analysis, including attachment, the nature of love, the ending of fear, and meditation. The point of the present exposition is merely to bring into focus sufficient material to show some of the scope and structure of Krishnamurti's approach to the field of psychology. His philosophy does not consist of mystical or spiritual images and ideals, but rather of factual observations of the dynamics of ordinary consciousness.

The discipline of psychology, however, includes more than theoretical frameworks and empirical findings. Central to the field is the issue of methodology. Psychology has progressed through several phases in its development, largely as the result of shifting norms and standards regarding what qualifies as verifiable knowledge. The father of the discipline in America, William James, employed the process of introspection, the inward examination of the contents and processes of his own consciousness. This method generated interesting results, but it has fallen into disfavor because it does not conform to the scientific imperative to produce findings that are independently verifiable.

Whether the field of psychology can ever become fully scientific is a debatable proposition. The data of the mind are inherently off limits to direct observation by others, and so the techniques for determining cause and effect are often contrived, artificial, and indirect. Nevertheless, psychology aspires to the model of scientific inquiry, and every effort is made to make experimental procedures explicit and consistent with accepted norms.

At first glance, Krishnamurti's work would appear to be quite hopeless in terms of methodological respectability. He does not perform experiments at all, much less controlled studies with multiple trials on randomly selected populations. In fact, he goes further and actively rejects any form of method or system as a means for verification of his observations. It would be hard to imagine a more unpromising point of departure from the perspective of normal standards for research.

On closer inspection, however, Krishnamurti's position may not be so indefensible. He strongly endorses two principles that are basic to science. First, he has little patience with beliefs or speculation; he insists upon factual observation. In addition, he strongly rejects the role of authority as a means for determining what is true; nothing is accepted on the basis of the status or reputation of any individual.

Krishnamurti's point of view is carefully worked out; he has not overlooked or neglected to consider difficult or problematic issues. His rejection of method, for example, was not arrived at in a casual, haphazard, or incidental manner. On the contrary, it represents a crucial element in his exposition. In the psychological field, he maintains, any method cannot be separated from the results it produces. Where there is a mechanical procedure, the outcome is in part determined by the means employed, and the results are distorted to that extent.

Although he rejects specific techniques for psychological investigation, Krishnamurti does recommend what he would call an approach, which may be considered a form of methodology in a larger sense. He advocates what he calls the choiceless awareness of thoughts and feelings as they occur from moment to moment. He describes this approach in detail. It is not something undertaken with a motive or the intention to achieve a definite result. It is choiceless in the sense that there is no judgment of whatever thoughts and feelings may arise. Such an awareness, he says, brings about "self-knowledge," which is a non-accumulative form of learning about oneself from moment to moment.

Conventional standards of research would automatically reject any suggestion that choiceless awareness can bring about self-knowledge. Such a process would be viewed as doomed to failure because it is subjective and therefore vulnerable to and potentially saturated with personal bias. The scientific method is specifically designed to establish procedures that eliminate the subjective element, and Krishnamurti's approach manifestly appears to fail this crucial criterion.

His methodology, however, does not disregard or neglect to acknowledge this objection; on the contrary, he confronts this issue fully and turns it on its head. In Krishnamurti's approach, the possibility that personal bias may influence or distort inward observation is not merely an annoying difficulty to be circumvented or overcome. Instead, he makes it the very object of the inquiry: judgments and opinions, acquired from family and society, are precisely what need to be observed. They form the background of what he calls conditioning; and choiceless awareness is intended to provide the opportunity to observe one's own conditioning in action. To learn about and expose the subjective element is part of the very point of his approach.

Ultimately, what Krishnamurti advocates is a form of inward observation without the "observer" participating at all. The observer, the psychological entity at the center of consciousness, is the source of subjective bias; and so to eliminate the observer is to eliminate the subjectivity that conventional research decries. If we combine this principle with the other elements of his approach—choiceless awareness, no method, no motive, and no authority—we can see that Krishnamurti has a comprehensive and consistent methodology after all. It differs from conventional standards in some respects and is similar in others. In any case, it represents a serious and original approach to the challenges endemic in the field of psychology. There is no basis for rejecting his work on grounds that it lacks an explicit and well-considered methodological foundation.

There remains the question of whether Krishnamurti's philosophy goes beyond the psychological field. What has been said so far is intended to show that he has proposed a comprehensive and revolutionary contribution to the study of consciousness as it is experienced by most human beings. Although he never intended to contribute to the discipline of psychology per se, most of his observations fall within the embrace of that field and warrant attention and exploration on those terms. But now we are asking whether he is offering something more; and, if so, what is its nature or content.

Throughout his career, Krishnamurti's castigation of organized religion was unrelenting. Not only is there nothing sacred, he said, in sacred books or places of worship; but the sense of belonging, of membership in a sectarian group, contributes to division, conflict, and war. And yet he acknowledged and endorsed the possibility of living with a religious spirit and discovering something truly sacred. Indeed, he considered religion in this sense to be crucially important.

Krishnamurti defined religion as "the gathering of energy to find out whether it is possible to be free." The accumulation of energy entails living with a sense of priorities, not squandering time and attention on entertainment, popular forms of achievement, or escape from the actualities of daily life. Psychological freedom demands an intensity of awareness in order to eliminate the conditioning and illusions in which we are trapped. Such a mind is open to a dimension that is beyond thought, beyond knowledge, and therefore in contact with something limitless.

Krishnamurti maintains that what is sacred is not a divine being, or a holy book, or an ancient destination sanctified by time. The most sacred thing in life, he said, is truth. But truth is not a fixed or static set of knowledge or ideas. He considers truth to lie in the realm of the unlimited, and he equates it with "reality, or God, or whatever name you like to give it." However, "truth is a pathless land," and it cannot be described. There is no road to it or any method of achieving it. For this reason, there is relatively little mention made of truth or the unlimited in the public talks.

The only way to come into contact with that dimension, according to Krishnamurti, is to put one's life in order—not only the practicalities of house, job, and finances, but within oneself. To do so means living without inward division and conflict. Order for Krishnamurti is "putting every thing in its right place"; and inward order entails, above all, putting thought in its right place. Only when the contents of consciousness, including thought, feeling, and the sense of self, are fully understood can the mind open up to something beyond the field of knowledge.

Krishnamurti's nature writing supplements and reinforces his religious philosophy. He does not draw a direct line between the two or make the connection explicit, but his attitude toward trees, clouds, mountain streams, and wildlife is imbued with an appreciation so deep that the religious feeling or spirit is manifest. On rare occasions, he goes further, as in the instances where he declares, "God is color." Comments of this kind suggest an underlying relationship between the natural world and what he means by truth or the unlimited.

Another element of Krishnamurti's religious philosophy consists of his approach to meditation. He reserves special scorn for every form of method or technique in the practice of meditation. He says that the selection of a carefully chosen mantra, for example, might just as well be replaced by repeating "Coca-Cola"; the net effect can only be to dull the mind. He associates true meditation with a mind that is quiet, still, and engaged in a form of attention without direction or boundaries. Such a mind is free from the burden and limitations of knowledge, and therefore open to the possibility of coming into contact with something timeless.

In *Krishnamurti's Notebook*, he acknowledges the active presence in his life of some kind of force, entity, or energy that evidently belongs to another dimension. It visits him at odd and unpredictable intervals, uninvited and without warning. He calls it "the other," and he attributes to it a quality of numinous benediction. In her memoirs, Mary Zimbalist confirms her own awareness of the other on rare occasions. She describes it as a palpable sense of something throbbing or vibrating, although it is not actually tangible, much less seen or heard.

Krishnamurti never actively inquires into the nature, source, or meaning of the other; he seems to feel that to do so would be improper or show a lack of respect. He allows it to remain as if it were behind a curtain and to reveal itself only on its own terms. Thus it remains a mysterious feature of his inner life, something vital and significant to him, but inaccessible to our understanding.

These religious elements of the teachings are vitally important. The fact remains that what Krishnamurti expressed from a public platform consisted almost entirely of secular, psychological observations about the structure and function of ordinary consciousness. One has to move outside his stated remarks to public audiences to discover the full religious dimensions of his work.

It is also important to note that Krishnamurti himself did not draw so sharp a distinction between the psychological and the religious as has been presented here. The analytical approach adopted in this chapter is intended to draw attention to the comprehensive, detailed, and coherent quality of his psychological views; but from Krishnamurti's own perspective, the two fields are part of a seamless whole. The manner in which he approaches the psychological field is not different from what he calls religious: the gathering of energy to discover if it is possible to be free. Only the religious attitude is capable of fully addressing the deep disorder in ordinary consciousness.

Chapter Nineteen

THE MIND OF KRISHNAMURTI

W e normally consider people to be more or less interesting according to the magnitude of their accomplishments. If someone exhibits exceptional talent or skill in almost any domain, we want to know not only what they are like as an individual, but also what circumstances brought about or produced their abilities. Is their particular form of genius acquired or innate? To the extent that it is acquired, what combination of conditions was most conducive to its cultivation? The greater the accomplishment, the keener is our curiosity to know what brought it about.

Mozart was born with exceptional gifts, but he also had intensive training from an early age. Nevertheless, it is difficult to account for his ability to conceive an entire composition in a single, effortless stroke, and require time only in order to write it down. Einstein was exposed to no more than the normal educational opportunities for a youth in his milieu, and his behavior in school was an uneven mixture of precocious performance and resistance to authority. What precipitated the depth and originality of his insights? Leonardo was well regarded for his artistry and his inventive talents during his lifetime, but he also had a reputation for failing to complete his projects, and no one anticipated the towering esteem in which he is held today. Each figure is fascinating in part because the roots of great accomplishment are difficult to discern.

The difficulty in assigning causes to accomplishments is compounded in certain cases by uncertainty in assessing the significance or magnitude of an individual's contribution. No one who knew of Van Gogh during his lifetime could have remotely imagined what his paintings would sell for today. Copernicus did not publish his revolutionary findings until the last year of his life, and half a century elapsed before others began to take his work seriously. Mendel died in complete obscurity.

All these uncertainties and more apply in any effort to understand the sources of Krishnamurti's achievement. He maintained throughout his lifetime that the teachings were what was important, not the teacher. Nothing he said should be accepted on the basis of any assumed authority; all that mattered was what each individual could verify through his or her own observation and understanding. "When the man says, 'Be a light to yourself' from morning 'til night, why do you bother whether that teacher is this, that, blue-eyed, purple-eyed, or long haired?"

But even Krishnamurti was not immune to wondering about the characteristics or quality of the teacher. In his talks with trustees in 1978, he repeated several times how much he would have liked to meet with people who knew the Buddha if he had lived during that period of time. When Mary Lutyens was finishing the second volume of his biography, she pointedly asked him to help her account for what had enabled him to produce his philosophy. He might have turned her question aside and said it was not important, but he did not. He explored the matter at length with her in two conversations.

For Lutyens, the question was vitally important because she entertained no uncertainty regarding Krishnamurti's importance as a world figure. For her, his contribution was a matter of supreme significance. The source or circumstances conducive to the expression of his teachings was therefore a question she inevitably had to address. Not everyone would accept Lutyens's premise. Even a skeptic, however, would have to acknowledge the exceptional scope of the teachings, their revolutionary intent, and the single-minded persistence with which Krishnamurti pursued his work. The world may choose to ignore his contribution, but those who examine it cannot fail to marvel at its originality, depth, and serious purpose.

Against this background, a suite of perplexing characteristics of Krishnamurti calls out for explanation. The unusual features of his life are not limited to the quality of his work. Several additional factors claim our attention, including the events at Ojai in 1922 and at Ootacamund in 1948; his "process"; his sense of being protected; the visitations from "the other"; his dialogue with death; and the extraordinary prophecy that was made about his life at an early age. Collectively, these characteristics represent a network of attributes unique and without precedent.

The most unfathomable feature of the entire set of circumstances consists of the close correlation between the prophecy proclaimed by Annie Besant and the events that followed. Krishnamurti's separation from Theosophy and his dissolution of the Order of the Star count for little in terms of assessing the accuracy of her prediction. She never said the World Teacher would act as a theosophist. What she foresaw was someone who would speak to all of humanity with a message intended to heal the chaos and conflict endemic in the individual and in society. Krishnamurti fulfilled that vision to the utmost degree.

We can examine the improbability of what occurred from either end of the bridge that brought the participants together. How lucky were Besant and Leadbeater to find the embryonic World Teacher, a youth of just the right age, playing in the sand on the very threshold of the headquarters of the TS? Alternatively, how fortunate was the young Krishnamurti to land on the doorstep of the very organization in all the world most conducive to facilitating the expression of his special point of view?

One way to make sense of this sequence of events—to turn the extremely improbable into something ordinary and reasonable—would be to suggest that Krishnamurti's life was not fortuitous, but rather the result of careful planning. One might argue that Theosophy created him—not only gave him the idea to travel around the world speaking to people about their innermost lives, but also supplied him with the content and themes that he expressed. Leadbeater and others exposed him to Hindu and Buddhist ideas, especially as these were filtered through Blavatsky and Besant, and perhaps he received these views and repackaged them as his own.

Krishnamurti insisted that he was not influenced by theosophical doctrines—"I was never a theosophist." He dismissed the letters he wrote and talks he gave in his youth as mere repetition of what he had been told—or even, as he put it in one of his dialogues with Bohm, "making noise out there." Nevertheless, one might argue that he absorbed more than he acknowledged, or that his ostensible independence of Theosophy was self-serving or illusory.

This case is easier to make if one regards the teachings as unremarkable or derivative. But the case falls apart with the recognition of the originality of Krishnamurti's work. Indeed, the pure originality of the teachings is among their most outstanding characteristics. Who but Krishnamurti would ever have made any of the following statements, much less all of them?

1. Thought breeds fear.
2. Ideals are brutal things.
3. Where there is the meditator, there is no meditation.
4. God is color.
5. It is the most undignified, inhuman thing to worship another human being.
6. Truth is a pathless land.
7. Where there is division, there must be conflict.

Although they are presented here as isolated fragments, these statements function in his philosophy as parts of a coherent, integrated whole. It is impossible, therefore, to conclude that Krishnamurti was merely a byproduct or somehow derivative of Theosophy or any other doctrine, religion, or philosophy. To be sure, there are some points of similarity with statements made by others, but nothing remotely approaching the deep, comprehensive, and nuanced nature of his point of view. As a result, the confluence of events that brought this adolescent boy to that beachfront property at that moment in time represents a mystery impossible to overlook or explain away.

Mary Lutyens addressed this issue in her own way by posing the question, "Who or what is Krishnamurti?" This question has a subtext that reflects the theosophical orientation implicit in or underlying her overall point of view. One would not ordinarily use the form of speech "what is" to inquire about the essential nature of a person. The fact that she did so tips her hand, as it were, and reveals the background from which her question originated: Was Krishnamurti really the World Teacher? Was he the manifestation of the Lord Maitreya? If not, what made him the unique individual that he was?

In the two conversations he conducted with Lutyens on this question, Krishnamurti's answers were not very illuminating. He examined the Maitreya hypothesis patiently, and he considered whether he might be a biological "freak." Neither answer was satisfactory or accounted for all the evidence. More to the point, perhaps, he said that he himself was not able to answer the question: "Water can never find out what water is." On the other hand, if either Lutyens or Mary Zimbalist (who was present and taking notes) could suggest an answer, he said, he could confirm or reject it.

Neither Lutyens nor Zimbalist was able to propose another hypothesis to consider, and the question remained unresolved.

However, Krishnamurti offered one clue for anyone interested in pursuing this issue. His most outstanding psychological characteristic in his youth, he said, was a state of inward emptiness—"the vacant mind." By this he seemed to mean a mind unclouded by problems, fears, desires, or thoughts of any kind. His most characteristic activity was to sit quietly and observe birds, insects, chameleons, and other features of the natural world. If one could understand what brought about the vacant mind, he maintained, one could discover the conditions that allowed his insights to unfold.

The central puzzle associated with Krishnamurti's life and career, therefore, is difficult to penetrate and resolve. It may be best to consider some of the other unusual features associated with him that may either add to or diminish the mystery of the primary one. Perhaps next in significance are the episodes that occurred in Ojai in 1922 and in India in 1948. The first event took place over a period of three days, while the second one lasted for an hour or longer on some evenings for two or three weeks. Both events were characterized by intervals of time when Krishnamurti's normal personality was absent and replaced by a childlike presence that called out for his mother and worried about whether or when Krishna would come back. These episodes were associated with intense pain, often located in the head or the back of his neck. Krishnamurti was not helpful in explaining what was taking place or what it all meant, and Leadbeater said that the Ojai event was outside the scope of his theosophical or occult knowledge. In both cases, the days of suffering issued in or produced a sense of deep serenity or purification.

Krishnamurti's "process" appears to be related in some indirect manner to these events. They have in common periods of intense pain in the head whose origin is unknown. In neither case, however, was the pain considered by Krishnamurti to be a medical event or to require any form of intervention. According to the entries in the *Notebook*, the process occurred almost on a daily basis, especially when he was not occupied with meetings or visitors. When asked about it by Bohm in their 1975 dialogues, Krishnamurti was unable to explain the meaning of the process, although he insisted that others would not have to undergo anything similar in order to share his insights. He also offered the suggestion that when intense pain is endured without any form of escape, it generates an unusual quality or intensity of energy. He seemed to imply that this result was helpful in his work.

Krishnamurti's Notebook also provides the most extensive, detailed set of references we have to the force or entity he referred to obliquely as "the other." That name is suggestive both for its lack of precision and for the general direction in which it points. It begs the question (which unfortunately no one evidently asked): "Other than what?" By its very vagueness, the name seems to indicate an answer something like, "Other than everything; other than the known, familiar world in which we live." In short, "other" seems to suggest "otherworldly." Its unseen, ethereal nature and its association with a transcendent sense of goodness strongly reinforce an interpretation of that kind.

The dialogue with death occurred in the hospital following an operation on Krishnamurti's prostate, and it features the intervention of an entity that he also referred to as "the other." The designation is rather confusing because this other does not appear to be the same as the one described in the *Notebook*. This other is more active; it participates; it engages in a lengthy and strenuous debate with the personification of death. None of this is characteristic of the other that appears in the *Notebook*, which never speaks or interacts in any way. Moreover, Krishnamurti clarified for Mary what he meant by this other: "the mind that is inhabited by K." The other referred to in the *Notebook* is something that comes and goes at irregular intervals; it is almost certainly not the mind inhabited by K.

The proposed distinction between Krishnamurti himself and the mind that he inhabited is unique to this dialogue and not entirely convincing for that reason. The lack of opportunity to question what he meant adds to the uncertainty. Nevertheless, the accumulation of mysteries forms a certain pattern that may provide a clue to the resolution of them all. We begin with the primary puzzle of what conditions produced or precipitated someone who expressed the wealth of insights represented by Krishnamurti's philosophy. This puzzle is compounded by the extraordinary prophecy that preceded his appearance, coupled with the uncanny discovery of the boy on the beach. Krishnamurti regarded the events at Ojai and Ootacamund as meaningful in his personal development, even if he could not articulate exactly what was happening. And he suggested to Bohm that his "process" was also conducive in some manner to his work.

If we entertain the possibility that all these events are inter-related in some subtle manner, perhaps collectively they begin to illuminate one another. Each one independently suggests that Krish-namurti may have been the object or recipient of some unknown kind or quality of force or energy. When viewed not independently but as various manifestations of a single mystery, the possibility of some other agency at work seems to warrant further consideration. The presence and participation of the two different forms of "other" tend to confirm and reinforce this hypothesis. Collectively, all of this evidence points in the direction of an explanation that does not rely upon known or familiar forces or phenomena.

It is important not to confuse this suggestion with the impres-sion that he was some kind of channel or medium being used by someone else—an idea that he strongly rejected, as he said when speaking to the KFA trustees in 1972:

"Are you a medium?" Of course, I'm not a medium. That would be too childish, too illogical, too immature. Because if he were a medium, K would be a stupid, trivial, low kind of bourgeois, and K isn't that.

So, he's not a medium. "Is he aware that he is being used?"—right? No. That would be like a petrol station that is being used by others. Impossible.

Nevertheless, the door seems to be open to the participation of some kind of quality outside the known parameters of everyday life. This hypothesis gathers strength and corroboration from comments Krishnamurti made at certain periods throughout his life. Foremost among these are references to "they," some kind of collective enterprise that took a special interest in him and actively managed events to a certain extent. He referred to "they" repeatedly during the Ojai and Ootacamund episodes; he said that they were engaged in a unique experiment, but they knew how much pain his body could withstand.

One is tempted to discount these statements because they occurred when Krishnamurti was not in his normal state of mind. But he also mentioned the participation of "they" in several conversations with Mary. He said his life had been carefully planned and they would know when it was time for it to be over. "It is all decided by someone else," he said. "There are enormous things that you don't know," and he added that he was "not allowed" to say anything more.

These comments are among the most explicit mention he made of specific entities at work regulating his life and affairs. The reference to enormous things, coupled with the prohibition against divulging more, is particularly provocative. These comments were not recorded, and they were heard by only one witness; for those inclined to be skeptical, their weight or significance may be diminished for those reasons or discounted altogether. On the other hand, the statements are consistent with other references to "they," and they lend further coherence to the larger pattern of unexplained circumstances and events.

Also consistent with this overall interpretation were the many occasions when Krishnamurti described some quality of protection that seemed to accompany him. In some cases, he referred to the sense of protection as if it were simply a feeling he had, a kind of intuition that may or may not have been valid. But the consistency with which he mentioned it may lend it greater credence; and, on one occasion described by Mary, he said, "Something has acted, something has looked after things. I don't think, I know that." In fact, the protection extended to her role in his life. She had been "appointed," he once told her, to serve as his "guardian."

All things considered, some of the circumstances surrounding Krishnamurti strongly suggest the possibility of unknown agents or energies actively participating in his life. For some observers, such a possibility will be a bridge too far. Why consider that there exists some mysterious domain of energy or intelligence just to account for events associated with a single individual? To do so may seem to violate prudence, rationality, and common sense.

Rather than forming a definite conclusion one way or the other, perhaps it is best to hold the proposed solution in suspension, for the moment, and consider whether additional factors or sources of information may contribute to this inquiry. One rather obvious source to consider consists of the teachings themselves. Perhaps we can find within this resource, if not some direct evidence bearing upon these questions, at least some set of clues or a way of orienting ourselves to this dilemma.

Although the teachings do not shed any direct light on the mystery, they may open a window into the mind of Krishnamurti and illuminate the background from which his teachings emerged. If we were to distill the teachings to their simplest terms, one of their central themes would consist of the following: The human mind is clouded with knowledge, thoughts, and images derived from the past. The entire field of thought and knowledge is limited in scope, and when it dominates consciousness, it keeps our lives and minds confined to a narrow area. The mind that is empty of thought is not dead or inert; on the contrary, it is free to give attention to something timeless and unlimited.

Did Krishnamurti's mind actually operate in this manner, and was it open to another domain? If so, this comports with his emphasis on the significance of the vacant mind of his youth. This does not mean that thought had no place in his consciousness; it must have operated as and when needed; but it did not spill over into areas where it was unnecessary or illusory. During periods of meditation in particular, thought must have gone into abeyance. The states of mind he described in the *Notebook* and the "ground" that he discussed with David Bohm would have been among the products or results.

In a seminar conducted at Oak Grove School after Krishnamurti died, Bohm provided the appropriate metaphor to describe this form of consciousness. In a city filled with artificial light late into the evening, such as one might find in Las Vegas, the entire night sky is obliterated. Only when the artificial lights are turned off is it possible for an observer on Earth to witness the stars, the countless stars whose light has traveled from incomprehensible distances. In this metaphor, the artificial light corresponds with the activity of thought, dominating consciousness, and illuminating what seems like a large territory, but in fact is very small. The light of the stars corresponds with the energy or intelligence originating in the unlimited.

Perhaps it stands to reason that someone who directed our attention beyond the limitations of thought was himself open to influences from sources not apparent to our present knowledge. In any case, the content of the teachings suggests or is consistent with what we have proposed to explain the puzzling features of Krishnamurti's life. The teachings and the teacher seem to form a coherent fabric of phenomena.

Krishnamurti alluded to an explanation of this kind when he discussed the concept of the World Teacher in the 1972 dialogues with KFA trustees. He had explored several possible ways to account for his life and career, and none was entirely satisfactory. In the end, he said there was an element of mystery involved that could never be fully explained—something too vast for the human mind to grasp.

> I personally feel it's something so immense that the brain saying, "I am going to find out," can't find out. But the intimation of it is really quite extraordinary for me—not that I'm mystical, or deceptive, or I want a great experience. I have a horror of that.
>
> But there is something extraordinary which happens, which shows, which occurs, which gives hints, and opens the door. And after that, I don't want even to open the door to say what all this is. I don't think the brain can understand it.

The limitation of knowledge may be easier to realize or appreciate if it is considered within an historical context. Only within the last two hundred years have optical instruments revealed the astonishing scope and variety of the single-celled microbial world, with all that it entails for our understanding of health, medicine, agriculture, ecology, and evolution. What entirely new dimensions of reality will the next hundred years reveal? Like the inhabitants of Las Vegas at night, we are so flooded with the artificial light of information that we lose track of Krishnamurti's central insight: thought and knowledge, however extensive they may seem to be, are limited in scope. They are merely a small corner, he said, of something much more immense.

By the principle of parsimony, we may be inclined to reject the hypothesis that Krishnamurti's life is best explained by the participation of an unknown entity, force, or energy. But when all the factors are considered together—the several mysteries, the comments he made, the implications of the teachings—the ratio of probabilities begins to shift. Objectivity does not demand that we remain with what is familiar. In the end, the principle of parsimony may require that we admit what otherwise might seem to be unreasonable.

We cannot conclude this inquiry without taking into account Krishnamurti's final recorded statement, in which he reflected at some length regarding himself. The primary theme of the statement consisted of the revelation of an "immense energy" that had coursed through his body for seventy years. He refers to that energy alternately as "immense intelligence" or "supreme intelligence." Only if someone "lives the teachings" will they experience or understand the quantity and quality of that energy and intelligence.

This statement dovetails with the hypothesis developed in this chapter. It not only affirms the active presence in Krishnamurti's life of some unknown force, but elevates it to a role of central significance. Whether such an energy can account for every element of the mystery surrounding Krishnamurti remains an open question; but the general direction in which he suggests we should look is unmistakable.

One of the most noteworthy features of the statement is that it would be possible to come into contact with that energy if one lived the teachings. This statement reinforces the proposal that the mystery and the teachings fit hand in glove. The statement as a whole represents a capstone to the wide array of evidence suggesting a common hypothesis: that the figure of Krishnamurti was the expression of phenomena that cannot be entirely accounted for by known facts or principles.

Perhaps further light will be shed on these mysteries if and when one or more people enter into the state of mind from which the teachings emerged. At the present time, that prospect seems, paradoxically, extremely elusive and yet also inevitable.

Chapter Twenty

BEYOND THE BANYAN TREE

The condition of Krishnamurti's health during the last weeks of his life was widely known within the Ojai Valley, but neither Rosalind nor Rajagopal made any effort to reach out or contact him or to say good-bye. He asked rather plaintively several days before he died whether there had been any message from "that person." Evidently he entertained until the end the hope that some sense of decency might rekindle in Rajagopal's heart, but the hope was in vain.

Rajagopal's first acknowledgement of what had occurred consisted of a phone call from his lawyer a week after Krishnamurti died. The attorney offered perfunctory condolences and inquired whether the KFA would now be amenable to settle the lawsuit on terms more favorable to Rajagopal. That was out of the question, and the case was set for trial on June 24. In the weeks prior to that date, a flurry of legal motions and replies were exchanged, culminating in a final settlement of all issues on June 21. The terms of the settlement called for the complete dissolution of the K&R foundation and the transfer of all of its archives and assets to the KFA. This entailed the recovery of valuable land and an office building, as well as nine hundred thousand dollars.

The KFA agreed in exchange to complete the publication of the Collected Works and not to contest the Rajagopal Historical Collection or the transfer of materials to the Huntington Library. In addition, they promised not to bring any future lawsuit with respect to any of the issues previously litigated and settled. Rajagopal recovered none of the nine million dollars he had demanded.

⌒

Erna made an effort to work with me in a cooperative manner for three or four months after Krishnamurti died, but the tension between us was too deeply ingrained to remain in abeyance for long. She found another psychiatrist, Lachsman Rasiah, to serve as her parental liaison to the school. She appointed him head of the school board with the understanding that he had a nebulous authority to monitor my behavior as director. Rasiah was far more intelligent and circumspect than Krause had been, but, in the end, he succeeded in annoying me almost to an equal extent. He had multiple medical credentials, three children enrolled in the school, and the tenacity of a terrier, so he was difficult to ignore.

The first fissure in Erna's commitment to work with me cooperatively appeared a few weeks after Krishnamurti was gone. She had taken the unusual step of inviting me to attend a meeting of the trustees to consider agenda items pertaining to issues other than the school. One of the items consisted of a memorandum she had asked Dr. Rasiah to prepare. It purported to show that Krishnamurti's clarity of mind was impaired during his final illness. Rasiah had marshaled his medical expertise to argue that the effects of the illness itself, as well as the pain medications, were sufficient to cast doubt on his mental competence; and therefore any decisions he made at that time should be disregarded. In particular, Erna wanted the trustees to consider whether the recorded statements he had made should be kept under permanent lock and key or even destroyed.

In the presence of Erna, among others, Krishnamurti had declared emphatically his certainty of his own soundness of mind.

In her presence, he had made Scott Forbes swear that his last recordings would never be altered or destroyed; and he made Scott swear it again with greater emphasis. For Erna now to call all that into question—and to enlist Rasiah to compose a memorandum to undermine what Krishnamurti had said—was tantamount, in my mind, to treason. I had been present when he made Scott swear to preserve the recordings, and I realized at once how extraordinary this proposal was. I solemnly warned the trustees that if they did anything to those recordings, it would become the single act for which they would be remembered above all else for all time.

I was not invited to attend any more meetings of the KFA.

Why Erna would want to undermine the authority of Krishnamurti's last statements was not clear at the time, but two possibilities suggest themselves. In his final remarks, Krishnamurti had said that nobody had "lived the teachings." Erna may have felt that such a statement would not be well received by the public at large. She was extremely sensitive to appearances, including the image and reputation of the foundation. To say that no one had lived the teachings might tend to discourage people or call into question whether there was any sense in pursuing something so unrewarding. She may even have felt that such a statement cast a negative light on the trustees themselves.

Erna may also have been unhappy with the resolution of the copyright issue. The primary source of friction among the foundations was Pupul Jayakar's insistence on maintaining control over the publications produced in India. But Erna may have had her own cause for concern. I was told by a reliable source that Erna engaged in a campaign of subterfuge to wrest control of a portion of the copyright from the English foundation. In order to settle the last lawsuit, she persuaded the English trustees to grant the KFA the copyright for all materials published before 1968. She did so based on the promise that after the lawsuit was settled, the copyright would be restored to the English foundation.

But she failed to follow through on her promise. After the lawsuit was settled, the secretary (the chief officer) of the English foundation requested the restoration of the copyright, and Erna refused. The secretary reminded Erna that she had promised; and Erna replied, "You were fools to trust me." One reason Erna enlisted Rasiah's help to cast doubt on Krishnamurti's mental competence, therefore, may have been to avoid having to deceive the English foundation so nakedly.

Erna's normal attitude of overbearing interference in the affairs of the school had returned in full force by the summer after Krishnamurti was gone. In October, I decided to bring matters to a head. I had no desire to continue in my role under those circumstances, and I took an action intended to "kill or cure." She needed either to back off or to let me go. And so I told her on one of our morning walks that her involvement in the school was having a "destructive" effect. I chose a word that was sufficiently strong that she could not ignore it or pretend it meant anything other than what it did.

Erna responded to what I had said by amplifying her involvement in the affairs of the school by another order of magnitude. She moved her own office out of the KFA facilities and into the very center of the school administration building, and she sat there throughout the school day every day. She even took to attending our weekly meetings with teachers and staff. Her presence was deeply unnerving to everyone, but she did it with ice in her veins and without the least acknowledgment that there was anything unusual about it.

In February 1987, one year after Krishnamurti had declared that I was to be "in complete charge" of the school, five of the seven trustees voted to relieve me of responsibility for the high school section of the school. (The KFA normally acted only on the basis of complete consensus among the trustees.) Mary Zimbalist and one other trustee voted against this decision. Two months later, after additional clashes with the trustees, I submitted my resignation from my remaining responsibilities. So the result I had anticipated in May 1985 came to pass two years later, a little more than a year after Krishnamurti had died.

Erna's record of defiance of Krishnamurti's wishes in the year following his death was now complete. First she attacked the credibility of his last recorded statements, after he had insisted on their authenticity. Then she reversed the decision that had been so carefully reached regarding publications and the holder of the copyright. And finally she had her way regarding me. It was a wholesale violation of the agreements she was charged to carry out.

Erna's willful disregard of her responsibilities must weigh heavily in any assessment of her overall contribution to the work of the KFA. On the other hand, her actions must be viewed within the larger context of everything she had done to create the KFA and to recover the assets that Rajagopal had stolen. She never would have had the opportunity to do so much that was wrong if she had not already done so much that was right. Her record was mixed; but, on balance, there is no doubt that the good outweighed the bad. She may have been a flawed warrior; but, without her contribution, Krishnamurti's work in America would never have flowered in the way that it did for the last twenty years of his life.

The Rajagopals waited until Krishnamurti was gone and unable to reply before they attempted to deliver a dagger to the heart of his reputation. The publication of *Lives in the Shadow* the year after he died represented a fitting capstone to their pattern of misconduct. Now their daughter served as the agent of their vindictiveness—Radha, the one whom Krishnamurti had raised almost as his own when Rajagopal abdicated that role. The guiding premise of her bitter memoir was Krishnamurti's purported duplicity—the charge that he exhibited one face to the public at large, and another face in private to those close to him. Her primary evidence in support of this charge was that he interacted in his personal relationships with no sense of entitlement, no pretense of superiority, no hint of consciousness of his lofty mission or reputation. His very humility, the ease with which he blended into social situations, represented for Radha some kind of contradiction of his role as speaker on the public platform. The absurdity of this accusation underscored how thoroughly she failed to understand the meaning of his philosophy.

The revelation that Krishnamurti had engaged in an intimate relationship with Rosalind served to reinforce the charge of hypocrisy. Nowhere in the book is there any acknowledgment of her complicity in everything that had taken place. She is presented as a passive vessel, with no sense of agency or responsibility for her own actions. There is no hint of what Krishnamurti testified to under oath: that the physical relationship began because "she wanted it." Rosalind, he declared under penalty of perjury, was "the aggressor." The laws of libel protect an author from statements made about someone who has died, no matter how false or misleading they may be. Radha took full advantage of that protection by waiting until after Krishnamurti's death to bring forth her perversion of the truth.

Anecdotal evidence suggests that Radha's narrative may have succeeded in spreading seeds of doubt and disinformation about Krishnamurti and his work. Serious students of his teachings are impervious to her efforts to malign him, in part because he himself negated his role as an authority more thoroughly than Radha could ever have done. One thing is certain: the teachings themselves are impregnable; they tower over Radha's malicious gossip like Everest over an anthill.

Numerous other memoirs published after Krishnamurti's death

paint a very different portrait of his character and personality. Sidney Field and Krishnamurti were lifelong friends. They met in Hollywood in 1925 when Field was twenty years old and Krishnamurti was thirty. Field came from a wealthy theosophical family, but his relationship with Krishnamurti was personal and direct, not filtered through theosophical ideology and images. The two young men talked easily together about cars, careers, and movie stars, as well as more serious issues. Field's friendship with Krishnamurti continued through the war years and beyond, into the 1970s. His observations, published as *The Reluctant Messiah*, are detailed, perceptive, and imbued with affection and respect.

Field met Nitya in 1925 and was fascinated by his quick wit and entertaining assessments of prominent political figures. "Nitya was very funny and had us all in stitches, particularly his brother, who would explode with his contagious, boyish laughter…. He had a special charm, and he made you feel at ease with him." Field describes the young Rajagopal as "a personable, good-looking young man of considerable charm…. He was a good organizer and a hard worker. He was also very bossy and could be inflexible and petty in his work rules…. I sensed an undercurrent of jealousy in Rajagopal toward Krishnaji."

Field consulted Krishnamurti occasionally regarding his relationships with women. Even in the 1920s, Krishnamurti had a well-developed attitude toward sex. "You bank your sex force," he said. "You don't let it disturb you…. Think of sex simply as energy, energy to be used to attain a goal. If you want to climb a mountaintop you conserve every ounce of energy." Field asked, "Does that mean a man who would attain the highest must be an ascetic?" Krishnamurti replied, "Not at all. Asceticism as a goal is destructive. There is the biological need for sex, and there is also the need to conserve energy in order to attain a goal."

Field had a brother with whom he was very close, who died

unexpectedly in 1972. Shortly afterward, he met with Krishnamurti and initiated a conversation about life after death. He said he felt as if his brother were with him at that moment, and Krishnamurti confirmed that in a sense that was so. He said that a strong personality leaves behind an "echo" that may remain for some time, even years, after the person has died. The conversation also explored the subject of reincarnation, and what emerged seemed so interesting that they reconstructed it in a recorded version a few days later. The transcript of the recording is included as an appendix to Field's memoir.

Whereas *The Reluctant Messiah* reveals Krishnamurti as a young man, *The Beauty of the Mountain*, by Friedrich Grohe, illuminates his final years. Grohe was a wealthy, retired corporate executive who met Krishnamurti in 1983. His memoir is similar to Field's in that it provides a record of Krishnamurti through the eyes of a friend and companion. Grohe was not a partner in recorded dialogues, but the two men shared a love of nature, long walks, and an appreciation for excellence in clothing and cars; they also shared an intuitive bond of mutual affection and trust. His many quotations of Krishnamurti's comments have the ring of authenticity; they aptly convey the perceptive and graceful manner in which Krishnamurti moved through ordinary events of daily life. Grohe was an avid and talented nature photographer, and his book is richly illustrated with scenes from many locations, including Ojai and Brockwood Park. Krishnamurti said that he and Grohe were brothers.

The Reluctant Messiah was published in 1989, three years after Krishnamurti's death; *The Beauty of the Mountain* came out two years later; and in 1997 there appeared *The Kitchen Chronicles: 1001 Lunches with J. Krishnamurti*, written by my friend Michael Krohnen. Michael served as chef in Ojai from the opening of the Oak Grove School in 1975 until the end of Krishnamurti's life. He writes with a gift for language, precise observations, and an immense, almost worshipful, appreciation of Krishnamurti.

Michael's memoir is more comprehensive than its predecessors. He not only prepared the meals but also served as Krishnamurti's lunchtime companion for as many as one hundred days each year. He must have kept meticulous notes, because his book records the exact menu served on specific dates, the number of people present (which varied from half a dozen to twenty or more), and detailed descriptions of conversations, with special attention to Krishnamurti's contributions. He was particularly fond of the jokes Krishnamurti told, each of which he reproduces with a richly descriptive style of narration. Most of these jokes featured the participation of world leaders, or God, or the devil, or St. Peter at the gates of heaven; and they had in common a distinctive sense of irreverence—such as the story of the young man with long hair and a beard who raced around heaven recklessly in his Ferrari; but no one could do anything about it, because he was "the Boss's son."

Michael skillfully conveys the tone and ambiance of the lunchtime interludes in the long dining room at Arya Vihara. These occasions lasted for an hour or more and often represented the social highlight of the day. A regular feature of the event consisted of Michael's summary of the news, received by Krishnamurti with interest, and often serving as prelude to further conversation. He also provides concise character studies of some of the many visitors to the lunch table, such as the professors Ravi Ravindra and Nobel Prize winner Richard Feynman.

Lunch was served buffet style. Krishnamurti often carried prepared dishes from the kitchen into the serving room, and he insisted on standing at or near the end of the line. Michael notes that Krishnamurti disdained chocolate on grounds that it was a stimulant, as well as the very curious fact that he said he did not experience the sensation of hunger, no matter how long he went without food. He only ate, he maintained, because otherwise he would become physically weak.

In each of these memoirs, a delicate balance exists between observations of Krishnamurti and the author's descriptions of his own reactions and interactions. A somewhat related issue revolves around whether the author is able to observe objectively rather than through the filter of unbridled admiration. Michael's memoir is intensely personal and perhaps can be criticized on both accounts; but those very qualities may have formed the wellspring of his creativity. In any case, his book provides an endearing portrait of Krishnamurti and a lasting contribution to the literature that documents his life.

My account of Krishnamurti's involvement in the first twelve years of the school did not appear until 2011. *The Unconditioned Mind: J. Krishnamurti and the Oak Grove School* represented an effort to record what had transpired in as factual and dispassionate a manner as possible, notwithstanding that my involvement was an inextricable element of the narrative. It was not easy to relive events that were challenging, confounding, and even humiliating, which may help explain the length of time required to compose it.

The line between observations of Krishnamurti and personal disclosure is not only crossed but obliterated in Mark Lee's book, *Knocking at the Open Door: My Years with J. Krishnamurti*, published in 2015. Although Mark refers to his book as a memoir, it is closer to an autobiography, a detailed accounting of his own experiences and points of view. His interactions with Krishnamurti played a prominent role in his life and therefore in his book; but these are subordinate to the larger narrative of his personal odyssey.

As he makes clear from the opening pages, Mark's worldview is permeated with a sense of the mystical, the paranormal, and the occult. He refers early on to his "etheric body" as if this is a normal manner of speech, requiring no elucidation for the general reader. He accepts astrology as authentic and reincarnation as an actuality. He even invokes an entirely new dimension of Krishnamurti's philosophy in support of all things esoteric: "The mystical and subtle are the meta Teachings, and then only alluded to, not explicated in detail as the Teachings were." To be sure, Krishnamurti considered that certain paranormal phenomena do exist; but he would have shuddered, in my judgment, at the suggestion that those phenomena formed any part of his teachings, "meta" or otherwise. And he flatly rejected the characterization of his work as "mystical."

Mark met Krishnamurti at the talks in Saanen in 1965, when he was twenty-five years old. He was invited to lunch repeatedly during the talks and groomed for his mission in life. Krishnamurti offered him a position as a teacher of English at the Rishi Valley School. Mark accepted at once, initiating a seven-year sojourn in India. He fell in love with the people, the cultures, the land, the colors, and the food of India, and he records his detailed impressions with an artful command of words and phrases. He has a well-developed appreciation for artifacts of every variety, from pottery and clothing to landscapes and architecture.

Less reliable are Mark's interpretations of his difficulties serving as an administrator in Krishnamurti's schools. He says Krishnamurti held "socialist views" regarding the treatment of faculty and staff. He even accuses him of hypocrisy in taking an interest in personnel matters "under the guise of concern." Mark's excellent memory for events took a holiday when he had to describe the circumstances that led to my appointment as director of the school. He said I had catapulted to the position of director straight from being a teacher—entirely overlooking the four years he and I spent as co-directors. He makes no mention of the Krause-Hidley faction that dominated the last two years of his tenure as director and ultimately brought him down.

Mark writes he "sensed coldness" from Erna and Theo Lilliefelt when he first met them. "Both projected wealth, position, and an intimidating, dry authority." He adds that they had an antagonistic attitude toward the school right from the beginning, even before it started.

The portrait of Krishnamurti that emerges in Mark's book is curiously devoid of the warmth and humor apparent in other accounts. The individual he describes is incompetent in personnel management; he is naïve and somewhat deluded in his attitude toward money; and he is highly susceptible to uncritical acceptance of disparaging gossip about those close to him. If Mark's negative assessments were more objective, they would carry greater weight; but they seem instead to be filtered through the personal hurt he suffered. Nevertheless, he has provided a deeply felt and sensitive account of a life dedicated to the service of Krishnamurti and his teachings.

A Jewel on a Silver Platter, by Professor Krishna, also published in 2015, represents a study in contrasts with *Knocking at the Open Door*. Whereas Mark's book is saturated with his own feelings and attitudes, the personal element is reduced to the barest minimum in Krishna's book. Almost half of the book is devoted exclusively to Krishnamurti's philosophy. The book is not arranged sequentially but rather according to categories, including anecdotes about Krishnamurti, his relationship to Theosophy, and words as Krishnamurti used them.

Krishna's father grew up in the Theosophical Society, and his aunt, Radha Burnier, later became president of the TS. Nevertheless, Krishna maintains he was not exposed to theosophical ideas and knew nothing about Krishnamurti until the age of seventeen. At that time he ran across a book of talks to students in his father's bookshelf. Two years later, a family friend invited him to meet Krishnamurti and join them for lunch. For the next two decades, Krishna attended the talks whenever possible, and he had numerous opportunities to put questions about whatever he found difficult to understand. His well-developed appreciation of the meaning of the teachings was cultivated over the course of his entire adult life.

Krishna took his PhD in Physics in 1962 from Banaras Hindu

University, where he remained on the faculty until 1986. His research into crystallography led to his election as a Fellow of the Indian Academy of Sciences. At the age of forty-seven, he was invited by Krishnamurti to serve as the director of the Rajghat Education Center, the two hundred-acre complex near Varanasi where the school had been founded in 1933. His book takes its title from the manner in which Krishnamurti described the offer he was making.

One of the highlights of Krishna's book is the complete transcript (fifty-five pages) of a two-hour dialogue he conducted in 1977 with Krishnamurti, David Bohm, and Asit Chandmal, a computer scientist and the nephew of Pupul Jayakar. Krishna introduced the main theme of the conversation: only insight, not a voluntary action, can bring an end to the ego; but the egotistical mind itself prevents such insight. How is it possible to break out of this vicious circle? Krishna's ability to engage on an equal footing with Krishnamurti and David Bohm distinguishes him from other authors. Today he is the foremost expositor of a philosophy similar to, and informed by his engagement with, Krishnamurti's work.

In 1997, a biography of David Bohm was published, written by his friend and fellow physicist, David Peat. *Infinite Potential* represents a competent account of Bohm's work as a scientist, but it fails to capture the quality and significance of his relationship with Krishnamurti. Partly for this reason, I felt it was necessary to compose a more comprehensive and accurate description of the work the two men conducted together. *An Uncommon Collaboration: David Bohm and J. Krishnamurti* appeared in 2017. The book describes the development of Bohm's career in physics, including his seminal contribution to the theoretical foundations of quantum mechanics. Bohm was led to understand and appreciate the work of Krishnamurti by extension from the issues he addressed in science. The book corrects the false impressions left by Peat's biography and attempts to capture the significance and outcome of their quarter-century collaboration.

After Krishnamurti died, Bohm continued to express his insights into psychological issues in a series of seminars he conducted on an annual basis in Ojai. These weekend seminars, held on the premises of the Oak Grove School and open to the public, provided the opportunity for Bohm to articulate many of the themes of Krishnamurti's philosophy with his own preternatural gift for language, colorful metaphors, and insights into consciousness. One of the seminars was transcribed and published in 1992 under the title *Thought as a System*.

Paul Howard is a gifted and highly regarded documentary filmmaker who is currently in the process of completing a film about the life and work of Bohm. The film takes its title, *Infinite Potential*, from the biography by David Peat, with whom Howard worked in the early months of the film's production, until Peat died in June 2017. The film's primary emphasis is on Bohm's work in quantum physics and cosmology, but it also includes his interest in consciousness and his work with Krishnamurti. For this portion of the film, Howard interviewed me in the large living room of Pine Cottage. His questions were astute and well informed. If the trailer for the film is any indication, the finished product will be original, colorful, and creative, much in the spirit of the mind and work of its subject.

Mary Zimbalist's memoir provides the most complete and intimate portrait of the private side of Krishnamurti, including comments he made regarding his inner life and states of mind. The greatest weakness of her work was her lack of understanding of events at Oak Grove School. The contrast with her deep involvement in Brockwood Park is striking and inexplicable. Perhaps the fact that she and Krishnamurti lived on the premises of the school in England enabled her to take a more active interest in its affairs. Perhaps Erna's dominance over events in Ojai left little room for Mary to play a more vital role. In any case, her memoir is far less helpful for understanding what took place at Oak Grove than it is for most of the issues within her purview as Krishnamurti's closest companion and confidante.

Scott Forbes's memoir of Krishnamurti's final year, *Preparing to Leave*, captures his personality on a day-to-day basis as well as any other record. Mary takes the eyewitness account inside Krishnamurti's house, as it were, but Scott provides the close-up. His book has been criticized for insufficient discretion regarding Krishnamurti's critical comments about various people, and the distinction between Scott's opinions and Krishnamurti's is not always entirely clear. Most of his book consists of notes he made contemporaneously with the events he describes, which reinforces its contribution to the historical record.

The memoirs cited here are the best among a larger literature surrounding Krishnamurti and his work. Each of these authors is a perceptive observer as well as a gifted writer; their command of language is skillfully deployed in conveying the subtle quality of a unique personality. The books represent a fertile resource for present and future generations. Krishnamurti said that once he was gone, nothing would remain of what he was; but these books beg to differ. Each one in its own way reveals the living flame that touched so many lives.

In the spring of 2019, the KFA celebrated the fiftieth anniversary of its founding, some thirty-three years after the death of its founder. Krishnamurti would have had reason to appreciate what had transpired in his absence. The east end residence now functions as an educational center for adults, with various activities in several venues. Arya Vihara serves as the Pepper Tree Retreat, with accommodations for visitors to stay overnight or for weeks at a time. An archive building houses an environmentally secure and profession-ally managed vault that contains the many thousands of documents, manuscripts, photographs, and audio and video recordings that constitute the physical record of the teachings. The large living room in Pine Cottage is a library and conference room for visitors through-out the year. Krishnamurti's personal living room and bedroom are preserved as they were when he lived there, affording guests the opportunity to partake of the atmosphere he generated.

Each year a weekend "Gathering" is held in early May, corre-sponding with the time when Krishnamurti gave public talks in the Oak Grove. Talks and discussions exploring the teachings are scheduled throughout the weekend. The foundation sponsors many additional conferences and seminars during the year, including selected speakers whose professions indirectly bear upon Krish-namurti's philosophy. An active and robust online presence makes the teachings available in every format, and search engines enable access according to topics, locations, time periods, audiences, and discussion participants. As a result of all these activities, the teach-ings remain alive and healthy, and a resource available to individuals throughout the world.

One of the reasons—perhaps the main reason—why Erna nurtured a negative attitude toward the school was that it represented a steady drain on the financial condition of the KFA. She had the mentality of a bookkeeper, which made her an effective opponent of Rajagopal, but ambivalent at best about the school. In a delicious irony—one that even she might appreciate—it is now the school that subsidizes the activities of the foundation, rather than the other way around. After running annual deficits for three decades, the school now operates in the black and generates a surplus that helps the foundation make ends meet. The relationship between the school and the foundation has been a chronic source of tension, but now the partnership is more stable and mutually beneficial.

Oak Grove School has always been blessed with a beautiful campus, dedicated teachers, and students from families deeply committed to the welfare of their children. Now it also has full enrollment (216 students), with waiting lists at each level from K through twelve, and a more coherent educational program. Whether the school fulfills the deep intention of its founder is not easy to assess; there is no metric for matriculation at that level. What can be said is that graduates of the school tend to embody or exemplify the principle of self-actualization: they seem to be fully themselves, in a sense, as if they have flourished in a place that allowed them to discover their own talents and identity and begin to develop them. They are highly qualified academically, as confirmed by access to the best and most selective colleges and universities.

The seed that Krishnamurti planted in America is well and firmly established. There can be little doubt that it will survive and grow for another hundred years at least. His message is imprinted indelibly in the fabric of civilization; the question that remains is whether the world will ever pay it the attention it warrants and humanity so desperately needs. He has opened the door into another way of living. Only we can enter it.

POSTSCRIPT

U pon the completion of this manuscript, I shared it with Jaap
Sluijter, the executive director of the KFA, for his comments
and corrections. Among his suggestions was a recommendation
to listen to and take into account a conversation Krishnamurti
conducted with members of the Krishnamurti Foundation of India
and with Mary Zimbalist in 1979. The conversation was initiated
by Pupul Jayakar for the purpose of exploring the meaning of the
mysterious events that had occurred in Ojai in 1922 and in Ootacamund (Ooty) in 1948.

The KFA kindly allowed me access to the recording within
the archive offices, and I was able to listen to it and take notes. A
preliminary transcript of the conversation was also provided to me,
but I found that it had errors and omissions that rendered it less
than reliable. However, through a combination of listening to the
recording, referring to the rough transcript, and making my own
notes, I was able to obtain a sense of the conversation sufficient for
my own satisfaction to report upon it here.

The dialogue does shed light upon the events at Ojai and Ooty,
as well as on related questions regarding the nature of Krishnamurti's consciousness. As a result, I debated whether to rewrite certain
sections of my manuscript in an effort to incorporate this new material. After some reflection, I decided instead to compose the present
postscript. I made this decision in part because I was concerned that

my report of the conversation might not meet the highest standards of research, since I have no access to a verified and verbatim transcription of it. Moreover, the new information does not materially affect the substance of the judgments and conclusions already stated in the manuscript.

The dialogue begins with Pupul's description of the events at Ooty in 1948. Her description closely parallels what she reported in her biography, but she adds that the events at Ooty were preceded by a somewhat similar episode the previous month in Madras. At that time, she and Nandini were staying with Krishnamurti when they were alarmed to hear him crying out in the middle of the night. When they went to his room, they found his normal personality had vanished and was replaced by the voice of the child that has been previously described.

The more extended sequence of events at Ooty lasted for two weeks. They began one evening after Krishnamurti, Pupul, and Nandini returned from their walk together, and he asked the two sisters to remain with him while he lay down on his bed. He told them to have no fear, no matter what happened, and not to call a doctor or let anyone else into the room. He said not to touch him except to close his mouth if he were to faint or become unconscious. Thereafter, his normal personality vanished and the childlike voice remained, calling out for Krishna to return. The pain commenced and was concentrated in his tooth, the back of his head, and the nape of his neck. When the pain became extreme, he fainted. These events continued for hours, but after they were over, Krishnamurti recovered and told Pupul and Nandini they could go to their rooms. The next morning, he was perfectly normal and acted as though nothing unusual had occurred.

Pupul gave special attention to one night when Krishnamurti went out walking by himself and said something unexpected and dangerous had occurred. His walk took him through a forest, where he reported that he lay down and, in order to protect him, "they covered me with leaves." What Pupul found most striking was that it was raining that evening, and she and Nandini went out in their car to see where Krishnamurti had gone. They could not find him, but he returned ten minutes after they got back to the house; and they were surprised to see that he was not drenched with rain. Pupul asked where he had been and he indicated the road on which they normally walked each evening. She asked how he had avoided the rain, and he said, "What rain?" Pupul stressed that she was reporting exactly what had actually occurred.

Krishnamurti responded to her account of these events with a degree of surprise bordering on incredulity. He interjected comments such as, "It all sounds very dramatic," and "That sounds cuckoo." When she described the childlike voice warning that he "might slip away," Krishnamurti asked, "What does he mean by that?" Pupul said she did not know what it meant—she was simply recounting what had occurred.

Krishnamurti emphasized that he had no memory whatsoever of what she had described—"not a scrap." Because he did not remember it, he was not at all sure he could explain it. He was very skeptical whether it had occurred as she described. He did not doubt her sincerity, but he wondered aloud whether she could have imagined or misremembered it. Mary Zimbalist pointed out that several people had witnessed similar behavior, including herself and Vanda Scaravelli. Since there were several independent reports that corresponded with one another, it was difficult to doubt the accuracy of all of them.

Krishnamurti asked Pupul and Nandini what was their impression of these events at the time. How did they respond to what they were observing? Pupul said she felt that she was witnessing something sacred; she called it "the holy of holies." Krishnamurti responded by saying that a sense of sacredness had been with him ever since the events in Ojai, with varying degrees of intensity at different times. He seemed to feel that Pupul's observation of this element gave some authenticity and support to the overall reliability of her description.

In view of the independent reports of several observers, Krishnamurti accepted the veracity of the accounts and proceeded to attempt to discern their meaning. He did not speak as though he had some exclusive knowledge or insight, but rather as someone investigating the most logical and probable explanation, in view of the totality of facts and circumstances. What follows is a summary that represents a distillation of the primary conclusions from a long and rather wide-ranging conversation.

The main theme that emerges from the conversation revolves around the relationship between Krishnamurti's brain and the energy that flows through him. The energy is enormous and requires a very unusual brain in order to manifest through it. Krishnamurti appeared to accept the Leadbeater interpretation that the boy on the beach exhibited little or no self-interest, and that was the crucial characteristic that allowed him to be selected for his role. Krishnamurti characterized the energy flowing through him as the force of "goodness," and the essential meaning of the events at Ojai and Ooty was that his brain was being prepared to receive that energy.

The kind of preparation that the brain required was described as "polishing" and acquiring increased "elasticity." Krishnamurti rejected thinking of it in terms of removing impurities. Rather, he said, the brain cells needed to "expand" or become more "free." This form of preparation was also related in some way to his process, including "the pain and all the rest of it."

Among the most perplexing of the puzzles associated with Krishnamurti's life were his references to an unknown "they" who interacted with him in various ways. The role of "they" was prominent at Ooty, where the childlike personality said "they" were "burning" him, "having fun with him," causing intense pain but "knew how much he could take," and had covered him with leaves during his walk in the forest. In these and other ways, the childlike voice unmistakably attributed to "they" whatever operations were taking place on his brain.

In the conversation with the Indian trustees, Krishnamurti offered no support or confirmation for the role or participation of "they." When asked specifically what he had meant by "they," Krishnamurti asked whether "the man on the bed" might have been in an "imaginative" or "hysterical" state of mind. Moreover, he offered an entirely alternative explanation for how his brain had been prepared, polished, or acquired greater elasticity. In a rather remarkable revelation, he offered the possibility that the brain had been changing itself. After considering the matter, he said, "I think that's right. I'll stick with that."

Krishnamurti knew this was an unexpected proposition. He asked, "Would you accept that? The brain can change itself?" He elaborated on what this implied or entailed. In order for the brain to change itself, it must experience no "friction" or "pressure" of any kind. When the brain has no friction, he said, it has its own "rhythm." These were the conditions that allowed the brain to polish or prepare itself to receive the tremendous energy of goodness.

Where did Krishnamurti's normal personality go when the procedures were taking place to prepare his brain? The childlike individual repeatedly called for Krishna to return and worried about where he had gone. In the dialogue with the Indian trustees, Krishnamurti rejected the idea that his normal personality had left the body and gone to some other location. Instead, he maintained, his normal consciousness had simply shut down for the duration of the procedures, rather like what happens when the electricity to a light bulb is turned off. When that occurred, there remained a residual form of awareness that was the consciousness of the body itself, and that was what produced the voice of the childlike individual. The body interpreted the disappearance of Krishnamurti's personality as if Krishna had gone somewhere; but that was not the fact; it was merely the expression of the body's experience.

These were the primary themes that emerged to account for the events at Ojai, Ooty, and somewhat similar events at other times and places. Several additional points were developed that were tangential to this theme. Why did these events occur only in the presence of one or two individuals with whom Krishnamurti was close or whom he trusted? Krishnamurti maintained, as mentioned in this volume, that there exist forces of evil that attempted to interfere with the manifestation of goodness through him. He said he was on guard against these forces all the time; it was the reason, for example, that he would not go out unaccompanied at night. When his normal consciousness disappeared, the body was left vulnerable and exposed to attack by these forces. But if there were people with him who cared for him, nothing could harm him. "Where there is love," he said, "evil cannot exist."

How is it possible for the brain to undergo healing or preparatory functions while the normal consciousness is absent? In order to repair an instrument or a piece of machinery, such as the device that was recording their dialogue, the instrument had to be switched off. Similarly, his normal consciousness had to go into "abeyance" in order for the preparation to occur. Krishnamurti maintained that the state of mind of emptiness is not really empty. It is full of energy, full of activity, but not the activity of thought.

One of the participants asked whether these events corresponded in some way with the theosophical doctrine of the periodic appearance of Lord Maitreya. According to Krishnamurti, that theory derived from a Hindu idea that events in human history precipitate the manifestation of Maitreya. He rejected the suggestion that the energy of goodness appears in response to historical circumstances. That was impossible, he said, because it implied an action that was "utilitarian." He seemed to be suggesting that goodness was not a product of cause and effect, but appeared without any form of motive or premeditation.

As an aside, Krishnamurti remarked upon the circumstances that kept him within the orbit of Rosalind and Rajagopal for so many years. He said Rajagopal had foreseen that eventually Krishnamurti would separate from him, and he had worried what would become of himself. Someone would always take care of Krishnamurti, he said, but he was worried about his own security. As a result, he and Rosalind "gradually wove a circle around" Krishnamurti; "gradually they closed the trap." They deliberately kept his influence and effect upon the public as small as possible. At the time he separated from Rajagopal, the mailing list they had accumulated after all those years numbered only two hundred names.

Krishnamurti remarked how strange it was that he had remained with Rajagopal for so long. He said he knew at the time that it was not right, but he was unable to do anything about it. He attributed it in part to his delay in arriving at full maturity. He also related it to his feeling that his whole life had somehow been arranged. Only when Mary Zimbalist and the Lilliefelts came along and "picked him out" was it possible for him to separate from Rajagopal. Their involvement contributed to his sense that his life had been arranged.

This conversation was conducted at an apartment in Bombay on January 25, 1979, and it lasted two and three-quarter hours. In addition to Pupul, Nandini, and Mary Zimbalist, it was attended by Sunanda and Pama Patwardhan, Achyut Patwardhan (Pama's brother), Asit Chandmal (Pupul's nephew), Radhika Herzberger (Pupul's daughter), and Dr. Parchure. The rough transcript of the dialogue occupies sixty pages. This report represents only a summary of the main points and does not capture much of the subtlety, nuances, and incidental comments and issues raised. I look forward to the day when a complete transcript of the conversation is made available to the public, and readers will no longer have to rely on this partial and approximate description of it.

BIBLIOGRAPHY

Albert, David Z. "Bohm's Alternative to Quantum Mechanics." *Scientific American* 270 (5) (1994): 58-67.

Bohm, David. *Causality and Chance in Modern Physics.* Pennsylvania: University of Pennsylvania Press; Reissue edition, 1971.

Bohm, David. *Quantum Theory.* New York: Prentice Hall, 1951.

Bohm, David. *The Special Theory of Relativity* (Routledge Classics). London: Routledge, 2006.

Bohm, David. "A Suggested Interpretation of the Quantum Theory in Terms of Hidden Variables I," *Physical Review* 85 (1952): 166-179.

Bohm, David. "A Suggested Interpretation of the Quantum Theory in Terms of Hidden Variables, II," *Physical Review* 85 (1952): 180-193.

Bohm, David. *Thought as a System.* London and New York: Routledge, 1992.

Bohm, David. *Wholeness and the Implicate Order.* London: Routledge and Kegan Paul, 1980.

Bohm, David. *The Essential David Bohm.* Edited by Lee Nichol. New York: Routledge, 2003.

Field, Sydney. *Krishnamurti: The Reluctant Messiah*. New York, NY: Paragon House, 1989.

Forbes, Scott. *Preparing to Leave*. SHF Publications, 2018.

Grohe, Friedrich. *The Beauty of the Mountain: Memories of J. Krishnamurti*. Krishnamurti Foundation, 2006.

Huxley, Aldous. Letters to J. Krishnamurti. March 1945; May 1945; January 1948. Krishnamurti Foundation of America Archive Collection.

Jayakar, Pupul. *Krishnamurti: A Biography*. San Francisco: Harper & Row, 1986.

Krishna, Padmanabhan. *A Jewel on a Silver Platter: Remembering Jiddu Krishnamurti*. Peepal Leaves Publishing, 2015.

Krishnamurti, J. *The Awakening of Intelligence*. New York, NY: HarperOne, 1973.

Krishnamurti, J. *The Collected Works*, vol. II. Kendall/Hunt Publishing Company, 1991.

Krishnamurti, J. *The Collected Works*, vol. III. Kendall/Hunt Publishing Company, 1991.

Krishnamurti, J. *The Collected Works*, vol. VI. Kendall/Hunt Publishing Company, 1992.

Krishnamurti, J. *The Collected Works*, vol. XVII. Kendall/Hunt Publishing Company, 1992.

Krishnamurti, J. *The First and Last Freedom*. New York: Harper and Brothers, 1954.

Krishnamurti, J. *Krishnamurti's Journal*. London: Victor Gollancz, Ltd., 1982.

Krishnamurti, J. *Krishnamurti's Notebook*. Ojai, CA: Krishnamurti Publications of America, 2003.

Krishnamurti, J. *Krishnamurti to Himself: His Last Journal*. London: Victor Gollancz, Ltd., 1987.

Krishnamurti, J. *Last Talks at Saanen, 1985*. San Francisco: Harper and Row, 1985.

Krishnamurti, J. *The Perfume of the Teachings: Krishnamurti in Dialogue with the Trustees*. Krishnamurti Foundation Trust Ltd, 2018.

Krishnamurti, J. *Truth and Actuality*. San Francisco: Harper and Row, 1978.

Krishnamurti, J. *The Wholeness of Life*. San Francisco: HarperSan-Francisco, 1979.

Krishnamurti, J., and David Bohm. *The Ending of Time: Where Philosophy and Physics Meet*. New York, NY: HarperOne, 2014.

Krishnamurti, J., and David Bohm. *The Future of Humanity*. San Francisco: Harper and Row, 1986.

Krishnamurti, J., and David Bohm. *The Limits of Thought*. London and New York: Routledge, 1999.

Krohnen, Michael. *The Kitchen Chronicles: 1001 Lunches with J. Krishnamurti*. Ojai, CA: Edwin House Publishing, 1997.

Lee, R.E. Mark. *Knocking at the Open Door: My Years with J. Krishnamurti*. Hay House Publishers India, 2015.

Lilliefelt, Erna. *KFA History*. Report on the formation of Krishnamurti Foundation of America and the lawsuits which took place between 1968 and 1986 to recover assets for Krishnamurti's work. Krishnamurti Foundation of America, 1995.

Lutyens, Emily. *Candles in the Sun*. Philadelphia and New York: J.B. Lippincott Company, 1957.

Lutyens, Mary. *Krishnamurti: The Years of Awakening*. New York: Farrar, Straus, Giroux, 1975.

Lutyens, Mary. *Krishnamurti: The Years of Fulfillment*. New York: Farrar, Straus, Giroux, 1983.

Lutyens, Mary. *Krishnamurti: The Open Door*. New York: Farrar, Straus, Giroux, 1988.

Lutyens, Mary. *Krishnamurti: His Life and Death*. New York: St. Martin's Press, 1990.

Lutyens, Mary. *Krishnamurti and the Rajagopals*. Ojai, CA: Krishnamurti Foundation of America, 1996.

Lutyens, Mary. *To Be Young: Some Chapters of Autobiography*. London: Rupert Hart-Davis, 1959.

Moody, David Edmund. *An Uncommon Collaboration: David Bohm and J. Krishnamurti*. Ojai, CA: Alpha Centauri Press, 2017.

Moody, David Edmund. *The Unconditioned Mind: J. Krishnamurti and the Oak Grove School*. Wheaton, IL: Quest Books, 2011.

Moody, David E. "Can Intelligence be Increased by Training on a Task of Working Memory?" *Intelligence* 37 (2009): 327-328.

Moody, David. "The David Bohm Biography." *The Link* 14 (1998): 20-22.

Moody, David E. "Gaia Comes of Age." *Natural History* 119 (3) (2010): 40-42.

Moody, David. "The Insight Curriculum." *Journal of the Krishnamurti Schools* 2 (1998): 13-15.

Moody, David E. "Review of *On Gaia*, by Toby Tyrell." *Progress in Physical Geography* 38 (1) (2014): 138-141.

Moody, David E. "Seven Misconceptions Regarding the Gaia Hypothesis." *Climatic Change* 113 (2012): 277-284.

Patwardhan, Sunanda. *A Vision of the Sacred: My Personal Journey with Krishnamurti*. Ojai, CA: Edwin House Publishing, 1999.

Peat, F. David. *Infinite Potential: The Life and Times of David Bohm*. Reading, MA: Addison-Wesley, 1997.

Sloss, Radha Rajagopal. *Lives in the Shadow with J. Krishnamurti.* London: Bloomsbury, 1991.

Smith, Ingram. *Truth is a Pathless Land: A Journey with Krishnamurti.* Wheaton, IL: Quest Books, 1989.

Zimbalist, Mary. *In the Presence of Krishnamurti: Mary's Unfinished Book.* SHF Publications, 2018.

Additional Source Material

Howard, Paul, director. *Infinite Potential.* A documentary film about the life and work of David Bohm. Imagine Films, 2020.

Krishnamurti, J., David Bohm, & David Shainberg. *The Transformation of Man.* Videotapes of the dialogues published as *The Wholeness of Life.* Krishnamurti Foundation of America.

Krishnamurti, J., David Bohm, John Hidley, & Rupert Sheldrake. *The Nature of the Mind.* DVD Set. Videotaped dialogues. Krishnamurti Foundation of America.

Zimbalist, Mary. inthepresenceofk.org. Transcripts of Mary Zimbalist in dialogue with Scott Forbes, discussing her diary entries of her life with Krishnamurti.

INDEX

www.ingramcontent.com/pod-product-compliance
Lightning Source LLC
Chambersburg PA
CBHW051848090426
42811CB00034B/2260/J